Identity Cards

Book Two

The Spawater Chronicles

Barry Tighe

Published by

Can Write Will Write

Published 2012 by

Can Write Will Write
Cambridge Lodge
Wanstead England

http://www.canwritewillwrite.com

A catalogue record for this book is available in the British Library

ISBN 978-0-9563028-0-9

Printed in the USA and UK by
Lightning Source

Typeface Georgia
12 Points
Margins 2.2 & 1.9
Width 22.86 & 15.24
Case Laminate

The Spawater Chronicles are a series of tales set in the old Roman City of Spawater.

Book Two

Identity Cards

Nothing to hide, nothing to fear?

Other books in the series

Book One

Youth Market
Chickens versus television

Book Three

Casino
Heads we win tails you lose

Book Four

Gone Fission
It's a power thing

Book Five

Vote Alison MEP
Booze cruise to gravy boat

Thank You

I wish to thank Cas Peace and Mark Atkins for their practical help, positive criticism and all-round encouragement.
I wish to thank Guy Herbert for the foreword and George Netley for his great help with the cover production.

I also wish to thank the British political Frankenstein known as *New Labour*, whose ability to be so wrong, so arrogant and so dishonest on so many important issues, has provided me with so much comic material. We shall not - fingers crossed - endure their likes again.

The Spawater Chronicles

Published 2012 by

Can Write Will Write

Foreword

I am delighted to be asked to write a foreword for Barry Tighe's book because what he has done in it is to dramatise what people rarely consider when they discuss the National Identity Scheme: its likely insidious effects in everyday life.

It is an occupational hazard of being a civil libertarian that one becomes preoccupied with pessimism. The temptation is always to look at the worst that could happen. Some opponents of the government's plans point out that their motivation is transparently distrustful monitoring and control of the populace, and leap immediately to visions of a dystopian surveillance state and what could happen if a totalitarian regime had use of such an instrument of state power. But while those are real dangers, they are distant ones, and may seem implausible panic-mongering.

The proximate problems of state 'identity management' schemes are not instant dictatorship. They are that they add friction to our lives; subject us to petty officialdom; expose us to criminals; diminish or remove our self-sufficiency; and gradually, perhaps imperceptibly so, make us steadily a little less free. Barry lets us see this gentle degradation of social life by official good intentions through his characters' experiences. Not everybody will suffer a disaster. But nobody will be untouched.

Now just as Spawater is not a real town, the ID database imposed on its residents is not the same as that currently being promoted by the British Government. Nor is the government of the real Britain prepared to undertake small-scale trials. It is pushing ahead with a National Identity Register regardless of technical doubts, and insists the social disadvantages (corresponding to those Spawater's residents discover) simply do not exist. The zealots in government want to lumber us with a system that cannot be conveniently abandoned, because government administration is already tied to it.

NO2ID thinks this is foolish as well as authoritarian. A badly managed, rushed, scheme is likely to do more damage before it can be stopped than a controlled one. We intend to stop it anyway. I hope that as someone who has picked up a copy of 'Identity Cards', you might be interested to find out more about the real thing - maybe even help us. If so, please visit our website *www.no2id.net* for more information.

Meanwhile, I hope you enjoy the story.

Guy Herbert
General Secretary, NO2ID

Identity Cards
Chapter One

After the lull comes the storm. Alarms reverberated through the Dark Lord's head awakening him to his colossal blunder. By concentrating his thoughts, strength and armies on the fleabite facing his unassailable fortress, he had committed the most foolhardy, dangerous and deadly folly. He had neglected the inhospitable highways and barren, ashen-pocked byways leading to Mount Doom.

His all-seeing eye swivelled from what was plainly Gandalf's diversion, his sacrificial force, onto Baggins wrestling with the creature Gollum. They, like the Dark Lord's future, hung over the precipice.

Simultaneously sensing their Master's imminent peril, the Nazgul bat-winged their way to Mount Doom's cavernous entrance.

Sauron, the Dark Lord, smiled the smile of victory.

The pitiful Hobbits were locked in their forlorn combat, fighting over his Precious. Soon they would be taken by his loyal Nazgul servants and the Ring would return to its rightful owner. 'One Ring to rule them all, one Ring to bind them'. Soon, very soon, all of Middle Earth would be enslaved; the dark shadow would envelope the land forever. Soon, very soon...

Not soon enough, fretted Sauron, as the Nazgul failed to report in with 'mission accomplished'. Where were they? Suspicion replaced complacency. The acrid bile of fear welled up sickeningly. What's keeping them?

The Dark Lord knew that his future, his very existence, depended on the Nazgul getting to Baggins before the Ring fell into the abyss. Where, oh where, were his Nazgul? Boys? Where are you?

The palantir rang. At last, thought Sauron, relieved; about time too. He clicked it open.

'Hello, Sauron, Dark Lord here.'

It was the chief Nazgul. 'Sorry, boss,' the Nazgul reported, 'I'm afraid we have a bit of a problem. A huge spider at the entrance to the Cracks of Doom won't let us pass unless we show her our identity cards.'

'Well show them, then!' cried out Sauron in desperation. This was no time to argue with arachnid doorkeepers.

'We haven't got them with us, boss. We were in a hurry.'

'What on Middle Earth!' hollered Sauron frantically. 'Tell her who you are! Tell her the fate of Mordor hangs in the balance!'

'She knows who we are, boss. We are easy to recognise. She says it cuts no ice with her. Rules is rules, she says, and if she made an exception for us she would have to make it for everyone and then where would we be?'

Sauron recoiled in despair. Those bloody identity cards! Ever since the Grand Council of Wizards introduced them, Middle Earth had been crawling with jumped-up jobsworths demanding identity cards all over the place. Everywhere Humans, Elves, Dwarves, Ents, Hobbits and Nazgul went, they were stopped by fixated flunkies demanding the production of little bits of plastic before they could go about their business. It was the wrong side of enough, flailed Sauron wretchedly.

Only the Orcs liked them; stealing cards and selling them or holding them to ransom was a nice little earner. Better than working for their former employer, thought Sauron bitterly. No wonder he could not get the staff needed to protect his borders from burgling Hobbits.

Too late! The delay allowed Gollum to bite the hand that didn't feed him and fall, gloating, into oblivion.

Sauron too, was finished. With ringing in his ears, he felt himself falling...falling...

Clump. Joanna woke to find she had fallen out of bed, her alarm ringing piercingly and her morning off to the worst possible start. When identity cards invade my dreams, she silently fumed, rubbing her elbows, they have got to go.

The last three months had been a strain for Joanna and her friends. She had returned from a well-deserved holiday to discover that an insecure government had selected her hometown of Spawater as the trial area for identity cards and a national database. Since then, life had assumed an unpleasant and serious atmosphere. Frodo and his fellow Hobbits felt the same when they returned to the Shire to discover their own insecure rulers had closed all the pubs.

Over a bleak, solo kitchen coffee - her partner Jady was not up yet - Joanna recalled how she had heard the barely credible news. The gang had met up in the Lifeboat Club, a nautically-themed establishment resembling a cruise liner down on its luck, after some time apart. Jady and herself, their great friends Jenna, Alison and Hanif, Farmer Tom and young Arnie, Hanif's assistant at the computer security company for which Hanif and Arnie worked, were in attendance.

It had been a happy occasion, drinks all round, with Farmer Tom getting the go-ahead from Spawater Council to get into the humane farming business and out of the battery hen Hell he had been forced into for financial reasons. It was a happy evening for Tom, but after he slipped his moorings the atmosphere had struck a reef.

Ron, the owner of Lifeboats' and a man as gloomy as Monday mist, had casually informed Jady that Spawater was to be the testing ground for the identity card and national database project. Biometric cards would be issued to all citizens in the Spawater area, compulsorily, to accustom the country to the idea prior to inflicting them on the entire population.

Far from enraging the gang, as Joanna had expected, the news split them several ways. She was furious, of course, as was Jenna, albeit for different reasons. Jady was against but not overly concerned as he expected the idea to collapse.

'It is just a fetish of the Home Secretary,' he deemed. 'His career is on the way down and as soon as he dies, politically, the scheme will die with him.'

Joanna was not so sure. Amongst her friends, Arnie did not care one way or the other, like Switzerland, and Alison made the simple and lacklustre observation that kind-hearted people often make about identity cards.

'If you have nothing to hide, you have nothing to fear.'

Lovely, trusting Ali, thought Joanna sadly. Betraying such trust was another thing that annoyed her about the business. Suspicious, cynical members of the government played on the fact that most ordinary people are innocent and willing to give others the benefit of the doubt. Living with Jady, Joanna knew better. Power abhors a vacuum, and once introduced, the information held on the public by their rulers would be used against them whether they thought they had nothing to hide or not. Alison was sometimes too nice for this world, but better a world fit for Alisons than a world fit for governments.

No, the real surprise was Hanif. Hanif was for them. Not only in favour but actually keen. He could not wait to see everyone stamped and filed, and honestly believed identity cards would make the country a better place.

'How will splitting the country from top to bottom make it a better place?'

'Wait and see, Joey,' Hanif replied. 'Once people get used to identity cards they will learn to love them.'

'Like Winston loved Big Brother? Hang on to Nurse for fear of something worse?' Joanna rounded on her friend, spilling her celebration wine over Ron's comfortable cruise ship's armchair. She was no longer in the mood to party. The others were quiet, sensing a private argument. 'I am shocked at you, Han, how could you favour such a terrible assault on the whole country? Why should you want to control everyone's lives? It is not like you at all.'

Hanif averted his eyes; guilty as a sheep-dog hosting a barbeque. 'You see, Joey,' he replied at length, 'while you were away my company obtained a big new contract. Here in Spawater. The biggest job we have ever had.'

'Morning, world.'

Joanna jerked herself back to the present to greet Jady at the breakfast room. The two of them lived in Chez Guevara, the downstairs half of a large old sprawl on the edges of town. Upstairs lived Jady's sometime sparring partners, Mike and Carole. 'Least said about them,' maintained Jady when asked, 'the better.'

Jady removed a fruit bowl from the refrigerator, smiled approvingly and tipped half its contents onto his plate.

'Good morning, Jady.' It was good to be back in the present. Remembering old arguments is no way to start the day. What a lovely world it would be if everybody forgot what they were arguing about!

Joanna and Jady were evidence of the old adage that opposites attract. Joanna was a worrier; she cared about the troubles of the world and cried when the world let itself down. Jady cried when the world let *him* down. After all, who was the world for? Joanna loved Jady enough to let him infest the flat with hideous, ancient heavy furniture giving the place the air of a used furniture emporium circa late nineteenth century. Jady loved Joanna enough to actually listen to her, at least when the wind was blowing in the right direction. As likely a combination as Red Riding Hood going into partnership with the Big Bad Wolf; 'Wolfie 'n the Hood Ltd. Organised picnic basket delivery and cottage management; text Grandma for directions. No woodmen.' Together they made a team as redoubtable as sand and cement.

'How are things at the anti identity card campaign?'

Joanna winced. She was a member of the 'Campaign Against Identity Cards', a national organisation opposing their introduction and the even more dangerous national database. It was struggling to raise the database up the league table of national consciousness, an uphill task.

The problem, she knew, was that people are intrinsically decent and wish no harm to others. Their mistake is that they assume governments are the same. So, when a government assures them that identity cards are a 'good thing', the government is believed. The truth will become apparent when it is too late. If only, she mused, there was a way to discredit identity cards before they could be imposed upon the whole country. That was her task; to discredit national identity cards before it was too late. Churchill had a similar problem; he failed and it caused no end of trouble.

'Not so good, Jady,' Joanna admitted. 'The usual protests, letters of complaint to the newspapers as you know, but the government anticipated all that before it started and, let's face it, they have the drop on us. We are losing the argument; not to counter-argument but to apathy.'

'Mmmm?' Jady munched his fruit. Have a good breakfast and the rest takes care of itself, was Jady's approach. Tall and slim, that's what kept his brain and body supple enough to morph through life.

'I said our enemy is apathy.'

'Yes, I suppose it must be,' Jady mumbled. He sympathised, of course, but found the idea of labelling the entire country so ludicrous that he could not get worked up about it. The whole nonsense would be quietly dropped as the impossibility of making such a scheme actually work dawned on the authoritarian control freaks that promulgated it. And the Treasury. And the voters. He had other business.

'You are not listening, Jady. This is important to me.'

Recognising the signs, Jady devoted the rest of breakfast time to Joanna. Placated, but no further towards solving her problem, Joanna pecked Jady goodbye and set off to her day job.

Jady relaxed. Discussing identity cards with Joanna, or listening, anyway, had reminded him of how his current situation had come about. Problems are opportunities, he mused. It was Joanna's problem that had given Jady just the opportunity he was looking for. Jady recalled the events leading up to the current position.

It was in Lifeboats' the evening of their return from holiday, he recollected. An argument had erupted between Joanna and Hanif. When the two of them started squabbling over identity cards, Hanif had been obliged to declare his interest.

'The biggest job we have ever had,' confessed Hanif.

'What do you mean?' Joanna challenged. She learned towards him angrily, violating his air space. 'What are you saying?'

Hanif was not a confrontational person. Birds of Paradise came to him for relationship advice. With the tortured anguish of a Hell's Angel confessing to wilful vegetarianism, he owned up.

'My company have the contract to oversee the introduction of identity cards in Spawater. I am liaising with the consortium that is running the whole thing from London on behalf of the government. It is my job to supply local knowledge in order to make the thing a success.'

Hanif reached for his drink and took a defensive swig. Hanif and drink were like Popeye and spinach. Emboldened, he continued. 'We are in the twenty-first century and it is time people realised it. For better or worse, identity cards are here and here to stay.'

A likely story, thought Jady complacently, people have got the twenty-first century on the brain. As if everything must be different because of a number. As though the taxpayer will bankroll an enormous army of mouse manglers poking their bureaucratic noses into other people's affairs when there are worthwhile things to spend taxpayers' money on. No chance.

Anyway, Jady mused, this Spawater experiment could be turned to his advantage. Strange how fate works; if not for the identity card nonsense, Hanif would not have fallen out with his Joanna, and Arnie, Hanif's assistant, would not have quit his job.

'Why?' asked Jady when Arnie told him in Lifeboats'

Pool room.

'Because Hanif has fallen out with your Joanna. We had a blazing row about it and I walked out.'

Young Arnie was the nearest thing Jady had to a fan club. A computer wizzo, Arnie had lacked confidence in the real world until Jady had shown him that it was the real world which had the confidence problem. The world had to justify itself to them, not t'other way around. The follow-on from this was that Arnie could not work for anyone who was at loggerheads with Jady's partner.

'Let me get this straight,' Joanna challenged Jady that evening, 'Arnie has resigned because Hanif and I disagree about identity cards? That makes it my fault. I still like Hanif, for goodness' sake, we just disagree on something, that's all. Tell Arnie to ask for his job back. I will tell Hanif that Arnie was only doing what he thought was right. Surely he will reinstate him?'

They were at home, parked on their enormous settee in front of the huge unlit fireplace, mulling over recent events armed with tea and biscuits Joanna's spat with Hanif caused ripples in their social lives, especially as Jady and Hanif were close friends, but Jady and Joanna were close friends too, so, unlike Hamlet and his uncle, all could be discussed and resolved.

'I'm ahead of you there. I spoke to both of them in Lifeboats' this evening. Secretly, they would like to let bygones be bygones but neither will back down and besides, Hanif's company is committed to this identity card and database nonsense so even if Han agreed with you, he would have to continue or resign himself. No, Jo, while Hanif's company are carrying out this trial, young Millado stays resigned.'

Joanna was mortified. Guilt comes easiest to those who deserve it least. Dick Dastardly caused the resignation of scores of assistants and didn't miss a heartbeat. 'What's that, Muttley? You don't want to fix the race? Tchaa!' Joanna inadvertently caused one assistant's resignation and couldn't sleep.

‘Don’t worry, Joey,’ Jady reached forward and dunked a consoling biscuit in her tea, ‘this was fated to happen. It so happens that I need Arnie to help me in a moneymaking project I have been thinking about lately. I need Alison as well.’

‘No, Jady.’ Joanna knew all about Jady’s moneymaking projects. Yes, they usually made money; they also made havoc. ‘I don’t mind you causing trouble again but I won’t have little Arnie dragged into something beyond his ken. Remember last time? If not for Alison, he could have been imprisoned. No, leave Arnie alone.’

Jady knew his Joanna. Protecting Arnie from him would assuage her guilt. He would agree with her for now and suggest the scheme to Arnie later. Arnie’s enthusiasm would ensure Joanna’s permission to proceed, if not her blessing. Machiavelli would approve, though he might think it a bit raw.

‘All right, Jo, we’ll leave it for now. Don’t worry about Arnie, Hanif wants him back and as soon as the identity card rubbish is dropped and things return to normal, things will return to normal.’ Jady squeezed her arm affectionately. ‘Now, fancy a nightcap?’

Identity Cards
Chapter Two

'So, Mr Singh, are you entirely happy and au fait with your assignment? It is absolutely vital that you are aware of what is expected from you and are both willing and able, no, enthusiastic and able, to carry out your responsibilities.'

Hanif bridled. Yes, he was in favour of identity cards, whatever his friends thought, but that did not mean he approved of the establishment bigwig infesting his office and treating him like a mentally deficient amoeba on a slow day.

'No worries, Mr Dauntliffe, I am, as you say, aware of the position and in total control of it.' Hanif was not going to give the intimidating Mr Dauntliffe the satisfaction of hearing him repeat the words 'au fait', like an impressed underling. 'I am in complete concord with both your plans for the implementation of identity cards in Spawater and the rationale behind them.' Hanif could speak faux French too. 'Compulsory identity cards and their controlling national database will be a step forward for Britain in its march to the future. The sooner everybody in the country is issued with a card, the better. Would you like another coffee?'

Mr Dauntliffe nodded importantly. Hanif had impressed him. He had made a wise choice in choosing Hanif's company to implement the identity card project trial. This Mr Singh, he considered, was just the man for the job; intelligent, knowledgeable and an enthusiastic supporter of compulsory Identification Cards.

Indeed, Mr Dauntliffe wondered, he might even be worth inveigling into the real project. Early days; time will tell if Mr. Singh is suitable or not.

'Ooh, that would be lovely. As it is on you, I will have a large one with added chocolate and a cream cheese bagel. You don't mind, do you?'

Alison was torn between desire and manners, and manners were having a hard time of it. Belying her svelte, concave figure topped to the north by a lustrous golden mane of hair that would be the pride of any lion, she would no more refuse a creamy bagel than Gollum would refuse the Ring. 'What'ssss that, Master? You say sod walking to Mordor for a game of soldiers, you are off to the Havens, so do I want the Ring? Sssss...give it to Boromir, he quite likesss it.'

She sat with Jady in a coffee emporium close to her place of work. Jady had telephoned her earlier and asked if he could meet her for lunch as he had something to discuss. So the treat was on him.

'Nothing's too good for my favourite Alison,' replied Jady pleasantly, rising to go to the counter. 'And my favourite advertising consultant.' He looked back at his long-time friend and smiled winningly. 'I want to pick your brains.'

Picking Alison's brains was not something many people outside her work did, preferring to take their chances with random fortune. Alison combined a warm and loving temperament and an industrial-strength sense of justice with a naivety that could have got her mugged in the Hundred Acre wood. Her relationship to reality mirrored her relationship to oxygen; she knew it mattered but did not let it ruin her day. All in all, Alison was a helpful, heart-warming person to call a friend, but you wouldn't want to be stuck in the jungle with her. 'Look at the pretty lion; shall we stroke it?'

This, of course, made her perfectly suited for a life in advertising, brand-building and promotion; and it was in this capacity that Jady wanted to pick her brains. Life, he reflected, he would handle himself.

He sipped his coffee in silence, eyeing the person opposite appraisingly, and waited. Susan, Hanif's secretary, removed the debris from the previous coffees, shot Hanif a disapproving 'who is this nasty man,' glance from behind his shoulder, and left, closing the door pointedly. Waiting a moment, Mr, Dauntliffe placed the coffee cup carefully on the centre of the place mat, and resumed.

'Well, Mr Singh, I am satisfied, so far, with this company's work and especially with your attitude. I need a man like you at the sharp end. As you know, identity cards are a controversial issue. They will happen anyway; it is inevitable. My objective, our objective, is to implement them with the minimum of fuss. It is vital for the smooth and steady transition to a knowledge-rich society that identity cards are implemented in Spawater with as little trouble as possible. In fact, no trouble at all.'

'There are bound to be hiccups,' Hanif replied, swallowing his resentment at Mr Dauntliffe's patronising manner and the implied suggestion that his assistant Susan could not be trusted. Hanif trusted Susan unreservedly - she disapproved equally of all his clients without fear or favour.

'Hiccups, yes,' conceded Mr Dauntliffe, sitting back, clasping his fingers together and twirling his thumbs, 'I can accept a few. That Luddite anti identity cards outfit, whatever they are called, is causing a bit of a fuss. This is inevitable when men of vision implement progress. However,' he raised his voice abruptly and sat up bolt upright, giving Hanif visions of vampires at sundown, 'it is your job to ensure that they are no more than hiccups. Any scandal could set the project back years. That must not be allowed to happen, Mr Singh -' Hanif felt Mr Dauntliffe would prefer to call him Igor '- and I am relying on you to make sure that it doesn't. Do I make myself clear? This must not fail.'

'Yes. It sounds like a great idea. Totally absurd, of course, but the best ideas often are. Handled properly, you could fool the whole country.' Alison giggled merrily and continued. 'Actually, the more I think about it the better it seems.' She leant forward, absently brushing her hair from her eyes. 'You see, Jady, the usual problem with promoting a product is that the better you make it appear to be and the higher you raise people's expectations, the more disappointed they are when they finally come across it. Of course, in your case, this doesn't apply. Yes, it is brilliant. If you handle it properly, it can't fail.'

'It will be a disaster. That's the one thing I am sure of; it will be an unmitigated mess.'

Joanna sipped her coffee, absently spilling the lukewarm liquid down her chin without noticing. 'You know what Jady is like; you know what Ali is like and as for poor Arnie...'

Joanna was not in the best of humours. Sitting with Jenna in the unfair-trade coffee bar adjacent to her workplace she was unloading her worries, or at any rate, talking about them. Jenna, familiar with the protagonists, was not entirely sympathetic. Lady Macbeth would have piped her eye, not Jenna.

'Honestly Joey, you underestimate your Jady sometimes. Yes I agree, any scheme that involves seeking advice from Alison sounds about as convincing as a drunk's promise, but Jady knows what he's doing. After all, Alison came up trumps with that chicken farming business a while back, and you have to admit, when it comes to advertising she knows her stuff. As for Arnie, he worships the ground Jady stumbles on.'

Joanna hardly ever expected sycophantic agreement from Jenna, and hardly ever got it. A smidgeon of empathy once in a while would be appreciated though, and she informed Jenna of this.

'Yes, I agree,' agreed Jenna, nonchalantly stirring her cup, 'and you have my complete support as always. My point is that you worry too much. Let's go over the thing again. Jady is up to one of his shady-Jady schemes to keep the wolf from the door and halfway down the drive. It is something to do with marketing, or promotion, or whatever it is that Alison does when she leaves the real world and enters her advertising agency. Ali must be good at what she does, or at blackmailing her boss - either is a good career move - so it is only reasonable that Jady would look to her for help. The more off-the-wall the scheme, the more Alison is the woman for the job. Which reminds me,' she dropped her spoon into the flower vase, 'what is the scheme, anyway?'

'That's just it,' replied Joanna miserably, 'I don't know. Jady explained it to me, how he intends to promote a brand and sell it for sacks of money, as he put it, using Arnie as the unique selling proposition, but it still doesn't make sense. I think I will just leave him to it as usual.'

Joanna was far too preoccupied with her fight against identity cards to get deeply involved in Jady's schemes. They were close, but kept a little bit of space for themselves. It worked for them.

'I see your point,' agreed Jenna. 'Ignorance is bliss, that's why you never see an unhappy turkey. Also it looks much better in court. No, seriously Joey, I shouldn't worry about it. Jady wishes to promote something using Arnie to help, and Alison -' Jenna couldn't suppress a giggle, '- Alison is generously donating her professional advice. I won't say it can't fail, but it will probably not do too much harm. I should leave them to it if I were you.' Jenna drained her own tepid cup. 'Now, time to go. I have got to get to the Hall.'

'Oh, how is that going?' asked Joanna, relieved by Jenna's reassurance and pleased to change the subject.

'Not so good,' responded Jenna, rising and grimacing simultaneously, like a deep-sea diver late for an appointment, 'I'll tell you about it tonight.'

Joanna rose too. 'See you at Lifeboats'.'

'See you at Lifeboats', and don't worry about the money, it is all on me.'

Jady put down his home telephone and smiled the smile of one whose plans are going according to plan. After a successful meeting with Alison, he called Arnie and arranged to meet him in Lifeboats' that evening to discuss his part in the scheme. As Jady expected, Arnie agreed with enthusiasm.

Arnie was going through a bad time. He had made the grand gesture of resigning on principle only to discover that his mother, with whom he lived, preferred rent. Mrs. Bennett was a great admirer of Hanif and persistently encouraged Arnie to apologise to him for his childish pique, as she put it, and earn some wages. Arnie had intended going to Lifeboats' that evening anyway, to play Pool and get some peace, so Jady's invite was an exciting bonus. His life was currently a mixture of melancholy and boredom, two emotions of which Jady could never be accused. Bugs Bunny, yes, Groucho, possibly, but Jady, no.

'Interesting chat?' Susan directed this remark pointedly to her boss as she cleared up the coffee paraphernalia. Recognising her tone of disapproval Hanif went on the defensive.

'All right, Susan; Mr. Dauntliffe is our most important client and must be humoured. I agree he is not the type I would care to socialise with but facilitators cannot be choosers. We just have to put up with it.'

Susan gave Hanif a look reminiscent of Rhett Butler bidding final farewell to Scarlet, and departed.

Hanif sighed despondently. Things were not going well at all. No, that was not true. The implementation was going according to plan. Identity cards were being distributed to the people of Spawater with remarkably little fuss; no mass card-burnings or protests, and the card readers were being installed in municipal and other buildings according to schedule. Soon, Spawater would be the first town in the country to be 'knowledge rich', as Mr Dauntliffe put it, so things were shaping up splendidly.

Why, then, was he so out of sorts? After all, he supported compulsory identity cards; he believed that people would eventually come to love them and wonder how they managed before. So why was he unhappy? True, Mr. Dauntliffe was an unpleasant person to have to work with - Stalin would be an improvement - but Hanif had worked with difficult clients before without the feeling that there was gloop where his soul used to be. It was not the job, which was going well and one he believed in; it was not the client, unpleasant though he undoubtedly was. So what was it? What was this worm of unease devouring his sense of worth?

Hanif looked out of the window at the pedestrians and drivers going about their affairs, apparently oblivious to each other's aspirations. In the bright, reflective sunshine, the street was lively and invigorating. The creative anarchy involved in total strangers on foot and in vehicles meandering seamlessly, seemingly at random, successfully negotiating their way through to their disparate destinations, inspired Hanif to creative and productive thought.

It was Joanna. And Arnie. And Jady and the gang at Lifeboats'. Hanif was upset at being at loggerheads with his friends. Stalin could wave his former comrades goodbye if they disagreed with him, or even if they didn't. Hanif was made of flabbier stuff. He believed in compulsory identity cards and they did not. It was an honest disagreement and one where opposing views could be respected. There was no need to let it ruin their friendship.

Hanif picked up the telephone.

'Hello? Mr. Pettifogg? Dauntliffe here. Mobile call so I will keep it brief. Yes, it is all going according to plan. The organisation in Spawater is doing a sterling job. The person in charge of local operations is a Mr. Hanif Singh, a good man. Believes in the project unreservedly.'

Mr. Dauntliffe was driving back to London. On his hands-free, he was reporting to his civil service and consortium subordinate.

'We can leave the day-to-day running in his hands; the bigger changes will come later. Much later.' Mr. Dauntliffe looked aside at the orderly row of cars in the slow lane, each equidistant from the next and travelling at exactly the same, sedate speed. This pleased him. Complete strangers co-operating together. The drivers in the slow lane had not met and probably never would, but they all knew the rules and obeyed them without fuss or protest. If only people could behave that way all the time; in cars or out of them. Well, it was Mr. Dauntliffe's intention that they would. Order and control, and an end to Anarchy; that was the way forward, the slow, sane, sensible way to run society, and he was the one who would implement it.

Without warning, not even a flashing indicator, one of the slow lane cars pulled out in to the middle and accelerated. Mr Dauntliffe was obliged to adjust his speed momentarily. A flash of anger contorted his features. 'Try that on a motorway in the future, my friend, and you will pay,' he thought. Mr. Dauntliffe eased back into the soft, imitation leather seat that, womb-like, held him in comfort as he accelerated. 'Oh yes,' he continued, a cold determined expression replacing his flash of anger, 'you will pay.'

'I will pay, so you need have no worries on that score.'

Arnie wondered if he had become a celebrity and was the last to know. First there was Jady insisting he go to Lifeboats', all expenses paid; now his former boss, Hanif, was making the same offer. What was a youngster to do? Simple really.

'Ok boss, or ex-boss, I will see you tonight at Lifeboats'.'

Identity Cards
Chapter Three

'Where is he? Where is he?' Ron passed Jady's white wine across the imposing, heavily varnished bar and answered his own rhetorical question. 'He is where he always is, of course, where he has decided to spend his life. It is not his second home, it is his first. I wouldn't mind, but since he lost his job with your friend Hanif he manages to make one drink last the whole evening. I lose more money in Pool chalk than I make serving him. Honestly, Jady, can't you get young Arnie a job? Or at least buy him some chalk?'

Ron, owner of The Lifeboat Club, was on his usual form. Upon leaving the catering division of the Navy at a rate of knots a few years back, Ron had sunk his severance pay into what he'd thought, with the optimism of a wasp issuing picnic invitations, would be an upmarket, sophisticated, social drinking club. Persuaded by the helpful estate agent's brother-in-law that a nautical theme was what was required, and also by the amazing stroke of fate that the aforementioned brother-in-law just happened to have the very fixtures and fittings to hand, Ron dived in. He'd sunk his all and was now marooned. Instead of sophisticated, affluent social elites, Ron found himself with a clientele that would be cosy doing deals with Arthur Daley, Del Boy and Bilko, as well as the likes of Jady and associates, including the now financially challenged Arnie. Ron would love to jump ship but nobody would board her; the combination of ready cash and gullibility being a rare thing in Spawater. Ron himself still reigned as the undisputed champion. He could not set sail into the sunset, laden up to the Plimsoll line as he was with debts. Given the professionalism, these days, of the Fire Service and the insurance actuaries, there was no choice for poor Ron but to continue splicing his customers' main braces, face pressed firmly to the telescope keeping a weather eye out for a rescue ship. Ben Gunn knew the feeling.

'Nil desperandum, shipmate,' Jady responded insouciantly, 'your troubles may soon be over. I have a proposition to make to young Millado that will enable him to drink himself stupid and fill the Pool room with chalk dust. In fact, pour him a lager, will you, I'll take it to him. Stick it on my account.'

'It won't involve the Club, will it?' Never one to look at the sunny side - where others saw treasure maps, Ron saw litter - Ron was continually disconcerted by Jady's breezy cheeriness. 'I do not want any underhanded flim-flam here.' Ron began pouring Arnie's drink in a suspicious manner.

Jady was used to such negativity, he could power new age batteries on it. 'Nae fret, laddie. This is all honest and above board. In fact, Alison is my agent. You don't get more honest than that.'

'Ye gods,' retorted Ron, handing him Arnie's lager and hurrying to adjust Jady's account before the slate ledger self-destructed in disbelief. 'I don't want to know.'

'Very wise,' conceded Jady amicably and sauntered off bearing liquid gifts to the Arnie-filled Pool room.

Ron returned to his routine Club manager activities, bickering with the members and generally carrying out his self-imposed sentence, and was neither surprised nor enthused by the arrival of some of those who he knew as the Jady gang.

Alison and Jenna, for that's who it was, strolled into the main quarters of the Club, selected a large table in the darkest corner, parked their accoutrements, jackets, bags, and in Jenna's case, Ron suspected, knuckledusters, and strolled barwards with a buoyancy that made Jady's sauntering resemble forelock tugging.

'Belay there, Ron old buddypal, how are things? Shipshape and Spawater fashion? Or as normal? Never mind, we are here now so things are looking up. Fancy a drink? My good friend Ali and I will have a bottle of your excellent house white. Give us three glasses. Joanna will be here soon. By the way, have you seen young Arnie? Joanna is looking for him.'

Ron reached for the wine bottle. Jenna might rabbit a bit, he reflected philosophically, as Plato did of his friend and mentor Socrates, but at least she always puts business across the counter. It compensated for the fact that despite being an original member, she had not once paid her Club dues. Swings and roundabouts.

'Your friend Arnie is with your friend Jady in the Pool room, or Arnie's room as I shall rename it. I think they are in conference.'

'Jady is always in conference,' chortled Jenna, reaching for the bottle. Jenna knew Joanna's partner of old, and liked and admired him, seeing in Jady a reflection of herself. Desperate Dan and Friar Tuck had a similar mutual respect regarding their appreciation of cow pie.

Alison brushed her hair aside and picked up the three proffered glasses.

'Hello, Ron,' she smiled sweetly. 'When Joanna comes in tell her we have her drink ready.'

'Cheers.'

'Cheers.' Jady replied to the toast. His timing was fortuitous, arriving in the Pool room just as Arnie finished off yet another opponent. Jady looked on admiringly and with satisfaction. Arnie was good. Very good. Chivvying him away from the tables, Jady sat him in a corner and made with the drinks.

'So, Millado, how are things with you these days?'

Arnie shuffled uncomfortably. He had resigned over Hanif arguing with Joanna. A Grand Gesture. The trouble, he was discovering, is that grand gestures are like grand binges. Great fun at the time; they do not seem so clever the next day. Ask anyone on Monday morning.

'It was a noble gesture of yours, resigning like that, I must say,' continued Jady seamlessly. 'Not employed yet? Good. Listen Millado, drink up, lots more where that came from. Now, I have a proposition to put to you.'

‘So what is this proposition? I bet it is something appalling and totally illegal. I also bet it will make Jady a big pot of cash. Am I right?’

‘Partly right, but no cigar.’ Alison took a dainty sip of wine, shuddered slightly, and continued to reply to Jenna’s question. ‘If it works it will certainly make Jady a lot of money, and it is appalling, but it is not illegal, so far as I know.’

‘Do tell then,’ tched Jenna impatiently, ‘What’s it all about?’

‘Hang on, Jen, here comes Joanna.’

Joanna approached them from the bar area, having been directed to the recess by Ron. Routine hellos over, the three friends settled down for a spot of enlightened conversation.

‘Jenna, are you free next Wednesday?’

‘Why?’

‘I want you to accompany me to London.’

‘So, what do you think of that then?’

Arnie was confused. Over a drink, Jady explained his idea, the scheme, and Arnie’s role in it. It was all a bit sudden and original for Arnie to take in, in one go; he was baffled.

‘I don’t quite get it. Could you go over it again? It seems a bit confusing.’

A serene man - Jady could give lessons in anger management to Buddhists - Jady related the idea once more.

‘You know your Jady is in the Pool room with Arnie, don’t you?’ Alison remarked.

‘Yes, Ron told me. Jady is drinking white wine and Arnie is on lager. Jady has gone to see Arnie about his latest project. He knows I don’t approve of Arnie getting involved in any more of his schemes but we have agreed to give him the opportunity to hear what Jady has to say. Well,’ Joanna continued dully, ‘Jady has agreed, anyway. Arnie is an adult, technically, so it would be patronising to veto the idea without giving him the chance to hear it, I suppose.’

'Yes, yes, yes,' cried out Jenna impatiently, 'but what the hell is the bloody scheme in the first place? If Jady can tell Arnie, can't someone tell me?' She giggled, slightly embarrassed. 'Not that I am nosy, you understand; call it professional curiosity.'

'Of course,' laughed Joanna, for the first time that day. This is what friends are for, she considered, to cheer each other up when things look grim. Good to be home.

'Actually,' she continued, 'I was rather hoping that Jady's technical advisor could explain it all to me.'

'Who is that?' asked Alison.

Jenna placed her glass on the table, looked deeply into Alison's eyes, grinned and whispered, 'I think she means you.'

'Me?'

Joanna nodded in confirmation and continued. 'Jady told me he saw you today to discuss his latest scheme, involving himself and Arnie.'

'Oh, that. Yes he did. He told me all about it.'

'So would you be so kind as to say to us what he said to you?' pleaded Jenna mildly. 'Before we all die?'

'Of course, I thought that was the idea.'

'Excuse me?'

The girls, absorbed in their own little world, looked up.

'Erm,' Hanif was slightly self-conscious in front of Joanna due to their strained relations. This had no effect on Jenna, of course, or Alison.

'Hi, Hanny Honey,' replied Jenna, recovering first. 'Draw up a chair and a glass.'

'Hello there, Hanif,' added Alison, smiling.

Not to be out-welcomed, Joanna joined in. 'Welcome aboard, Han.' She was not going to let their difference of opinion ruin their long-standing friendship.

'Yes, I will be glad to join you, but first I am looking for Arnie. Is he in the Pool room, do you know?'

'Where else?' replied Jenna. 'Why, are you going to give him his job back?'

Jenna's direct approach and raising of an awkward issue disconcerted Hanif, as she'd known it would. Experiencing a hot flush and hoping it was not obvious, Hanif replied.

'I have kept his job open for him. He can have it back at any time. Excuse me, I'll see you later.' Hanif departed hurriedly.

'Jady is on white wine and Arnie wants lager,' teased Jenna after him. 'Anyway,' she continued unabashed, 'where were we?'

'Alison was just about to explain Jady's latest scheme.'

'So that's the scheme, pure and simple.' Jady sipped his wine in a satisfied manner. Explaining such an abstract idea as his scheme to a computer programmer such as Arnie entitled him to both drink and satisfaction.

Arnie did not share Jady's satisfaction; in fact Arnie still couldn't grasp how on Earth the scheme could possibly make Jady money, but he did not wish to endure another explanation. Fermat's theorem, yes; Jady's machinations, no.

'I would hardly call it simple,' he replied daringly, drinking his lager with considerably less satisfaction, 'but I think I have got the hang of it. My part in it anyway. And if it works, I get twenty-five percent?'

'After expenses, yes. I will pay you a stipend, that's a basic salary plus beer money, which will ultimately be deducted from your cut. Should the scheme fall flat,' Jady frowned, 'then I will take the loss. You win either way.'

Before Arnie could drink to that, Hanif arrived, clutching three flowing glasses.

'Hello all.' Hanif placed the drinks on the table. 'Peace offering. May I join you?' Jady smiled and Hanif relaxed. 'Well, well, young Arnie, how are things with you?'

'Hello, ex-boss,' grinned Arnie cheekily. 'Things are just jim dandy. The chief and I have been discussing a business proposition.'

'Pull up a seat, Han old boy,' contributed Jady gaily whilst accepting the proffered white wine. 'Welcome aboard.'

Hanif obeyed gratefully. After what had occurred between him and Jady's Joanna as well as young Arnie, he could have been cast adrift. As Helen of Troy was oft to remark, it is good to be amongst friends.

'So, Arnie, Jady, tell me about this business proposition.'

'Here's to Jady. A man after my own heart. At least, he would be if he thought it was worth a buck. Well, Joey, I have to hand it to you. Living with Jady must be a laugh a minute.'

Alison had explained Jady's scheme to Joanna and Jenna. Quicker on the uptake than Arnie, they grasped the idea in one shot.

Joanna was tired. Much as she loved Jady, this was quite enough of him and his clever-clever schemes for one day. Time to change the subject.

'Anyway, Jen, what's all this about trouble at t'mill?'

'T'mill?'

'Trouble at the Hall, I mean. You said things there were not so good.'

Metaphorical storm clouds darkened the atmosphere. The anguished howls of twenty werewolves opening their vets' appointment letters rent the still, fetid air asunder. Frightened villagers lit their torches and honed their stakes, eyeing their first-borns quizzically.

Joanna had opened a wound.

'So that's it?' Hanif laughed. Jady never failed to astonish him. After swearing a trustworthy Hanif to secrecy, Jady had given him the gist of the scheme. 'I must say, Jady, this time you excel yourself, using identity cards to your advantage. And Arnie too. Take the money and run, Arnie. That's my advice.' Hanif drank some of his wine. 'While we're on the subject, this identity card trial won't last forever. There is always a job waiting for you when it is over.'

Arnie blushed uncomfortably. He was not used to being in so much demand. The two adults who had shown more confidence in him than legions of schoolteachers, social workers and therapists combined were buying him drinks and offering him work. Like Tinkerbell, people believed in him. Life was full.

'Thanks, boss; when the chief and I have finished our project,' he looked ingratiatingly at the condescending Jady, 'I might well take you up on that, but you are embarrassing me now. Can we drop the subject?'

'Let's change the subject, shall we?'

Jenna had explained to the girls exactly what the problem was between her and the Town Hall. She had much more to say on what she proposed to do about it, but Lifeboats' was not the proper place for that type of discussion. Jenna was as fond of a drink as the next dipsomaniac, and as such knew that after a few liveners her discretion often went west with the wagons. Her solutions to the slings and arrows of outrageous fortune that occasionally made the elementary error of coming her way were best discussed in private.

Ever ready to change any subject any time, Alison chirped inquisitively, 'What was that you were saying, Joey, about going to London?'

'London? Wouldn't touch the place with a bargepole. What do you want to go there for?'

As the owner of the Club, Ron felt he had carte blanche to join in any conversation he wished whilst doing the rounds. As he whisked Alison's and Joanna's nearly empty wine glasses onto his tray - Jenna's had diplomatic immunity - he gave them his two pence worth. 'What has London got that Spawater hasn't?'

'Privacy,' countered Jenna, offering up a silent prayer to her favourite god, Bacchus, and thanking Alison for so recently changing the subject.

'Actually, Ron,' said Joanna in a placatory manner, 'if Jenna is up for it, we will be going to London next Wednesday for a meeting of the national Campaign Against Identity Cards and the national database. You are welcome to come along too.'

'You mean you are still fighting against identity cards?' questioned Ron from behind Joanna's shoulder. 'Why bother? You know they are inevitable so why not make the best of it? You carry identification anyway, driving licence, credit cards. So why bother causing a fuss?'

Joanna bristled like an electrified hedgehog. Normally a peaceful, easygoing person, the compulsory implementation of identity cards drove her to distraction. The only thing that annoyed her more was the way so many people meekly accepted them as though there was nothing they could do about it. What was the point of being alive, she thought, if only to live as robots? Forcing people to justify their very existence to the State, the same State that should be the servant of the people and not the other way around, made her madder than a scorned hornet. Abruptly she turned and faced him.

'What the Hell do you know about it? If you think we have made a fuss so far, you ain't seen nothing yet. If you won't stand up for yourself, make way for those who will. And give me back my wine glass.'

This was a side of Joanna Ron had not encountered before. Come to think of it, he didn't much want to encounter it again. Returning the wine glass, plus Alison's for luck, Ron muttered that it wasn't *his* idea to have identity cards and it was no use taking it out on *him*. Joanna remained unmoved. Chastened and with head bowed, Ron skulked away. Right, he thought, I think the Club subscriptions should go up again this year. Cheered by this happy notion, he straightened up and continued about his business.

'I say, that was a bit strong, old gal!' said Jenna, impressed. 'But right on, sister.'

'You should not let it get to you, Joey,' clucked a concerned Alison. 'After all, he is right. It is not his fault; it is the fault of the government. You should blame them.'

'That's right, Ali; you tell it like it is,' agreed Jenna enthusiastically. 'Now Joey, book the tickets for Wednesday. It is time to fight back.'

Identity Cards
Chapter Four

Michael was a clever man. Born in Austria - Germany lite - and educated at a minor British public school, he was equally at home in either country. From his early schooldays, his teachers reported that he would go far. As the years progressed, Michael did not disappoint. His import-export businesses - smuggling, some would say - ensured that his mind was broadened. He traversed the longitudes and latitudes of the globe, often at high speed, narrowly leading a field which consisted of a disparate and sometimes desperate group of followers straddling both sides of the legal divide.

To put it simply, which is something he never did, Michael was a crook. A dishonest man whose saving grace was that, like Robin Hood, he did not bother stealing from the poor.

A relaxed and amicable mastermind, Michael sat drinking a meditative coffee al fresco in the sunshine at the café opposite Spawater Town Hall. The Hall itself, however, was not occupying his highly developed brain. No, the object having that honour was encased within the large, semi-open air building next door: the building housing the Spawater Baths.

The Romans had constructed the Spawater Baths in the good old days, before rising villa prices and the realisation that Rome sold better wine obliged them to leave the Baths to the locals. They had long since become Spawater's pride and joy; like Loch Ness and Nessie, a symbol of Spawater's superiority over other towns. 'And how many monsters does your town have, the noo?' Rival areas might have bigger cinemas, or busier bypasses, bluer skies or cheaper pubs, but none of them could match Spawater in the Spawater Baths stakes. Mention Spawater in any company and immediately people would refer to the world famous Spawater Baths.

Michael intended to steal them.

'Are you serious? You mean now?'

'Oh yes, if you can. You see, we do not stand still in this business. If someone has an idea, it is considered immediately. If the big cheeses approve, they act on it straight away. If they do not, they reject it straight away. Quite logical, really.'

Jady agreed that it was quite logical, really, though what acquaintance was shared by Alison and logic, he was at a loss to imagine. Still, there it was; Jady had asked Alison to act for him and she had. It was all a bit sudden, though.

'You really mean now? Right away?' Jady was rarely nonplussed, normally being very plussed indeed, but Alison's ability to move events without really noticing astounded him.

She ran her hair idly through her fingers. 'If you are ready, of course. I told my bosses that you have an idea to promote a brand using the fact that Spawater is the first town to introduce those identity cards that Joanna and Jenna are so annoyed about. They are in London for a couple of days, aren't they? Attending that meeting. Anyway, I told them that you had a plan whereby we could use this identity card thing to our advantage. The big cheeses, I mean, not Joey and Jenna. That would be silly. Of course they are interested, Jady. The big cheeses, I mean. We are all interested in the brand-building world; turning things to our advantage is what we do. It is how we make our money. So, can you come in today and meet the big cheeses? If you can, it will have to be at six this evening, just when it gets quiet.'

Could he? Jady mused. Never at a loss for long, he recovered his equanimity and replied. 'Jolly good, Ali, I will be there. I won't bring Millado though; I think it would all be a bit sudden for him. Can I meet you outside in the coffee bar at ten to?'

'All right Jady; ten to six in the coffee bar; this meeting should be fun.'

'It was a very useful meeting. Things are going well. I am favourably impressed.'

'And you approve of this Mr Singh character? You said as much on the telephone.'

Mr Pettifogg passed the silver tea tray to Mr Dauntliffe. They were in a discreet corner of their London Club, discussing progress.

'Yes, he is very keen on the project.' Mr Dauntliffe looked up from the tea tray and stared into Mr Pettifogg's eyes. 'What he thinks is the project, anyway.'

'Quite.'

'The introduction of Identification Cards in Spawater has exceeded expectations. The man in the street does not mind - or hardly minds - another piece of plastic in his pocket. When we double it up as a driving licence and passport, he will be queuing for it. What resistance we have encountered has consisted only of the usual suspects; the unholy alliance of the extreme, loony anti-globalisation hippies and the libertarian, Little Englander Right. The average man in the street could not care less.'

Mr Dauntliffe paused, poured his tea out of the silver teapot into the middle of his cup, set the teapot down in its proper place, carefully added the milk in a clockwise direction, no sugar, and continued. 'We are winning, Pettifogg, we are ahead of the game. At this rate we will be able to move to stage two ahead of schedule.'

Mr Dauntliffe was a man of limited emotions and furnace-forged control of them, but the excitable child that resides in us all escaped momentarily. He thumped the table, making a storm in his teacup and falsettoed, 'I tell you, Pettifogg, we are going to win!'

'Keep your voice down. Where do you think you are?'

Mr Dauntliffe regained control, a little irked that his junior should rightly reprimand him, like Robin reminding Batman to lay off the bat juice before driving the Batmobile.

'Yes, you're right, Pettifogg. We must be calm and calculating at all times. Now, how are things at your end?'

'Just great, Michael, exactly how you said it would be.'

‘Excellent.’ Despite being right nearly as often as Nature, Michael still got pleasure from being reminded of the fact. His lieutenant had returned from his public tour around the Spawater Baths with the message Michael had hoped for.

‘Get yourself a coffee and tell me what happened while it is still fresh in your memory.’ Michael switched on a discreet recorder so he could pour over the account at leisure. He was a meticulous and organised planner who, whilst being realistic and therefore aware that the difference between success and failure is often down to chance, nevertheless believed in stacking the odds. Monte Carlo would not have liked him. It was his attention to detail and his consequent reputation amongst the cognoscenti that had landed him this assignment. His biggest and, if successful, his last, this would pay him enough to retire to a life of ill-earned leisure. Jason felt the same way about pilfering the Golden Fleece.

His assistant returned with a latté.

‘All right, Erich, tell me in your own words, but with discretion, precisely what happened from the moment you queued up for a tour of the Baths. This is being taped so that our colleagues hear the same account. Don’t let that bother you but please bear it in mind and speak clearly but quietly.’

‘I cannot remember the precise details, of course, but this is a rough outline.’ Alison placed her empty coffee cup carelessly on the edge of the table. ‘The big cheeses are always looking for new ideas. New angles, they call them; or blue sky thinking outside the box, all that old toffee. I told them that you had a new idea based on those identity cards. They are interested and would like to meet you. That is it, really.’

That was good enough for Jady. After his initial surprise that things could move so quickly, Jady was back on top of his game. Putting down his dead orange juice glass, he stood up and graciously lent his arm, unnecessarily, to Alison.

‘All right, Ali, shall we go? Once more unto the breech.’

When Michael accepted his assignment, he took a large down payment in order that it should not fail due to underinvestment, and to enable him to hire the best accomplices. This was no problem; money was one thing his client had in abundance. He was a fixture on the world's unofficial rich list, regularly pipping King Midas to the post. With money no object, Michael hired the best. He assembled a team of English-speaking Germans with enough brains and expertise to put Ali Baba and his gang to shame. All experts; two women and, himself included, two men. Strictly professional, they could pose as two couples where necessary, fitting in as unobtrusively as zebras in a bar-code factory.

'So that's how it was, Michael,' reported Erich. 'I had to show my 'Visitor to Spawater' temporary identity card just to get into the queue, and then stick my eyeball into their biometric iris scanner. When the scanner accepted me I was given a permit to explore the Baths, but I had to sign for it and have my thumb read by a biometric thumb reader.'

'How was this done?'

'By putting my thumb on a small glass screen.'

'Was the screen cleaned between users?'

'Yes, using alcohol, I think. It slowed the whole process down. They are really, really thorough.'

'What was the permit for?'

'I had to show it to a uniformed official to enter the Baths, then to one when I was leaving. They scanned it using some kind of portable scanner.' Erich paused for breath. 'They also had an official asking people at random to show their receipts.'

'At this rate they will be asking visitors to take off their shoes,' Michael laughed.

Erich grinned knowingly. 'Not quite, but they were nearly that paranoid. It looks like a close run thing.'

'Did anyone object? The public, I mean.'

'They grumbled at bit but they did what they were told.'

‘How about people with bags?’

‘Bags were put through a scanner like the ones at airports.’

‘Excellent, excellent, couldn’t be better.’ Michael was delighted. The whole setup was obviously a ruinously expensive administrative nightmare, which would appear, to the bureaucrats who ordered it from their headquarters in the clouds, totally secure. And so it was, if people played by the rules; clearly the control freaks were not expecting cheats.

‘Did you find out who runs the place?’

Erich patted his inside pocket. ‘It is all in here, Michael. They give out loads of literature bragging about how security is the watchword and just let the terrorists try it on in Spawater and they will get what is coming to them. They have wasted a couple of rainforests on this glossy bragging and the guy responsible seems proud of himself. There is a picture of the ‘Security Controller and Amenities Facilitator’ on the front of each booklet. He is a rulebook hero and thinks he’s fighting on the beaches.’

Michael laughed. ‘After the weekend, we work. Tonight, we celebrate.’ This was just too easy.

‘It won’t be easy,’ intoned Mr Dauntliffe portentously, ‘but it will be done. Now, if you will excuse me, Pettifogg, it is time for me to leave.’

Reaching for his leather briefcase, Mr Dauntliffe clicked it open, straightened his papers, and placed them in the correct file. It was this attention to detail that ensured his success in all his projects. Nothing was left to chance. He and his colleague, Mr Pettifogg, successfully completed their progress report meeting to their mutual satisfaction.

‘So,’ summed up his colleague, ‘for the immediate future we leave Spawater in the capable hands of your agent, Mr Singh, while we continue to gather details for the national database.’

‘That’s correct. Unless there are any unforeseen hitches we can simply continue with the plan.’

Mr Pettifogg halted, struck by a thought. 'That reminds me; you are aware that there is a meeting in the local university by the Campaign Against Identity Cards?'

Mr Dauntliffe frowned. 'Of course; one of my employees is attending. You see,' he leaned forward conspiratorially, 'the difference between our side and theirs, and one of the reasons why we will win, is that their activities have to be carried out in the public eye, whereas ours take place in secret.'

Mr Pettifogg smirked in agreement. 'It is quite ironic, really. Here we are arguing that the State should know everything about the activities and views of its citizens, whilst making sure that none of its citizens know our activities and views; the activities and views of the State. We work in secret to discover their secrets and they try to keep their secrets by acting openly.'

Mr Dauntliffe nodded wisely. 'And it is for the good of the State, and consequently the good of the subjects of that State, that it should remain so.' He stood up and tucked his briefcase under his arm. Turning to leave, he added, 'Remember, in order to succeed, we must be in complete control at all times and the public must be kept in the dark. That is the recipe for success.'

'So in order for the scheme to work, everyone must know about it. As always, publicity is the key. Yes, I like it. I like it.'

Jady had spent the best part of two hours explaining his idea to Alison's big cheeses. They had discussed it in private and decided unanimously to go ahead. This was hardly surprising. Not only was it a scheme that pressed all the correct buttons - simple, lucrative, local and cheap - but it had a plausible advocate. Jady could have persuaded the judge that the Big Bad Wolf only blew the house down because he suffered from hay fever, or that the Seven Dwarfs were work-shy gold diggers.

'All right,' decided the cheeses, 'phone Alison and tell her that we are going with it and that she is to liaise between

Jady and ourselves, letting Jady have whatever he wants within reason and the allotted budget.'

Alison took the call in Lifeboats', where an anxious Jady and a relaxed Alison were sharing a bottle of house white.

'Ok, ok, all right. I will tell him. I will make the arrangements. Yes, it should be fun. Bye.' Alison smiled winningly at Jady and glanced at his wine glass.

Jady breathed out in relief and reset his blood pressure to one hundred and forty over ninety. After all, telling him it was no go would hardly come under the heading of 'fun', even for someone who found reality television entertaining.

'Tell all,' he said, raising his glass in anticipation. Jady's big fear in life was that one day he would run out of things to celebrate and have to admit that he drank because he liked it.

'Congratulations, Jady, they think it is a great idea and they want it to run. I am your liaison officer as agreed. We start on Monday. This could be quite fun. Oh, we had better tell young Arnie, hadn't we? After all, he plays a big part.'

'No worries, Ali, I'll tell him; now, how about some champagne?'

'No, I'm sorry, I cannot serve you. It is against the rules.' Looking the happiest he had all day, Ron shook his head in sham sadness at the well-dressed foursome requesting a table. 'Members only, you see. Non-members have to be signed in. Sorry.'

Happily, Ron turned aside. Owning the Club had some compensations and Ron enjoyed hiding behind 'rules is rules' when it suited him. He mainly used it to keep out the losers residing at the Spawater Refuge Centre on the opposite side of the block - known to all as Losers Corner - but elegant looking winners were not immune when Ron's back was playing him up.

'Hi there, great to see you. Shall I sign you in?' Jady was in the mood to celebrate and his rule was 'when I am celebrating, everybody is celebrating'.

'Do you know these people?' asked Ron doubtfully. 'Anyway, you can only sign in two.' Not for the first time, Ron suspected he was being put upon by Jady. With justification.

'Ali and I will sign our old friends in. Two each as arranged. And then I would like some champagne. Ali and I are celebrating. Oh, and send a glass to the Pool room with our compliments.'

Ron reached for the guestbook, dropped it onto the bar and sloped off to the cellar with the dignity of a punctured butler. So Jady was on the bubbly again, he thought morosely. Ours not to reason why, just accept the profits.

Jady proffered the book to the foursome. 'A boring formality, I'm afraid.'

'Thank you, er...'

'Jady. Pleased to meet you, er...'

'Michael. And that champagne is on us. We are celebrating too.'

Identity Cards
Chapter Five

'How often are you stopped by the police? How much more often do you think you would be stopped if they could demand to see your identity card? Ask the people of Belgium. They have a basic form of identity card and the police have developed into a universally disliked organisation due to their officiousness. As a result, the public are reluctant to cooperate with them and crime goes undetected. Everyone loses. And that's just with an old-fashioned card. The modern ones that threaten us are linked to a national database and would be demanded by every policeman, parking warden, postman, Council officer, doctor, butcher, baker, candlestick maker, Uncle Tom Cobleigh and all.'

Joanna and Jenna were in London, at a London University, attending a debate arranged by the Campaign Against Identity Cards. If they had not been against them before, they certainly were now. Joanna stole a glance at Jenna. She was looking at the stage knowingly, like Pythagoras in a geometry lesson. Joanna had not seen Jenna look so concerned since she was on antibiotics and had to knock off the drinking for a month.

'Surely you will only be stopped by the police if you have done something suspicious?' asked a voice from the floor.

'Suspicious in whose opinion?' came the reply. 'After all, if you were really acting suspiciously the police could stop you now, without identity cards. No. The words 'Can I see your identity card please,' or 'Show me your identity now!' will become the commonest words heard in the country; and you won't have to act suspiciously to hear them.'

Joanna agreed. She had come across people who would just love to say those words. And many more like herself who would be driven to distraction by them. The country would become a waking nightmare. There would be no shortage of people acting suspiciously then.

'Identity cards are the best thing ever to happen to us. If it is not blasphemous to say it, they are a godsend.'

So spoke Michael to his colleagues Erich, Marlene and Louise at the office hired for their operation. They had had an enjoyable evening in Lifeboats' the night before and were meeting up for an informal briefing and question and answer session prior to getting down to business the following Monday.

'Of course,' Louise agreed with a knowing smile, 'if people trust identity cards they will trust the holders of them. And, as you know, identity cards can be faked.'

Indeed they did know. All of them were carrying fake identity cards. While Erich nipped out for coffees, Michael mused contentedly on the situation.

The fledgling national database being introduced by a gullible Home Secretary had already accepted their fake identities. He smiled at how easy it was. Obtain false identification in an offshore tax haven that the government dare not investigate too closely, and use that as identification in the UK. How to fake a biometric eye scan? Specially designed contact lenses will deal with that. Use one set of lenses for each false identity but for heaven's sake, don't get the sets mixed up.

On completing their mission, the four would simply leave the country, destroy their fake identities, do their laundering using other biometric-inspired aliases to evade tax and awkward questions, go back to their real identities and spend the cash.

The Three Musketeers in the latter stages of a pub-crawl with the Laughing Cavalier could barely have competed in the guffawing stakes with this merry band. 'All for one and one for as many identities as we like.' Michael grinned. And identity cards were meant to make things more secure!

'Identity cards will make things more secure. I will give you some examples.' Hanif was holding a meeting in the Town

Hall with the principle business people and Social Services chiefs of Spawater. As part of his crusade to insinuate biometric readers into Spawater, he was obliged to give such talks.

'For example,' he continued, 'identity cards will prevent illegal immigrants working on the black market and make it easier to prosecute employers who use them,' - a pair of restaurant owners exchanged glances - 'as all visitors to this country staying three months or more will have to register for biometric residence permits. Using multiple identities is a typical practice of terrorists and other criminals. This will prevent them from entering the country under false names more than once. Identity cards will also ensure that the Social Services are not used by people who are not entitled to them; illegal immigrants and so forth. This will lead to great savings which can be used for investment in the Social Services or other good causes.'

Hanif smiled encouragingly. He did not feel too encouraged himself; he sensed that he was not really gripping his audience. When in doubt... 'Any questions so far?'

'What is to stop criminals making fake identity cards?' asked one of the audience.

'Good question,' replied Hanif, reassured. This was an easy one. 'We take your biometric details, for example an iris scan from the eye, and enter them onto the national database. A copy is on your card. When you wish to enter a building such as a hospital, Town Hall or place of work, you will put your eye to a biometric scanner which will read your details. This information will be sent to the national database centre for confirmation that it is you. It is impossible to fake this information.'

'How does the information get from the eye scanner to the national database and back?'

'Via the telephone lines, like the internet. That makes it almost instant so it will not delay you by much.' Hanif noticed some tittering. 'And I know what you will say about the internet but let me assure you that it is totally secure. Next question please.'

'What is to stop criminals making fake identity cards?' asked a member of the audience.

'I am glad you asked that,' replied one of the Campaign Against Identity Cards people on the podium. Joanna and Jenna listened intently.

'The fact is, not a lot. To begin with, what identification do you need in order to obtain a card? Passport, driving licence? Telephone bill? These things can be faked. The authorities claim that as they develop the national database they will make things harder for criminals. What they ignore is that criminals learn too. This is a great opportunity for drug Barons, for example, to invest in biometric readers and card producers of their own; for money laundering and political reasons.' She smiled around the audience, catching their attention. 'The Barons cannot believe their luck. Just as they would be devastated if drugs were ever legalised, and bribe politicians to ensure they are not, so they are delighted at the scheme to give everybody in the European Union - Britain is just the start - a number, electronically linked to a file holding everything there is to know about them. Health, age, opinions, IQ, likes and dislikes, friends and associates, criminal records from birth, anything blackmailable, of course, and so on. Any technical innovations the government can produce, the Barons can copy. Any expertise the government can hire, the Barons can intimidate or bribe. There is nothing technical governments can do that drug Barons cannot. The only reason they do not forge perfect banknotes is that they do not wish to upset the world's financial system, as it would screw up their own investments.'

Pausing to let this sink in, she went nuclear. 'Criminals will milk our welfare state dry. They will hack in to the national database, plant fake names and claim full benefits. How? Simple. When people from abroad wish to become British citizens, top criminals will take their DNA, carry out biometric scans, copy fingerprints and other details and create a false identity on the database, indistinguishable from genuine British citizens. They will obtain genuine identity cards containing their true biometric details alongside their new identities. They will become British citizens overnight. The gangs will become even richer and Britain will become poorer.

'Drug Barons and top criminal gangs have more money than governments and no more scruples. Oh yes,' she concluded. 'The introduction of biometric identification will herald a new, golden age of crime and corruption. It will make 1930s Chicago seem like the Garden of Eden.'

'How will identity cards prevent terrorism?'

'Well,' replied Hanif, 'it will make it much harder for known terrorists to enter the country.'

'What about the ones we don't know?'

There was more tittering. Hanif could see this was not going down too well. That was the trouble, he thought ruefully; any system is only as good as its operators. If people took the threat of terrorism seriously they would be halfway to defeating it. Take the manager of the Town Hall and the Baths, he thought, perking up. Now there was a man who took his responsibilities seriously. The place was as secure as a tortoise's freehold. Checkpoints everywhere, biometric scanners on display, everything X-rayed and random checks throughout. Of course, it caused delay, but that was a small price to pay for security.

'Even if we don't know them, we may know their friends. The national database will be able to cross-reference people so that if someone is connected with just one terror suspect, we can and will refuse access or even arrest them on suspicion.'

'That lets out the politicians then,' laughed a wag to some applause. Hanif sighed.

'Isn't that a bit scary?' asked a serious voice.

'If you have nothing to hide,' Hanif parroted the official mantra, 'you have nothing to fear.'

'What about British-born terrorists who have proper identity cards?'

'Look, I did not say it was perfect, but it is better than nothing. Now let's take a short break.'

'How will identity cards prevent terrorism?' asked someone from the floor.

'They won't,' replied one of the speakers. 'Well, they might, if the terrorists obeyed our rules. For example, visitors to this country can stay for three months before they need to apply for an identity card, so we could ask the terrorists not to strike for the first three months.'

Some laughter. Another speaker joined in.

'The government claim that this new system would prevent known terrorists entering at all. Except through the proper points of entry, perhaps, as they do already. Trouble is, the government cannot even keep drugs out of prisons; to expect to keep people out of the country by introducing identity cards is just absurd. How will that guard the beaches? All they will do is falsely persuade people that they are being protected so that people will be off their guard, making things more dangerous. The whole thing is counter-productive.'

'This is all heavy going,' said the earlier speaker; 'how about a break?'

'Michael?' asked Erich.

'Yes?'

'What are you going to do after this job?'

'Me? Well, once we collect, I intend to retire from active service. With my money safely in the bank,' he smiled winningly, 'I would like to own a bar. Not to manage it, you understand, but to own it and employ a good manager to do the managing. I would just lounge around looking important and mixing with the customers. Actually,' Michael warmed to his theme, 'I wouldn't mind a club like the one we were in last night. A good size, friendly atmosphere and not too crowded. After all, I would not need it to make a profit; just to break even or thereabouts.'

He stretched yawningly in his spacious office armchair and gazed out at Spawater basking lazily in the sunshine; as pleased as a cat with ten lives. 'Nice town, this.'

'Shame it's going to lose its main tourist attraction.' Marlene snorted, raising her coffee cup in triumph.

They all joined in the laughter. There is a unique camaraderie in professional crime; just knowing that you and your comrades are about to put one over on the authorities gives you a feeling of being truly alive, and the more absurd the authorities, the juicier the feeling. In this instance, the government in all its overblown self-regard had decreed that its subjects were to be biometrically recorded and listed in a foolproof database, if you please. The entire population was to be filed, cross-referenced and measured at incredible taxpayers' expense according to the whim of an overweening group of nondescripts who could not even make the trains run on time. Michael and his gang were going to expose these tin-pot emperors for the nakid fools they truly were.

Pricking politicians' pomposity is always a tremendously liberating feeling; it put the Lucky in Luciano, the Merrie in Robin's men and the bullets in Bonnie and Clyde. Now it was going to make Michael and his colleagues rich. Good old biometrics!

'And so,' concluded Hanif wearily, 'we owe all this to the advances made in biometrics. Now, I am sorry but I do not have any more time to answer questions today. I am happy, however, to address any issues you may have. Please feel free to email me at any time with any question and I will get back to you. Now, thank you for coming here today; I am sorry about the hold-ups getting into the meeting due to security checks but the new system will take time to bed down and at least it is good to know that we are safe.

'Once again, thank you.' Hanif walked off the stage where several months earlier he had dragged Alison away from the riot she herself had started. A quieter exit this time, but no less upsetting. People kept asking him awkward questions that he knew he could answer, given time, but were impossible to address on the hoof.

No, he'd replied to the Hall in general, he did not know how much the whole thing would cost, or what would happen if you lost your card, or would iris scanners work on blind people. He did not know about Irish citizens, or what the Scottish and Welsh assemblies, which opposed the scheme, would do, or what would happen if a Nazi government took over and got control of the files.

No, he'd stressed, he could not explain what would happen if terrorists blew up the national database centre, or if a computer virus struck, or a power failure disabled it. Nor did he know how to counter the database harassing Muslims all the time and turning them against the State, or Hindus being mistaken for Muslims by idiots and being harassed too, or the general public turning on Big Brother and pulling him limb from control-freak limb.

He could not prevent national database input clerks selling confidential information, or taking bribes to tamper with files, or putting incorrect data on the records, or a hundred other things, Hanif considered resignedly.

And no, he did not, he insisted finally, worry about someone discovering Spiderman's secret bloody identity.

Hanif sat down in a dressing room backstage, let out a sigh of relief that he could now relax, and decided that what he needed was a drink. For the first time he wondered whether identity cards and a national database were worth the candle. Alexander the Great had entertained similar doubts. 'What's it all about, Bucephalus?' he would moan to his soul mate. 'Sometimes I wonder if people really want to be civilised by us at all.'

What had seemed, originally, to be a sensible move in the twenty-first century against terrorism and crime was turning out to be a jolly sight more complicated than he'd thought. There were any number of practical obstacles to be overcome at goodness knows what trouble and expense, before a national database combined with identity cards could become a practical proposition. And would the people wear it? He was beginning to have doubts.

Hanif put his mouth under the cold tap over the sink. His mouth was so dry that the lukewarm water tasted refreshingly cool. Sod it for now, he decided. He was off to Lifeboats'. One consolation, he realised; at least chasing Spiderman and other superheroes for their secret identities was not an issue.

That was all he knew.

'Let's go to the pub.'

The words creaked throatily out of Joanna's mouth like a village elder stretching up from a rickety wicker chair. Five hours in a dry, claustrophobic lecture theatre listening to speakers making her blood alternately freeze with fear and boil with rage like a teenage thermometer did not do a lot for the vocal cords. Jenna was not up for Eurovision either.

'Good idea. The Three Nuns, they said it was. Let's go.'

The Campaign Against Identity Cards was not a dry organisation. After the formal debate, the discussions could continue in the local student bar. Joanna and Jenna were eager participants. Staying with friends in London for a couple of days, their time was their own with no national database yet to record where they were going and what they were doing, and therefore no-one to be held accountable to.

Not yet.

'Tell you what,' said Michael, languidly, 'as there is not much we can do until Monday when the electricals arrive,' he nodded towards Marlene who nodded back, 'why don't we return to The Lifeboat Club? That Jady fellow said he would be there tonight and he seems to know everything in this town.' Michael looked over at Louise. 'He might be able to help you hire a local firm to remove the goods.' He beamed like sunshine on silver. 'I do like to hire locally; it feels like I am giving back something to the community.'

‘To make up for what you are taking away from it,’ laughed Erich.

‘That’s right,’ agreed Michael, laughing in agreement. ‘All perfectly fair and above board. Spawater fashion, the locals call it. Seriously, we need to hire a good local contact and we can pay top dollar. Somehow I think Jady is our man. So, off to Lifeboats’?’

They all agreed.

‘Lifeboats’ it is.’

Identity Cards
Chapter Six

'That's better.'

Jenna placed the pint glass on the table and wiped her mouth theatrically. 'I needed that. It's not Bacchus's Best but it will do. Well Joey, the ordeal is over; what did you make of it?'

Joanna and Jenna were in The Three Nuns, a student bar adjacent to the university lecture theatre enjoying a well-earned pint of student best. The bar was full of meeting attendees; like-minded people who opposed identity cards and the national database as Rip Van Winkle opposed alarm clocks. 'Morning, Rip old buddy, rise and shine.' 'In your dreams.' They were amongst friends.

Joanna matched Jenna's swig of bitter. 'Whew!' she replied, and meant it. After five hours in a crowded lecture theatre watching the future painted as a picture Dante would have rejected for being too depressing, 'whew!' after the first swig of bitter was putting it mildly.

'Yes, that is much better.' They sat for a moment in contemplative silence, like a pair of ancient philosophers after an unexpected eclipse, and then started the debriefing.

'I don't know where to start. What did you think yourself?'

'Put it this way, Jo. I was mad before. I am bloody furious now. As the Campaign people were talking about all the practical objections to the scheme that will occur in the future, all I could think of was that interfering idiot at the Town Hall who is costing me my livelihood right now by making it so difficult for my clients that they stop coming to my classes.' Jenna smiled apologetically and continued.

'As I might possibly have mentioned before,' - Joanna laughed briefly at the recollection - 'I am having a tiny spot of difficulty at work. Curse the dark day when Spawater Council entrusted that meddlesome moron with the smooth running of the Town Hall and environs! He has decreed that nobody can move in the place without submitting to impertinent checks on their bona fides. As a result, people have stopped attending events in the Town Hall rather than put up with the hassle. Consequently, people are leaving my aerobics and dance classes. Accordingly, I am losing money and because of that I am going to ram one of those biometric iris scanners down that toe rag's throat.'

She paused and took a satisfied swig of her subsidised beer, like a cat that had just finished its first course of mouse pie and needs something to wash it down. 'But you knew that already. Now Joey, you are the voice of reason; what do you think?'

Joanna breathed out like an athlete warming up. She knew what she wanted to say but was not quite sure how to say it.

'Well Jenna, I certainly agree with you about that jobsworth in the Town Hall. Jady has spent weeks trying to hire the main hall itself for a tournament he hopes to arrange with Ali's employers now that they are going for his latest scheme. He said the idiot you have just referred to,' she took a pull at her pint and giggled, 'has been making him jump through hoops to get the Ok. Jady would happily insert the scanner into him when you have finished with it.'

They both laughed merrily. Public houses; where all the world is set to rights for the price of a pint.

'But,' Joanna placed her glass carefully on the solid, student-resistant table, 'the practical objections to imposing identity cards and the national database are only half the equation. The real reason I oppose them is far more important than that.'

'The main objections to the national database and identity cards are practical. Overcome them and Bob's your uncle.'

Hanif was trying to explain to a less than interested Ron that identity cards would be good for his business. Subconsciously he was using Ron as a sounding board for his own nagging reservations.

'You see, Ron,' Hanif persevered, 'you would not have to check people in every time they turn up at the door. They could just swipe their card through a machine reader and it would let them in if they were members and reject them if not. It would save you time and increase your productivity.'

Ron had heard it all before. Every day sales reps accosted him and wasted his time telling him of their grand innovations that would free up his time for more productive activities. Like shooting sales reps, he thought morbidly. Besides, he had just received a threatening letter from the Health and Safety people. They wanted to inspect his kitchen and Ron doubted the kitchen could stand the strain. With the world-weariness of an elderly sea turtle greeting yet another shipload of mariners claiming to have discovered its island for the first time, he replied.

'What would I do when the machine went wrong?'

Hanif had not thought of that. 'They won't go wrong; they are state of the art scanners.'

Ron eyed him pityingly. 'Won't go wrong? Do you remember what happened to the ATM cash machine I installed in the foyer? The one some of the members thought was ripping them off?'

Hanif did. He also had a shrewd idea who'd been the brains behind its downfall. Least said the better.

'And the television in the Pool room?' continued Ron.

'Well, it was wrong to put a television in the Pool room. The members objected.'

'And you think the members would not object to swiping a card through a machine every time they popped out to do one of their dodgy business deals?' Ron absent-mindedly wiped the portion of the bar in range. This inspired him to greater curmudgeons. 'And what if they lost their cards?'

'That's all right,' Hanif replied, happy to get the discussion away from messy real life and back to clean technology. 'They could put their eye to an iris scanner which would establish their identity.'

For the second time that year, Ron laughed aloud.

'Are you quite serious? What do you think Jacko, or Bullet or Mullin's lot would do to a scanner that annoyed them after they had had a few? And your friends too; I can just see your friend Jenna bowing down to a piece of delicate machinery. You must be mad if you think people will go along with all that.'

Hanif was at a loss. Somehow it all seemed so different when he was discussing it with Mr Dauntliffe. It appeared that the technology was fine; it was the humans who were a disappointment. They just did not fit in. Admittedly, some people were less human than others; those members named by Ron tended to be on the simian end of the scale. He bucked up. This was a challenge; where was the fun if it was all too easy?

On that note of determination, Hanif espied Jady and Arnie entering the main bar area and decided that this conversation had reached its argue-by date.

'We will see, Ron, we will see. Look, here are the boys. Get them what they want, will you? And have one yourself.'

'Jenna, just suppose for a moment that they managed to overcome all the practical and financial objections to their national database and Identification Cards scheme.'

Jenna guffawed. 'Don't put the bacon on the top shelf, it will get vertigo.'

'No, seriously; about half the objections raised in the meeting were of a practical nature. For example, before satellite technology, if the police were suspicious of a motorist they would stop the car and search it. Now they would just check the driver's identity card. If it were valid the car would not be searched. So a criminal with a valid or convincing fake identity would escape.'

'Yes, I know. I was there too.'

'Sorry. But my point is, just suppose it was somehow magically possible for all the impracticalities to be ironed out and for the national database system, along with identity cards, to work the way the government wants. How many people would oppose them then?'

'You mean, how many people are against them because they don't work, as opposed to how many people are against them on principle?'

'Yes.'

Jenna thought for a moment. 'It is your round.'

'My round.' Hanif greeted Jady and Arnie ebulliently. Their arrival meant it was time for him to clock off and relax. Hanif certainly had no intention of locking horns with Jady over identity cards or anything else; he had had a rotten day and it was now time to get good and drunk, or at least sufficiently squiffyoomped to forget his cares for the duration. He wondered idly if elephants were able to drink to forget, or did they have to join the Foreign Legion. Ming the Merciless had days like this; when he put interstellar conquest to one side and kicked his shoes off with a large one. Robin Hood would sometimes use the proceeds of a day's bushwhacking to book into a luxury hotel - 'stuff the poor, where's my room service?' - and Wil. E Coyote every so often settled for a sandwich. Hanif was at one with them all.

'Hi there, Han. Grab a table, would you, Millado; I will help Hanif carry the drinks.'

'Hello there, Jady, Arnie. Am I glad to see you; I fancy a really good drink tonight.'

'Well, you have come to the right place. Hasn't he, Ron? Hello there. And on the right occasion too. Millado has got something to celebrate. Ron, your Pool chalk need no longer take the strain. Millado is back in the world of the wage slaves.'

'I am delighted to hear it,' answered Ron, looking as delighted as Captain Hook hearing tick tock. 'Now, what are you having?'

'This one is on me.' Michael smiled winningly at Jady and Hanif whilst waving his three companions through to the heart of the Club. 'I seem to recall you bought the last round the other day. I am grateful for your help in getting us accepted here, Jady, so if you and your friend just name it?'

Ever the gentleman, Jady made the introductions.

'Hello there, Michael, this is Hanif. Han, Michael.'

'Hello, Hanif.'

'Hello, Mike.'

'Michael, sorry; I was called Mike at school and never got over it. Now, what are you having?'

With Ron's reluctant assistance they sorted out the drinks and went to their respective tables. Just before parting, Michael lowered his voice and beckoned to Jady.

'You couldn't spare me a moment of your time, could you, Jady? I have a proposition that might be of interest to you.'

Jady was quite wrapped up in his latest project with Arnie and Alison but he was never too busy to listen to a proposition. Had he been born a little earlier he would have considered a proposition from the ancient Britons to build Stonehenge while planning the pyramid job. 'What's that? You want a large, airy building, made of stone and built like a bunch of football goalposts? The object being to confuse people of the future? Well, I am a bit tied up with the artificial ski slopes in Egypt at the moment, but I'll give it some thought. How about a concrete lion instead? No? You sure?'

'Is it confidential or can you talk in front of my friends?'

'Oh, no worries, it is all respectable and above board. I am looking for someone intelligent to help me with my latest assignment. Just for a few weeks; easy work and good money. If I might join your table for a moment, I will tell you about it.'

'Sounds interesting. OK, join us and tell me about it.'

They made their way to the table currently occupied by Hanif and Arnie. After introducing Arnie to Michael - Jady and Michael both being firm believers in observing the proprieties - they all sat down again and collectively drank some of their drinks. The correct rituals observed, it was time to get down to cases.

'Michael has an interesting business proposition to make, isn't that right, Michael?'

Hanif groaned inwardly, like an inhibited bullock. Business was the last thing on his mind this evening. Jady, of course, never closed.

'There is something about you people that always looks suspicious. Honestly, if I were a policewoman looking to up my score, I would come here and arrest the lot of you just for sitting in the corner without due care and attention. Oh, hello, I didn't notice you there. Sorry, have I interrupted anything? I do apologise.'

'Hi, Alison.' Jady rose. Alison had caught sight of them sitting at one of the many corner tables - the best clubs are those with the most corners - and joined in before noticing their guest. Upon realising her faux pas she faltered, unsure what to do next. Hamlet would have understood.

'Allow me to introduce Alison, one of my dearest friends. Your associates the other day were signed in on her ticket. Alison, this is Michael, one of my newest friends.'

'Charmed, I am sure, and please don't say sorry, it is a pleasure to be interrupted by such a melodious voice as yours,' replied the courteous Michael. Cornball stuff in this cynical age, but Michael knew better. The old world manners are the best; they worked wonders for Dracula. 'May I introduce the Count? Dracula, is it not?' 'Charmed, I am sure, and such fetching jewellery. Never have I espied such a dazzling necklace; may I take a closer look?'

'Now, may I get you a drink?'

'I will get it,' interrupted Hanif brusquely. Hanif was very protective of Alison and did not care for knights in shining armour queering his pitch. Courtesy only impresses its recipients; bystanders tend to feel left out.

Hanif went off to the bar whilst Alison settled in and Michael got back down to business.

'Well, my name is Michael Lehmann and I am an historical architect specialising in the Roman Empire.' He smiled. 'You could say? I am an ancient architect.'

Arnie laughed and the other two grinned, as Michael hoped they would. Keep it light, he reflected, and you will be all right.

'My team and I, that's them over there,' he nodded in his colleagues' direction, 'have been asked to make a close examination of the Spawater Baths. That is our assignment. As you probably know, Spawater Council are anxious to promote your fair city and the Baths are the obvious tourist attraction. The trouble is, they appear to have suffered the ravages of time, like us all eventually, and if they are exposed to more tourists, they may suffer from irreparable erosion. It is my job, and that of my team, to make a thorough study of the Baths and then decide what, if anything, we can do about it.'

Hanif returned, bearing Alison's wine, and sat down quietly.

'How fascinating. Thanks, Hanny. Oh, I do love all that historical stuff, especially the Romans. Is it true they invented wine?' Alison was enthralled. Michael was interesting, presumably important, and courteous. A rare combination.

Michael laughed. 'No, that was much earlier.' He mentally made a memo to self; find out who invented wine. He was supposed to be the historical expert and ignorance of such trivial things could raise suspicion. If Napoleon had not been so ignorant about the range of a British musket, we would all be speaking French.

'And you need help?' asked Jady, who was interested in anything connected to the Council.

'Yes. We are not exactly overstaffed and will be coming and going all over the place. We may have to hire various specialists and general helpers. We need someone on our side, on the spot full-time, to handle routine enquiries and generally keep people off our backs. While we are going about our business we would prefer not to be disturbed.' And how, Michael added privately. 'What we require is a troubleshooter; someone who knows the area, the type of people likely to be around, and in particular, the workings of the Town Hall. They must be able to liaise between whoever is working at the coalface and us, the ones in charge, whilst keeping busybodies at arms' length. That means both the public and the Town Hall busybodies.'

'How long will it take?' asked Alison.

'We hope to finish the job in about two months.' He paused, and looked keenly across the oaken table. 'Well Jady? What do you think? Would you be interested in taking the job?'

Jady always considered himself a lucky person. Lucky in love, lucky in life, lucky in scheming. What goes around, comes around, he thought with self-justification. After all, it was his act of kindness, signing Michael and his colleagues into the Club, which had led to this remarkable proposition. The immediate obstacle to Jady's latest scheme was the obduracy of a certain jobsworth at the Town Hall. The paranoid, bureaucratic bonehead who demanded to know people's private details all the time even if they were only there to ask for directions. In the war against the Town Hall troublemaker, Michael had opened a new flank.

Jady grinned like Churchill the day America entered the war against Hitler.

'Well, Michael, I am not able to take the job myself as I am much too busy, but I know someone who can.'

Identity Cards
Chapter Seven

'Ok, this is how I see things.' Joanna's second drink loosened her communication logjam and she felt able to get her point across to the world.

'I read a book once a about the refugees who came to Britain to escape Hitler before World War Two, and Stalin after it. One of the main themes that illustrated their joy to be in this country was that for once in their lives they were not on anybody's list.'

'How do you mean?'

'Well, in totalitarian states everybody is classified by various means; religion, ethnicity, behaviour, opinions etc. Everyone is filed; everyone is on a list. Just think what Hitler or Stalin would have made of the biometric nonsense that this government supports? They would have loved it. Ok, they had databases of their own, but nothing to match what is being threatened in this country. If the national database ever becomes a reality in this country it will be the start of an inevitable process that will turn this country, and Europe, into the kind of totalitarian Hell Orwell could only dream about.' Joanna sipped some liquid reinforcement. Churchill would have approved.

'This meeting has got to you a bit, don't you think?' interrupted Jenna. 'I entirely agree, of course, but if you start shouting the odds from the rooftops people will just call you paranoid. They have heard these dire threats before and they have never come to pass. This will just be another one.'

'Oh yes,' Joanna agreed. 'These things would occur slowly, one small, harmless step at a time, usually in the name of security. When our brave rulers in Parliament took up the cudgels against terrorism, they first voted themselves a big wall in the House of Commons to hide behind. When it was not foolproof, they erected a bigger one. At our expense, of course. They will do the same throughout the country. First, carrying identity cards will be voluntary. Then, after a minor incident, it will be compulsory. After all, if you have nothing to hide... Then it will be needed for many more things. As you heard today, when they introduced identity cards in WW2, people only had to show them for three reasons. By the time Churchill got rid of them in 1952 there were 39 reasons why you could be forced to show them. It is called 'mission creep' and it is the inevitable outcome if identity cards are imposed on us.'

Jenna nodded thoughtfully. 'So Hitler and Stalin loved identity cards and Churchill abolished them. That shows which side our government is on. They really must be stopped.'

'But it is worse than that. There is an old, pessimistic phrase that says, you are born, you keep your head down and you die. In other words, do not take risks. Keep your head down and keep out of trouble. What do you think life will be like if everybody is watched, all the time? Not actually spied on every minute of the day, but traceable at all times. What will that do for enterprise? For risk taking? How will it affect people trying to increase the quality of life, happiness, health and wealth of the world? How would you behave if you knew your movements were being traced and your actions recorded? Sure, you would not commit many crimes, but you would not achieve anything radical or worthwhile either; you would stagnate.'

Joanna took another swig of beer and continued.

'Why has Britain produced some of the best musicians in the world? Because they have been allowed to exist on the odd gig, cash in hand, to pay the bills and buy new guitar strings and all the while they were learning their art. That was not just about the money; living that bohemian lifestyle, living a life of relative freedom, allowed them to write from the heart, write from the soul about life as they encountered it. Take away the ability to do the odd unofficial, tax-free gig for peanuts and you take away their creativity. Musicians could not develop at their own pace and in their own manner. The only music, if that is the word, that would appear is that from organised companies or promoters;

winners of talent competitions on the television who would be managed, shaped, sponsored and cast aside after one season for the next group of botoxed beauties, to repeat the mindless, commercial pap the following year.'

She clasped her beer glass like a baby clasps a rattle.

'And music is only one area,' she continued. 'All creativity would dry up. Art, music, literature are at their best when at their most subversive. Freedom feeds the imagination; oppression starves it. Knowing that everything you do can be held against you, you would do nothing that might be, or even seem to be, in the least way challenging to the State. With no opposition to it, the State would become ever more intrusive; for our own protection, of course. We would surrender our freedom in the name of security. The motto of the State would be, 'better to live on your knees than die on your feet.' No, it would be 'existing', not living. The motto would be, 'better to exist, securely, on your knees than live life to the full, risks included, on your feet'.'

Joanna stopped once more to oil her vocal cords. Satisfied, she continued. 'Except that it's supposed saving grace, security, is false. We would lose our freedom and our security together.'

Jenna sat back, the better to enjoy the show. There are times when it is advisable to interrupt, and times like this.

'We would have the midnight knock. The government are attacking our rights to a jury trial, trying to set up a national Police Force under the direct control of the Home Secretary, allowing suspects to be held without charge or their next of kin being informed, and lowering the burden of proof in terrorist trials. Combine this with a national database and identity cards and you have all the mechanisms in place for a Police State. Spread this virus across Europe via the European Community and it looks as though the British government will succeed where Hitler failed; the British government will put the lights out all over Europe. They will wither our souls. As Orwell foresaw, identity cards and a national database produce a boot crashing down on a human face. Forever.'

'Who is paying for all this?' asked Hanif, just to be awkward. First a rotten day at work, now some smoothie dominating the conversation and holding Alison spellbound. It was too much for a mild-mannered Information Technology expert.

'Good point, Hanif,' replied Michael pleasantly. 'The British Heritage people and the Society for the Protection of Rural Britain, along with the British Museum, the Museo Italiano the British Tourist Board, the National Lottery and one or two other interested parties have formed a consortium in conjunction with the European Union. They have produced the company that I work for, 'Ecochtrust.' The idea is to bring together various organisations with a similar agenda; in this case to protect our European Heritage by preserving the Spawater Baths. This is our first outing.'

'I have never heard of you,' countered Hanif suspiciously.

'Hanif!' cried a dismayed Alison. This was no way to speak to such a polite man, especially one they hardly knew.

'It's all right, Alison,' Michael laughed. 'Hanif is quite right. Nobody has heard of us.' Michael lowered his voice. 'That is the trouble. You see, the reason why the groups I have just mentioned needed to form a separate entity - us - is that most of the money is coming from the European Union and if word got out, the voters in other countries would want Britain to pay for the whole thing. Also, if the Italians got wind of it they might claim ownership, like the Greeks with the Elgin Marbles.'

Hanif snorted quietly. It all sounded too pat to him. Well, Hanif was just the man to check out Michael's story. To work in Spawater since the identity trials began, Michael would have to have obtained a temporary Pass. This was a visitor's identity card and was necessary to allow Spawater to interact with the rest of the country. Of course, when the identity card system went nationwide, such visitors' cards would only be available to temporary workers from abroad. To get his visitors' card Michael's details would have to be on the fledgling national database. Strictly speaking, these were confidential and Hanif should not really have access to them. In reality, Hanif knew perfectly well how to obtain any information held on the national database that he wanted.

Right my lad, thought Hanif. Tomorrow I will find out if you are telling the truth or are some kind of conman. If you are I will nail you. Or blackmail you out of town. We will see how much Alison likes you then.

Michael shrugged his shoulders to illustrate how helpless decent people were in a world of deviousness and bureaucracy. 'That is why we are very much on our own. We have a good budget, thanks to the European Union.'

'Thanks to our taxpayers' money, you mean.'

Hanif was becoming belligerent. Normally so mild-mannered that people mistook him for Clark Kent, the combination of a bad day at the coalface, his special friend Alison being drooled over by an out of town Lothario, and a good helping of alcohol, was proving combustible. Any half-decent Health and Safety officer would have slapped on a demolition order soon as look as him.

'Are you keeping up with your Pool practice, Millado? It is very important, you know. How about giving Hanif a game? Alison can play the winner. You don't mind, do you Ali?' Jady recognised the signs and decided that what the lounge area of Lifeboats' required was less Hanifs. In the Pool room nobody would notice, of course. He hated taking liberties with Alison but knew she would understand.

She did. Attuned to people's emotional states she was aware that Hanif was cruising for a bruising and that the best way to get rid of him was to hold out the possibility of a game of Pool alone with her. As a hopeless romantic, Hanif would ignore the fact that Arnie would beat him hollow.

Alison clapped her hands. 'Good idea. Arnie, you set up the table and I will play the winner.'

Arnie needed no encouragement. He loved thrashing his former boss at Pool. It beat Prozac all to pieces. 'Ok chief,' he said, referring to Jady, 'c'mon, ex-boss, let's go for it.'

Hanif was placated. He was not very good at losing his temper, having had such little practice, and trying to be argumentative was becoming a strain. Besides, Alison had smiled at him.

'All right, Arnie, you carry the drinks and I will get a table.'

He and Arnie left

Michael was undisturbed. He had noticed Hanif's latent hostility but did not consider it prejudicial to his assignment. It was just some local issue and of no concern to him.

'So, Jady, you say you might have the person for the job?'

'Oh yes,' Alison answered for him. 'We know exactly the right person, don't we?'

'You know a good troubleshooter?'

Troublemaker more likely, thought Jady. Aloud he continued, 'Yes, I know just the right person.'

'So,' said Hanif to Arnie as they chalked the cues, 'how is your project with Jady getting on?'

'Haven't you heard? Alison's company have given it the go-ahead. I am now officially self-employed, working for Jady.'

The relaxed atmosphere of the Pool room had mollified Hanif's irritability. He had simmered down to his normal size and was his usual good-tempered, unexciting self once more. The Incredible Hulk would have thought they were related.

'Well Arnie, old chap, I hope you enjoy being self-employed working for Jady. Remind me, what exactly are you going to be self-employed doing?'

Lining up behind the cue ball, Arnie paused.

'Ah. Well, you see boss, or ex-boss, Jady told me not to tell anyone. He said that if people found out it could ruin the whole thing.' He hesitated guiltily. 'Sorry boss, but I promised I wouldn't tell anyone.' Distracted, Arnie's poor shot left Hanif an easy target. Despite their conversation, Hanif's real objective was to win the match and thereby win his reward of a game with Alison. St George was like that. A pacifist at heart, he only went a'jousting in order to win fair maidens. Had St George been happily married, the country would still be teeming with dragons.

Hanif didn't mind Arnie not cooperating. He knew Jady would tell him soon enough and Jady's account was likely to be more comprehensive.

'Good for you, young Arnie. I can see why I hired you for my company's computer security business. You know how to keep a secret.'

'You don't mind, do you? I will tell you if you like. I am sure Jady would not mind you knowing. He just does not want it to be known by everyone.'

'No, that is all right. I am sure Jady will tell me in his own good time. Let's get on with the game.' Hanif lined up for an easy one.

'Ok boss. Anyway, Jady says that with this identity card stuff, soon nobody will have secrets any more. He says that the people controlling the national database will be so corrupt they will find out anything about anybody they dislike and blackmail them. We should all keep whatever secrets we have and not let the police State find them.'

Hanif miscued.

Jenna's mobile rang. The slight twinge of embarrassment that this always caused her was outranked by the feeling that she was saved by the bell. She could not fault a word Joanna said, but it was most disconcerting that they were said at all. Could this really be Britain in the early years of the new century? The world's biggest and most successful promoters of the Nightmare State?

Absurd though it would once have seemed, Joanna's argument was difficult to refute. Hours spent listening to unpleasant facts in the lecture theatre were accurately summarised by Joanna's outburst in the pub. Things have come to a pretty pass, Jenna reflected, when being hassled in the pub by a mobile call is an improvement.

'Excuse me, Joey,' muttered Jenna apologetically as Joanna heard Jenna's call sign and simultaneously recalled that she needed to inhale occasionally. 'I will just nip outside where it is quiet and answer it.' Jenna got up and exited quickly.

Joanna eased and adjusted her adrenalin production to ticking over. Getting her fears out of her system made her feel so much better. The very feat of saying aloud to a sympathetic listener exactly why she truly hated the elected baboonery that believed in enslaving the country in the name of a bogus 'security', the security of the Gulag, was cathartic.

These people dreamt of turning Britain, and Europe, if not the world, into a prison without bars. One identity card to rule them all, one national database to bind them. Well, she thought, they can dream on; the human spirit cannot be crushed. Even if it could, the spineless toadies in Parliament would hardly be the ones to crush it; the ones who protest that they will stand up to terrorism and who then hide behind a wall.

No, to crush the human spirit would take a spirit yet mightier. One we will not encounter in our lifetimes but may have to account ourselves to afterwards.

It must be the drink talking, thought Joanna, as if awakening from a reverie. When Jenna gets back I will switch to a weaker beer.

Too late. Jenna returned to the table via the bar, complete with another two foaming pints of the strong stuff, her face alight like Father Time's birthday cake.

'That was your Jady on the telephone; he sends his love and will call you later.' Jenna sat down and laughed uproariously. 'Joey, you are not going to believe this. I mean, you are just not going to believe it.'

Identity Cards
Chapter Eight

Harold Wood was an important man; the most important man in Spawater. This was not just his opinion, though it was one he shared, it was the opinion of Mrs Wood and all the staff at the Town Hall. At least he assumed it was. Mrs Wood regularly told him how much he was needed there and the staff certainly took notice of his pronouncements. This was to be expected, he knew. After all, Mr Wood was the Town Hall manager, or Security and Amenities Facilitator as he preferred to be known, in charge of all aspects of running the civic amenities both in the Hall itself and the Spawater Baths adjacent; the main aspect, of course, being security. Mr. Wood was an important man and everyone in Spawater knew it.

This had not always been the case. For the first two or three years that Mr Wood had control over the Hall and Baths he was virtually ignored outside of his immediate work colleagues, and even they did not pay him the respect a man in his position self-evidently merited. Councillors, general public and staff alike treated him like a glorified caretaker. Ron would have understood if Harold Wood had deigned to confide in him; they could have swapped hard-luck stories like Jonah and Dick Dastardly.

No, he admitted to himself, the first few years had not seen him make his mark.

The trouble was, in his early days as Amenities Facilitator, or general manager, people had a relaxed attitude to security. 'What is there to steal in a Town Hall?' they would say complacently. 'The fire extinguishers?' This upset Mr Wood as only derision to an important person can. What he needed, he confided to Mrs Wood constantly during their ballroom dancing classes, was some kind of shock, some kind of wake-up call that would show the people of Spawater their peril. Something to show that the world was a dangerous place, in need of the kind of security he was able and willing to provide, if only they would stop laughing at him and start to take security as seriously as he did.

And he got it. He got it on that unforgettable day, fittingly in the first year of the new century, the spectacular mass murder that woke the western world.

On its own, the attack on New York would not have been enough to turn Spawater Town Hall and its environs into the terrorist-free zone of which Mr Wood dreamed. 'After all,' people would say, 'what has that terrible event to do with us?' However, there was more. Following the attack and the insane wars of vengeance it launched which played into the attackers' hands, a frightened witless parliament was railroaded into giving the ok for a national database and compulsory Identification Cards, with the trial run taking place in Spawater.

Harold Wood's day had come.

Just as Harold Wood could scarcely believe his luck, neither could Jenna as she listened to Michael telling her the job requirements. It was Jenna, of course, who Alison and Jady had in mind as the ideal person to supervise Michael's work at the Spawater Baths. Jenna was a regular at the Town Hall, hiring rooms for her aerobics and dance classes. She knew the Town Hall activities inside out, in particular the security arrangements inflicted on Councillors, the general public and Town Hall staff alike by that bane of humanity, the jobsworth with a bit of authority, personified in this case by Mr Harold Wood.

'Honestly, Michael,' stressed Jenna, distractedly accepting the proffered coffee in his office, 'that guy Wood is well named; thick as a forest, and dense as mahogany. He is carrying out his own personal war on terrorism by spying on anyone who comes near the Town Hall or the Baths. If you are hiring outside contractors you will find they spend more time getting in and out of Wood's little empire than they do working. That guy is a menace.'

'That's where you come in, Jenna. Jady tells me you are somewhat of an expert in Town Hall affairs and that this

Mr Wood knows you very well. Jady also tells me that you have a habit of refusing to show your identity card to his security staff when asked. What does he do about that?'

'Do? Why nothing, of course. Well,' amended Jenna, 'he huffs and puffs like the Big Bad Wolf having a coronary but he doesn't try to throw me out of the building. He tried once...' She smirked at the recollection. 'The staff know me and leave me alone.' She scowled. 'No, it is my clients who get the hard time. He is costing me money and anything I can do to annoy him is fine with me.'

Michael was delighted. They had chatted briefly on Alison's mobile two days earlier and Michael had been favourably impressed. Now they were meeting for the first time and this impression continued. Jenna was just the sort of person to keep their biggest threat, a meddling manager, off their backs while they got on with the job in hand. Knowing Jenna, the manager would not suspect terrorists or, more importantly, professional criminals. He would simply be furious with Jenna's blatant flouting of his absurd security precautions and would direct all his energies into being outraged at her insults to his self-importance. The perfect diversion.

Michael smiled the smile of a person happy with the way things are progressing. Noah felt the same when he finished waterproofing the Ark's hull and shooed the lions away from the zebras on 'C' deck.

'All right, Jenna, welcome aboard. Officially, things start on Monday when your friend Mr Wood will be informed that the Spawater Baths are to be inspected by my company to ascertain whether or not they need renovation work. You won't be needed right away but I have your number and I take it you will be in the area with one of your classes, so you will be available when needed, probably later in the week?'

'Suits me,' replied Jenna. 'Just give me the call when you or your colleagues meet your first non-architectural problem. Knowing that pillock Wood and his security goons, I am sure it won't take long.'

Michael laughed.

'I am sure you are right.'

'It all sounds a bit melodramatic, are you sure you are right?' Jady passed Joanna a well-earned cup of tea and sat down with his just as well-earned orange juice.

He had spent a long and wearying day at Alison's place of work. Escorted by Alison and a couple of Alison's big cheeses, he first met the bean counters to discuss the financial side of things, a boring necessity that left him in no doubt that the eleventh century monks who'd invented double entry accounts did so as a penance. They must have committed one hell of a sin, thought Jady through his ennui.

More fun was the marketing department. Selling things that are worthless is what good marketing departments do, and Alison's colleagues were the best. Being brand builders, they had to be. Admin next. Then the design team. They designed the posters, newspaper advertisements and publicity stunts that kept their clients' in the public eye. They existed to hoodwink the world. Jady liked them.

Finally, Jady introduced Arnie to the cheeses. It was one thing to laugh about his assignment over a lager or three in Lifeboats', but now that the reality of what he had let himself in for sank in, Arnie was becoming anxious. Meeting cheeses was a novel experience for Arnie, but flanked by Alison and Jady he muddled through.

A long day but a productive one, was Jady's judgement at the debriefing with Alison and Arnie in the coffee bar afterwards. He would have liked to celebrate in Lifeboats' but he had promised a tired Joanna a quiet night in.

Joanna had arrived back from London earlier that day and gone straight to her day job. Home at last, she and Jady were having a quiet night in with a downloaded Charlie Chaplin film, his downtrodden persona in a threatening world matching hers.

They rarely watched live television these days, Jady objecting to the inexorable growth of irritating graphics and egoistical logos spreading like hogweed across the screen.

Downloading old films without graphics was the future of television in so much as it had one.

'Thanks, I needed that.' Joanna took a stimulating quaff of the reassuring brown liquid. Ignoring the film glowing in the corner and gazing into the friendly fireplace, she continued. 'There is no doubt about it, Jady. The national database being constructed is even more threatening than the Identification Cards. The cards themselves will be used to trace us, as we will have to carry them at all times. In conjunction with RFID - that's radio frequency identification - global satellite positioning, geographical information systems and microchip technology, it will not be long until the government can keep tabs on the entire population. In the name of security we will all be traced all the time. The government will naturally assume that it represents the will of the people and therefore anyone who disobeys it, or criticises it even, will be seen as an enemy of the people and dealt with as such.'

Jady was concerned. Up until now he had believed that the obvious practical flaws in such a scheme would be enough to crush it. However, if it could deliver the thing that governments, by their very nature, desire, the ability to remain in power and keep governing, then they might override the blatant absurdities inherent in having half the population checking up on the other half instead of being productive, and adopt it.

They would reason, subconsciously perhaps, that an ordered, stagnant society led by them was better than a disorderly society led by a government elected by a whim of the public; whosoever they preferred at the time. He put this to Joanna.

'Exactly,' she replied, pleased to get Jady off his complacent fence. 'For 'disorderly' read 'free'. A watched society can never be a free society. Nor can it be a productive one. Progress is often achieved through protest. That's how women got the vote and slavery was ended. Governments hate protest and therefore are the enemies of progress. A government that knew where we were all of the time could stop all protest by arresting anyone who opposed it; in the name of the people, naturally. They would stop all protest and thereby stop all progress. In time we would forget what protest was. Future generations would simply accept that that was the way things should be. History would be falsified, of course, to show that before everyone was stamped and filed the world was a violent, terrible place. Thank Heaven, therefore, for the government and for instant identification of malcontents. Any historian or brave citizen who opposed such lies would simply disappear. This is not just paranoia, Jady, this is fact and it is happening now. That's why we must act now to prevent it.'

Joanna took a deep breath, followed by more tea. Even as she spoke, she realised how fantastical her claims sounded and how impossible it would be to persuade large numbers of people that it was all true and happening now. Did her Jady believe her? If he didn't then nobody else would. She looked at him pleadingly, her expression belying her brave words of a moment ago.

Jady looked as serious as she had ever seen him, then leaned forward and kissed her gently on the brow.

'How can we prevent it? What is the best way?'

'You believe me?'

'Of course.'

'You believe me about how serious it is?'

'Joey, I know just how serious it is. Up until now I thought that it would be dropped because of the impossibility of making it work. Now I am not so sure. The government would put up with the waste and nonsense identity cards would cause if it meant they could stay in power perpetually. However...' Jady gulped his juice, '... I am not as pessimistic as you. All we have to do is expose the scheme for the nonsense it is. Not so much of the Armageddon, Apocalypse Now, more of the bureaucratic nightmare approach plus a bit of mickey taking. The best way to crush pompous politicians is to laugh at them.' He looked into her eyes and smiled winningly, reassuring Joanna with more than his words.

Jady was right, of course, she considered. Who do these politicians think they are, trying to control us all? It was not as if they were all that impressive themselves. If they were, they would not be turning Parliament into a fortress surrounded by ugly concrete blocks, stark as their souls, and issuing words of defiance whilst cowering behind bulletproof screens. So did the weasels defy the Badger. Well, if those parliamentary weasels thought they could impose their control-freakery on the people, those weasels had another think coming.

Joanna took the orange juice glass gently out of Jady's hand and placed it on the mahogany table. Taking his hands in hers, she gazed silently, and by the flicker of the silent screen their eyes reflected each other.

'You put my heart in the sky.'

'All clear? Any problems, you know where I am. Roger and out.'

Harold Wood watched the guard close the outer Hall door carefully and listened to the required number of 'clicks' thereafter, denoting the correct locking. It was with a slight pang of regret that Harold left work every day. He knew he had done all that was necessary to secure the area and had personally vetted the security staff to the extent that the rate of staff turnover had tripled, but he always felt that the place was safer when he was there personally to supervise it. Still, he sighed sadly, even he could not be at his post twenty-four seven, as his computer manager put it, so it was up to others to do their duty. He was on call, of course, if needed, and would often find an excuse to turn up unannounced for a subtle security check. For now, it was home to Mrs Wood.

As he trod the early evening path leading alongside the Baths, across the river Fons and up the steep hill heading homeward, he speculated on what a good job he was doing and how proud Mr Dauntliffe was of him.

Casting his mind back, he recalled how delighted he'd been to learn of Spawater's honour in being selected for the identity card trial, and how thrilled he was subsequently to receive a visit from the organiser in person. Mr Dauntliffe had come all the way from London to ensure that things were going according to plan and had, of course, inspected the Town Hall. How honoured Harold had been, demonstrating the new security systems introduced with the funds made available by the consortium. And how proud when Mr Dauntliffe congratulated him on a job well done! Mr Dauntliffe, head of the consortium, all the way from London, had congratulated him! Hercules, on finishing his seven labours and an extra one for luck, could not have been more satisfied.

Happy times, thought Harold, smiling distantly like a mobile telephone user and attracting looks from passers by, happy times. From the top of the hill Harold looked down across the river at the Hall and the adjacent Baths. Nothing amiss. Nor would there be, with Harold on sentry-go. The spirit of Captain Mainwaring surged through his veins like a flash flood through a sewer. Terrorists would not get away with anything in his Town Hall. Just let them try. He was ready for them. He had righteousness on his side and an infallible weapon.

Biometrics.

Identity Cards
Chapter Nine

When Harold Wood received the summons to the offices of the Head of Spawater Council, his spirit fell like an anxious barometer. Harold always disliked such summonses; they reminded him of who was really in charge. Not that Harold accepted his subordinate role. The voters elected the Council Head, nominally, to lead in Council affairs, true enough. Harold could, with reluctance, accept that. When it came to the Town Hall, however, Harold Wood knew his place; which was running it. It seemed to Harold that the Council Head did not know his own place at all, which was voting through Harold's ideas and the money to fund them.

Sir Humphrey Appleby looked down from that great Civil Service department in the sky, and smiled approvingly. 'Plus ca change, plus c'est la meme chose,' Sir Humphrey memoed happily. 'St Bernard.'

'Yes, St Sir Humphrey?'

'Stop calling me that. Memo to Upstairs: When Harold Wood reaches his final reward we could use him at the Pearly Gates running the admissions administration.'

'Pardon me, Sir Humphrey...'

'Yes, St Bernard?'

'Won't that slow things down? The man is a bureaucratic nightmare.'

'Exactly, Bernard.'

Bernard looked confused.

Sir Humphrey sighed, dimming his halo.

'With the greatest of respect, St Bernard, sometimes your dogs appear quicker on the uptake than you; and they are always good for a drink.'

'I don't understand.'

Sir Humphrey explained. 'The slower the admissions, the longer the queues and the more angels we can employ to minister to them.'

'Minister?'

'Yes, Minister. At this rate we will have a bigger department than the Seraphim and Cherubim combined.'

St Bernard gazed upon Sir Humphrey in awe. Some things never change.

So it was with slight apprehension that Harold presented himself to the Head's secretary and took his place on the visitors' couch, hands on knees like any junior job applicant, and waited.

'The waiting is over, Millado me lad. The show starts on Monday. It should be fun.'

Arnie disagreed, knowing that Jady's idea of fun was seeing how close to the wind he could sail without Zephyrus sending him to Neptune's basement.

'Let's hope so, anyway. What is happening about my costume?'

Arnie was at Jady's place, along with Alison and Jenna. Joanna was at work, trying to concentrate.

'You go for your fittings now. A car is on the way from Alison's company to collect you with one of their promotions staff. Alison is going too so things will be fine.'

Alison smiled reassuringly.

'And after the first fitting, this afternoon, it will be back to our studio for the posters. They will go up first thing on Monday morning. Afterwards your costume can be adjusted so that you are comfortable with it.'

Unreassured and uncomfortable, Arnie wondered about Jady's definition of words. 'Fun' and 'Fine' were a matter of opinion. Arnie was about to be taken by Alison and one of her colleagues to an expensive bespoke tailor who regularly undertook such assignments for the film and advertising industries. Arnie would be measured upright, sitting down, in repose, in action, stretching, walking and - just in case, said Jady alarmingly - running. All this to produce a costume complete with full-face helmet which would allow him unrestricted vision and mobility yet would disguise him so that his own mother not only would fail to recognise him but would call the police if he as much as bid her good morning. The outfit would make him look taller, broader and yet unhampered in movement. It was the ultimate masquerade, enabling Arnie to appear in front of crowds in complete anonymity.

Anonymity was the only part of the plan he approved of. It was just his faith in Jady's star that kept Arnie's heart out of his mouth and in its moorings, supplying drums n'bass for his stomach butterflies to dance to.

'Are you sure this will really work, Jady?' doubted Arnie, like a French Aristocrat half-heartedly enquiring after his eleventh hour reprieve.

'No worries, young Arnie,' grinned Jenna, metaphorically knitting merrily and booting a tumbrel, 'it's all arranged. Aren't you excited? I would be. I would jump at it, given half a chance. If I had your skill I would be in there like a shot. In years to come your adventures will be the stuff of legend and song; Arnie, the man himself, and his amazing adventures.'

'I thought no-one is supposed to know who I am?'

'Well, there is that,' replied Jenna, resignedly. 'Still, you are a lucky so-and-so, aren't you?'

Arnie was not convinced but he was in far too deep to back out now. Besides, Jady, Jenna and Alison in go-for-it mode raised the spirits like a Hogmanay toast.

Alison's phone rang. 'All right, Arnie, the car is here. Are you ready?'

'As I'll ever be,' he laughed. It would be all right. Jady was in charge, what could go wrong?

Once upon a time he would have telephoned the Heritage society or similar body for confirmation that everything was above board and Spawater fashion, but in the twenty-first century it was much more efficient simply to scan the relevant identity card.

Scanning plastic is so quick and simple; it removes the need for human suspicion and doubt. If the card reader says yes, all is well. In the land of the database, humanity can dispense with its evolved critical faculties. I have seen the future, the Head of the Council reflected, and it works.

'Welcome aboard, Mr Lehmann,' smiled the Council Head, handing Michael back his identity card with an apologetic shrug. 'Sorry about the formalities but you cannot be too careful these days.'

'Call me Michael, everyone does,' replied Michael disarmingly. 'You are right, of course, you cannot be too careful in this day and age.'

'Won't you sit down?' The Council Head waved him through to the comfortable area. 'Now, er, Michael, what can I do for you?'

'I want to know all the security arrangements for the Town Hall and how best to overcome them.'

'Then you have come to the right place.'

Jady and Jenna were in the right place, in their opinion. Lifeboats' in the afternoon was quiet, discreet, and sold liveners. Just the way they liked it.

'Seriously, Jady, thanks for getting me that job with Michael. Easy work, good money and a chance to kick our friend Mr Wood so hard even the bears would feel sorry for him.'

'Cheers.' Jady raised his glass in acknowledgement. 'What I need to know, Jenna, is how to get Millado in and out of the Town Hall without anyone knowing his identity; in particular, the main hall itself where Alison's company and I have booked a series of nights.'

Jenna clucked derisively.

'Come off it, Jady, this is Jenna you are talking to. Don't tell me you don't know how to get hold of false identity. Every mugger in town has half a dozen up their sleeves for sale. In some of the pubs they will transplant your picture onto anyone's card for a tenner.

'As for the biometric iris recognition, the machines are so fragile your accomplice bumps into them accidental like, spilling their soft drink everywhere, and the doormen just wave you through on flashing the card. I wave a supermarket loyalty card at them half the time. They are so fed up of checking everyone all day they just don't bother. It is easier to get into places now than before the control freaks went crazyapebonkers and introduced their lunatic database scheme. So what's your problem?'

'Well, sir, may I first impress upon you the vital need for complete confidence. What I say must not go outside these walls.'

Flattered and intrigued, the Head nodded his head. 'Of course, do go on.'

'In that case, sir, the position is this.'

Michael went down the well trodden highways and byways of deception, explaining for the nth time how he represented a firm called Ecochtrust, a subsidiary of the national Heritage Trust, the guardians of the Baths, and just about every heritage-related organisation in Europe, as well as the European Union. He and his team, Michael explained, had been appointed by the aforementioned body to closely examine the Baths for signs of erosion and general wear and tear. These, if found, might necessitate immediate action to preserve the Baths for Spawater and the nation. If so, Ecochtrust was empowered by its owners to carry out whatever remedial action was deemed necessary. Ecochtrust would pay whatever was required, being funded by its parent organisations.

'I see,' said the Head, importantly. 'Well of course you will have my fullest cooperation, and that of my staff. But why the great need for secrecy?'

Michael sighed ruefully, his manner as a good man, saddened by the needless unhappiness humans inflict on one another.

'Why indeed, why indeed. You see,' he said, leaning forward confidentially, 'things are not quite as straightforward as I may perhaps have implied.' Michael turned to the window as if expecting to see eavesdroppers. 'First of all, as an historical architect specialising in the

Roman period, I want, with every fibre of my being, to see the Spawater Baths preserved in perpetuity and looked after by those who appreciate them most.'

'Well,' stuttered the Head, 'I am sure we all do.'

'Ah, but not everyone at the Commission wants the Baths to survive; or Ecochtrust to succeed. There is a movement afoot throughout the now enlarged European Community to join all of Europe's national Heritage Trusts and related organisations into one European-wide conglomerate. The latest countries to join the EU want their slice of the heritage pie. When they get it, national treasures such as the Baths will be at grave risk of losing all of their funding and even heritage status.' Michael looked the Head in the eye. 'The bottom line is this. When the conglomerate is formed, if they decide that the Spawater Baths are suffering from terminal erosion, they will not be saved. Money available will be spent instead on Heritage projects in the new member countries.'

He paused to let this sink in.

'You mean..?'

'Yes.'

'Surely they can't do that?'

'Just watch them. It is all in the treaties of accession. Not in so many words, of course, but as a non-attributable carrot thrown to the new countries entering the Union in return for keeping quiet about the truth of the proposed European Constitution.'

Michael continued as the Head looked on, aghast. 'Oh, it won't be for a couple of years and everyone will deny it if asked, but it is coming. It is as inevitable as European Union identity cards.'

This was appalling; like a kick in the teeth from a Werehorse. On his watch! The Head was no mathematician but he could put two and two together; Head of Council plus demise of Spawater Baths equals End of Career.

'A couple of years? Are you absolutely certain?'

Michael nodded grimly; a nod the Reaper himself could hardly have bettered.

The Head was in shock. He knew what he was hearing must be true because the person opposite saying so was authorised. The card reader said so. He turned pleadingly to the man he had known for less than one hour.

'What can we do to stop them? Can you help?'

Michael smiled encouragingly, like the Sun cracking the ice and letting the flowers through.

'Courage, this game is not over by any means. It will not be easy, but yes, together we can stop them. If we succeed,' Michael added, adopting a more optimistic tone, like the Big Bad Wolf offering Bo Peep shares in a mint sauce factory, 'success will lead to grants for Spawater as a place of architectural importance. As Council Head, you will be in line for the European gravy boat. However,' Michael resumed his voice of doom, the Grim Reaper taking notes, 'and I cannot emphasise this strongly enough, I will need your total, unquestioning support, cooperation and assistance.'

Michael paused theoretically. Gielgud could only look down in awe. 'See that Larry? Now that is what I call acting.'

'Do I have it?'

Had Michael demanded the Head's house, he would have got the garage thrown in.

'Of course.'

'Are you with me totally?'

'Totally.'

Michael looked at the Head nobly, like a cow rescued from an abattoir. 'May I shake your hand, sir? You have just decided the fate of the Spawater Baths.'

'The Spawater Baths, of course,' said Jenna confidently. 'They are the key; that's your answer.'

She rewarded herself by pouring out some wine. Jady had explained his problem and an amused Jenna, processing the data faster than any computer, had produced her reply.

'So he has got a fake identity card but must not use it to enter the Town Hall. We can get round that by using the Baths.'

'How do you mean?'

Jenna raised her glass, sipped a satisfied sip, and explained.

'You see, Jady, the Spawater Baths are connected to the Town Hall. Not the actual baths, of course, but there is a corridor between the two buildings. Mind you,' she t'ched, 'it is locked usually.'

A flush of inspiration spread across her face, spreading enlightenment like a battalion of Missionaries on a roll. Archimedes had the same feeling on bath night.

'Eureka! I know the buildings pretty well, and I know they share the same heating system. There is a whole labyrinth of connecting tunnels containing the electricity cables, gas pipes, water and heating. The whole thing was rebuilt in the nineteen fifties, after World War whichever one it was, and everything connects. If you get young Arnie into the Baths, he can nip into the changing rooms, open one of the vents, crawl along the connecting tunnel and emerge out of the caretaker's door at the back of the stage. It will be a doddle to lose himself in the general throng.'

'Not in his outfit it won't!' laughed Jady. This was better than he could have hoped. A 'secret' tunnel connecting the buildings; what could be better? However, first things first. 'It was World War Two, by the way, Jenna. Show some respect for the fallen.'

Jenna looked suitably contrite. She knew Jady was a stickler for the proprieties. Some things could not be joked about in his presence.

'Anyway,' Jady continued, 'about this tunnel..?'

'Mr Wood? I would like to introduce you to Mr Lehmann.'

The Head of Spawater Town Hall, now a true believer in Michael and his cause, explained to a distinctly underwhelmed Mr Wood that for the next few weeks he was no longer the undisputed king of his castle. At any rate, that is how poor Harold saw it. Being sworn to secrecy, the Head could only say that Mr Lehmann was an historical architect and was here to carry out an in-depth study of the Spawater Baths. He had carte blanche to do whatever he deemed necessary and it was Mr Wood's job to ensure that he got whatever help he asked for. Also, added the Head, knowing Mr Wood's proprietary attitude to the Hall and the Baths, there was to be no hindrance or he, Mr Wood, would answer to him, the Head.

Harold was none too pleased. Anyone who undermined his authority automatically came under the chapter titled 'interloper' in Harold's book. Michael was already one down for this reason, and a potential threat to Harold's ordered existence and thereby to the security of the Town Hall and environs. In the final analysis, anyone who undermined Harold's position posed a threat to western values and civilisation itself. He took these things seriously. Harold was having a bad day, but there was worse to come.

'One other point,' interjected Michael to the Head and his resentful underling. 'To assist my team in its endeavours, I have engaged a local agent to represent our interests, deal with deliveries of tools etc, liaise with the various parties and generally act as a trouble-shooter in the event of problems. You know the sort, members of the public or over enthusiastic staff, that sort of thing.'

Harold bristled. Any passing badger would have greeted him as a cousin.

'She's a local woman,' Michael continued, 'one familiar with the Town Hall and its workings. It is vital that she receives full cooperation and attention from everyone concerned.'

Harold had never experienced a nameless fear before. If you had asked him, he would not have known what a nameless fear was. He knew now.

'Of course. What is her name?' asked the Head.

'Jenna Wilkinson-Baart.'

The nameless fear had a name. Somehow Harold just knew it would be her. That unspeakable woman. Harold's consciousness sank reluctantly to that dark, dusty dungeon in the pits of his mind; an unpleasant place, seldom visited by choice, where he kept that which he could not categorise. That woman might just as well be its gatekeeper. Unable to realise the peril Spawater was in from mad terrorists everywhere, and unwilling to make the sacrifices of personal liberty required in order to be secure, she just would not take Harold's security bandobast seriously. Calling him Double-Oh-Zero and asking if he was shaken not stirred. She was the bane of his life, and now he was expected to cooperate with her!

The woman laughed at him, ridiculed his security checks, refused to evacuate her class for his terrorist alert drills, refused to supply registers giving him the names of her dance or aerobics students, any of which could be saboteurs, and incited others to rebel too. Cooperate with her? Over his dead body.

'Do you understand, Mr Wood? Full cooperation and attention.'

Harold retrieved himself. 'Oh yes, Head Councillor, I understand perfectly.'

He did too. Harold understood that this Mr Lehmann and his damned assistant were threats. They would get no cooperation from him. 'Full attention, you say? Of course, everyone involved in this will receive my fullest attention.'

Identity Cards
Chapter Ten

'S'long, Jady, see you tonight. And thank you for a most illuminating discussion.'

Jenna and Jady went their separate ways; he, home for more planning and she, home to relax. In the evening Jenna was to meet Michael in Lifeboats' to discuss the state of play, and then with Jady, Arnie and Alison to discuss their project. Joanna and various others would be in attendance. It is a tough life, Jenna groaned to herself, but someone has to keep things functioning outside the office.

The nine-to-five mentality that has made the world what it is, like the Rings of Saturn, had no place in Jenna's orbit, nor Jady's.

Hanif felt the same about Michael. He had no place orbiting around Alison and the rest of the Lifeboats' crew. Employing Jenna to do his dirty work for him! Michael was more of a rogue meteor; burning brightly but briefly and deceiving the gullible and the honest into thinking he was the Sun, then fading into nothingness. Well, thought Hanif, he could burn elsewhere, and probably would, but he was not going to take Hanif's friends for a ride in his slipstream.

It troubled his conscience at first, but inevitably Hanif decided that there was only one thing he could do. It was wrong, Hanif conceded, and against his principles, but needs must when the Devil drives. It was the lesser of two evils and therefore, logically, the right thing to do. This Michael character was some kind of impostor; Hanif had convinced himself of that. Now he was going to prove it.

If people's ears really did burn when others thought bad things of them, sunglasses would never trouble Michael again. Harold Wood was considerably less intelligent than Hanif, but what he lacked in grey matter he more than compensated for in suspicion, doubt, and bile.

Harold was in charge of security, Health and Safety, administration and general running of the Town Hall and the Spawater Baths. Now the Head of the Council, out of the blue, had ordered him to jump to the command, not only of some foreign so-called architect, but also of his nemesis, that Jenna woman. Jenna whatshername, her name was; an enemy of security, control and stability, a disrespectful woman who laughed at him and his attempts to impose order on the public. Laughter is the slayer of pomposity, and Jenna was a metaphorical sword swinger.

Well, thought Harold determinedly, I am not going to take this lying down. This is clearly some kind of plot, some scheme to undermine my authority and make me a laughing stock. She might have fooled the Council Head, Harold fumed, but she is not going to fool me. That foreigner and that Jenna whatshername are up to something and I am going to find out what it is.

Unlike Hamlet, who Harold would not have got on with, Harold was a man of decision. Having decided to investigate the foreign architect, or whatever he really was, Harold took steps through the proper channels. Calling his assistant, he ordered, 'Get me the police, will you?'

'It went like a dream. Even better than I could have hoped for. Marlene, you are a genius. He was suspicious at first, but once he put my card through the scanner and read my 'details',' Michael twiddled two of his fingers is time-honoured tradition, indicating inverted commas, 'I just sailed through. He could not do enough for me. I have said it before and I will say it again, God bless biometrics.'

Marlene smiled. She was totally confident, of course, being just about the best in the business, but it is always nice to be complimented. That's why all the best gods demand sacrifices. 'Hey, Zeus!' 'Yes, Thor?' 'What sacrifices have you received lately?' 'Only the usual, nectar, ambrosia, gold, that sort of thing. How about you?' 'All I get is umbrellas. I think I will go and start a few storms.'

'And Louise,' rejoined Marlene generously, 'she has the database totally under her control.'

Louise returned the compliment with a generous nod. After all, they were all in it together, for equal shares. Michael insisted on fair shares all round in order to prevent petty squabbles. His employer could afford the best, and got it.

'You make it sound simple,' added Erich curiously. 'It can't be that easy really, can it?'

'It is if you know what you are doing,' replied Marlene with another smile, an enigmatic one this time. 'In fact, almost anyone could do it. As you know, all you need is to find the footway box and intercept the local loop.'

'Sounds loopy to me,' laughed Michael. The happiest crooks in town, they made the Laughing Policeman sound miserable.

'Yes,' continued Marlene, happy to recount her cleverness. 'The local loop is the bit of telephone wire that connects a building to the rest of the world. It travels to a footway box, a mini telephone exchange contained in a green box on every British High Street. These are not secure and with the right kit people can get in and tap telephones. Once we control the wires we can direct them to our own, private, little telephone exchange.' Marlene opened her bag and held up a small screwdriver. 'It is amazing what you can do with one of these.'

'Low tech beats high tech,' remarked Erich. 'So much for biometrics, eh, Michael?'

'So much indeed.'

'But you must thank Louise for the next stage.'

'Standard database work, any computer genius could do it,' cackled Louise immodestly. 'I just monitored all traffic, ignoring the rest until it flagged up your card, as Michael Lehmann, the world famous historical architect employed by Ecochtrust, a subsidiary of the world's heritage organisations and the marvellous, incorruptible European Union. I verified it exactly as the real database would have done. If it had not been a pack of lies, of course.'

They all laughed; the Laughing Policeman, had he been eavesdropping, would have turned in his badge. 'I am not arresting anybody as happy as that, ho ho.'

'What do we do next?' asked Erich the practical.

'Next? Next we celebrate a job well, if only half, done. I am meeting that Jenna in The Lifeboat Club tonight and I suggest we all go. Partly business as it looks good if we are all there, and partly pleasure.'

Michael looked at Louise. 'I take it our system will automatically verify any of our names should that Council Head or anyone else make enquiries?'

Louise nodded. 'And it will ring me up and inform me what the enquiry was.'

'Why not ring all of us?' asked Erich.

'And have all our phones ring at the same time?'

'Oh yes, sorry.'

'But only, of course, if they check from the Town Hall local loop. Anywhere else and they will get the real database, which will simply say that we applied for temporary identification as historical architects and that we work for Ecochtrust. It will not say that any heritage trust or the EU employs us. As you know, it was too risky to lie about our employers. We could be found out.'

'No problem,' said Michael complacently. 'It will say we work for Ecochtrust and that is good enough. We can tell anyone else that our true employers are commercially confidential. Now, I suggest we go back to our hotels for a meal and a shower, then off to the Lifeboat Club for business and pleasure.'

'So it is off to Lifeboats' then.'

'For a change.'

Joanna accepted the proffered cup of tea and relaxed back in her comfortable armchair. Much as she disliked Jady's choice of furniture - woodworms shunned it for fear of being thought dated by other woodworms; 'So nineteenth century' - she had to admit that it was comfortable. It reminded her of Lifeboats'.

'It is business and pleasure,' continued Jady, ignoring the sarcasm, 'I need to discuss the project with Alison and make sure Arnie is happy with his costume. Alison said that the photographs are fine so it is just a matter of approving the proofs and the posters can go up. Then we can all have an early celebratory drink.'

'This must be your idea of perfect happiness, Jady. Skulduggery washed down by champagne.' Joanna at the office had had one of those days.

'Helped by you fighting the good fight against a control freak government and its fascistic database threat.' Jady winked. 'I think we both do rather well, don't you?' Jady recognised the storm clouds a'rumbling on the fringes of Joanna's temper, but knew how to disperse them. Humour works better than crystals.

Joanna laughed the cares of the working day behind her. 'I just can't get over you, Jady. No matter how well I think I know you, you still manage to amaze me. Here am I, fighting the good fight, as you say, against an emerging totalitarian State, and here are you, hopefully about to make a fortune by turning their control freakery to your advantage. If you win, you will show up this identity card fetish for the farce that it is.'

Jady stood behind her armchair and put his arms around her neck. 'Drink your tea; we have to fight the good fight together in Lifeboats'.'

'Let me get this straight, Mr Wood. Your boss, the Head of Spawater Council, has instructed you to cooperate with a team of architects who are here to give the Baths a going over to check for signs of erosion and repair any damage they find. You are suspicious of the architects and want the police to check out their credentials. Just one question; what makes you suspicious?'

Police Inspector Josephine Brewe was no stranger to Spawater Town Hall. It had been the scene of her greatest career misfortune; when she had crossed swords with Jady and finished up on the wrong end of Spawater's first riot since Caesar's leaving do. She had been new to Spawater at the time and saw it as a stepping-stone to greater things in the Police Service. Or Police Force, as she preferred. The weight of the can she'd carried following the riot had slowed her ascent through the ranks. What Inspector Brewe dreamed of more than a White Christmas was a period of peace and calm. What she did not want was yet more nonsense from that self-appointed guardian of citizen security, Harold Wood.

'Well, Mr Wood,' she repeated, in that incredulous 'so you are asking me to believe?' tone of voice that police officers do so well, 'what is it that makes you suspicious when your boss is not?'

This disconcerted poor Harold. As the Town Hall manager he was unused to having to explain himself. Of course, he had no real evidence; just pique that his boss, that German and especially that Jenna woman, were undermining his authority.

Harold was no barrister, but he knew enough to realise that his suspicions would not stand up in court. They were too weak even to climb up the steps to the witness box.

When in doubt, try being pompous.

'Look, Inspector, as security overseer for these important buildings it is my job to be suspicious of everybody until proven otherwise. We live in dangerous times and it is for the well-being and security of everybody that no-one is trusted. How do we know this man is who he says he is? What I would like from you, Inspector, as we are both in the business of protecting the public from themselves, is to check up on this man. Who is he? What is his background? That sort of thing. Can I have your support in this matter?'

Inspector Brewe took a deep breath. She had learnt to do that in anger management courses. The Town Hall was a priority for the police and as such she was obliged to respond immediately to any request for assistance. All very well in theory, she supposed, but the police High Command did not have to deal with the likes of Harold Wood on the ground.

Silently promising greater autonomy for intelligent police inspectors when she took her rightful place in the higher echelons, she replied, 'Did the man show the Council Head his identity card?'

'Yes, I suppose so. Besides, he would have to have it scanned to enter the building. We can't risk assassins getting at the Councillors.'

'You think they are at risk?'

'We are all at risk. Who knows where the terrorists will strike next? Let me assure you, if they start anything here I will be ready for them.'

Harold Wood at the helm. That was all Inspector Brewe needed. If Harold's forbear had been helmsman to Christopher Columbus the world would still be flat.

'Look, Mr Wood, if this gentleman produced his identity card and it confirmed he was authorised to inspect the Baths, and if that is good enough for the Head of the Council, then it should be good enough for you. If people do not trust identity cards there is no point in having them. Now, one more time; do you have any evidence that all is not what it seems? Yes or No.'

Harold had to admit defeat. 'Not exactly, but I still think something is wrong.'

'We are busy people, Mr Wood. If you find any genuine evidence that something is wrong, then get in touch. Not before, understand?'

Harold nodded, shamefaced.

'Come on, Sergeant Mathews, we have work to do.' With that she turned to go.

Detective Sergeant Mathews was amused. He agreed wholeheartedly with his boss that Harold Wood was a timewaster, but anything that annoyed her amused him. He was easygoing and laid back. Dixon of Dock Green would have despaired. On the other hand, Inspector Brewe wore her ambition on her sleeve and was contemptuous of those who didn't.

'Do you think there is anything in it, Ma'am?'

'Of course not, Sergeant; now let's get on.'

Harold disagreed. He was more convinced than ever that something was amiss. Now he had been made to look a fool just for doing his job with a diligence sadly lacking in the local police service. Well, if they would not take the terrorist threat seriously, then he, Harold Wood, would.

Just as Hamlet and Harold lacked the divine spark, so Hamlet, Harold and Hanif would hardly rival the Three Musketeers, d'Artagnan, Athos, Porthos and Aramis when it came to mutual assistance. Nevertheless, Hamlet notwithstanding, Hanif and Harold were working to the same end: discrediting Michael.

At the end of the working day the office was quiet and Hanif had some time to himself for private research. Discrediting Michael was the objective and if Michael was exaggerating, or better still, lying, Hanif knew how to find out. He knew the gang would be at Lifeboats' that evening and he would enjoy showing Alison and the rest that Michael was the fraud Hanif suspected. He would not reveal how he'd found out, of course; the good detective, like the magician, never reveals his methods. Sherlock would approve.

Hanif was an honest man. He knew it would, of course, be unlawful for unauthorised personnel to check up on individuals recorded on the national database. Apart from civil servants, council officers and their agents, who would of course have legal access, others would just have to bribe the poverty stricken data entry clerks to check up on people illegally.

That being the case, plus the national database not yet being nationwide, Hanif felt justified in checking Michael's credentials. His normally ironclad, sinewy conscience raised one eyebrow, shrugged helplessly and gave up the ghost.

As a senior database administrator, Hanif had the necessary passwords, or protocols, for accessing all the database files. Working alongside Mr Dauntliffe, who, of course, knew nothing about the technical side of database security, Hanif was perfectly positioned to find out everything the database held on Michael.

He sat at his machine, codes at the ready, expert fingers poised. 'Well, Michael,' Hanif crowed vindictively, 'now to find out who, exactly, you really are.'

Identity Cards
Chapter Eleven

'No, don't tell me; let me take a wild guess. You are celebrating your latest coup and you want champagne. Am I right?'

Early evening, twilight zone of social clubs the world over. The evening shift was yet to arrive and the matinee drinkers had fled. Had the boy who stood on the burning deck been in Lifeboats', he could have saved his matches. Lifeboats' at six thirty made the Marie Celeste look like Noah's Ark at feeding time.

'Right you are, Ron,' Jady conceded amicably. 'It is a good barman who understands his customers. You should go far.'

'I couldn't agree more. What is it then? Champagne and two glasses?'

Jady looked over at Joanna who was establishing base camp at the north-western end of the well-furnished lounge. On reflection, as Snow White learnt to her discomfort, it was not always wise to show off. Joanna was hardly in the mood to celebrate; best perhaps to keep it low key until the others arrived. She could join in then.

'Not yet, Ron, I am waiting for the others. Make it your excellent house white for now. Two glasses.'

'Three, and make them large ones. And hi, Ron, Jady.'

Ron mumbled Ron-like.

'Oh, howdy, Jenna,' replied Jady. 'Good to see you. Jo is over there.'

'Righty ho.' Jenna embarked on her voyage to Joanna's table. 'Here we are again, then,' she called jauntily as she hove alongside, 'I must say, things are looking up. Well Joey, how are you?'

'Awful, since you ask. And you?'

'Me, fine. But what is all this about feeling awful? Has that Jady of yours been beating you again? Or has he stopped beating you? Which is it, yes or no?'

Joanna laughed knowingly. Good old Jenna; staying miserable when getting the Jenna treatment was like wrestling octopuses without getting ticklish. Or octopi.

'Oh, it's nothing really. I am just fed up of this identity card and national database business. I can't help thinking that it is just going to happen anyway and there is nothing we can do about it.'

'Hmm, yes, I know what you mean. Well, start at the bottom. Let's force whoever turns up tonight to discuss ID cards and what we should do about them.'

'Force?'

'Yes, force.' Jenna laughed. 'If we are talking about ID cards they will have to join in, won't they? Not all evening, of course, but let's insist that everyone who joins us tonight gives us their opinions on the subject.'

'Ok' agreed Joanna, brightening as embers in a gentle breeze, 'and if we do not approve we will give them our opinions.'

'That's the spirit. Oh good, here comes your Jady with the refreshments. We can practice on him.'

'Oh look,' added Joanna, pointing towards the entrance, 'there's Alison and Arnie.'

She waved encouragingly to them and was acknowledged by an unselfconscious cry from Alison that had Arnie reeling like a landlubber on his maiden voyage. Joanna and Jenna laughed.

'Things are livening up, Joey; the main thing is, we have plenty of support. We are certainly not on our own.'

Oh, what tangled web we weave, thought Michael light-heartedly, as he awaited the taxi collecting him and the others for their evening out in Lifeboats'. The business part of the evening consisted of briefing Jenna, letting her know that the manager, Mr Wood, was under instructions to cooperate with her. He smiled at the thought of Jenna punching the air in delight and vowing to make Mr Wood's life the misery he deserved. After all, Mr Wood and his delusional, petty constraints on individual freedom in the name of a bogus 'security' were making Jenna's working life a misery. Yes, he deserved everything that Jenna could throw at him.

This would, of course, keep Mr Wood occupied defending his territory and his monstrous conceit, and thus ensure that he had no time to do anything actually useful; like his job protecting the Town Hall and the Baths. Not, Michael considered complacently, that he was ever likely to anyway.

Laurel and Hardy looked down upon Harold and shook their heads, Stanley getting his halo entwined with Ollie's and bumping his noggin.

'Now look what you've done,' complained Ollie.

'I can't help it,' whimpered Stanley, on the verge of tears, 'but that Harold Wood is dumber than we ever were.'

'He sure is,' Ollie agreed, 'I'd hate to push a piano up a hill with him.'

'And I'd hate to push it back down again,' Stanley agreed. 'Why he has more brains in his whole body than he has in his little finger.'

'I couldn't agree less.'

'Neither could I.'

They clashed heads and ruffled their feathers, happily ever after.

As he left his hotel and instructed the cabbie to drive to the one where the others were staying, Michael mused on what the aftermath of this adventure would be. He had conceived a liking for Jenna and hoped she would not face too many problems at the inquest. True, she could look after herself, but the embarrassment the operation would inevitably cause could leave the authorities seeking scapegoats. Jenna might just be unlucky. Michael considered donating a bonus into her bank account - she had given him the details of her business account for payment purposes - he would certainly be able to afford it when his paymaster stumped up on completion, but chuckled inwardly when he realised that the prosecution would seize on that as proof of Jenna's complicity.

No, he concluded sadly, as the taxi made its way through the pleasant streets of Summer Spawater, Jenna was on her own.

'Here we all are then,' announced Jenna to the assembled crew when they eventually settled down. 'Glad you asked, glad you asked. Joanna and I were discussing the threat of compulsory Identification Cards spreading like cancer from our humble town to the length and breadth of the country. We wondered, didn't we Jo, what your opinions were. So, who's first?'

Alison, Jady and Arnie looked at each other enquiringly. Jady alone knew the thinking behind Jenna's no-nonsense approach; it was to cheer up Joanna. This being the case, he decided to start things moving. Had he a ball he would have rolled it.

'You know my opinion; obviously it is a stupid idea. The excuse, as you know, is that it will fight terrorism, prevent crime and cure cancer. It won't of course; it will do nothing of the sort. It is what's known as displacement activity. Real problems are too hard to solve so let's focus on easier issues. ID cards give the impression that something is being done - about terrorism, crime, immigration and so on - and that is how it is sold to the public, sold being the operative word. Sold a pup.' Jady took a sip of wine and continued. 'The national database, if it ever happens, will take responsibility for people's security out of their own hands and into the hands of the government. Given the records of governments the world over when it comes to safeguarding their people, we can be sure that people will be in greater danger than ever. Mainly,' Jady surmised, 'from their governments.'

He looked around the table. Everyone looked serious; now for a bit of mischief. 'What do you think, Millado?'

Arnie spluttered. He had been pushed from proverbial pillar to post all week; being prodded, poked and measured all over in the most embarrassing way by tailors who might just as well have asked him to cough while they were about it.

What side did he dress indeed! His costume designed, he had to pose in it for publicity pictures and then re-sit for the tailors so they could add the finishing touches. He had been coached on how to conduct himself while on duty, as it were, and finally informed by a gloating Jenna that he was expected to crawl along a ventilation shaft or something from the Baths to the Hall, in full costume before he even began!

Arriving at Lifeboats' the last week before the storm broke, Arnie expected to get splifficated in peace. Now people were asking him about identity cards; people who, as he knew perfectly well, hated them. It was too much.

'I like them. I think they are great.'

'Of course you do, Millado. We all do.'

'Well *you* certainly do, chief; after all, if it wasn't for ID cards you would not be about to make a fortune with me as the Masked -'

'Shut up, you idiot,' stage-whispered Jenna urgently, simultaneously clasping her hand over his mouth. 'It is supposed to be a secret. Like Batman.'

Arnie's rebellion crumbled. 'Sorry Jenna, sorry chief. I have had a tough week.'

'No, Arnie,' interjected Joanna, 'I am the one who needs to apologise. You see, I have been depressed about the national database and ID cards and how people don't seem to realise just how dangerous they are. Jenna was trying to cheer me up by getting everybody to talk about them. Sorry. Let's just forget about that rubbish and have a good time.' Joanna picked up her glass in a 'let's change the subject then' manner.

'Identity cards? A fascinating subject, tell me more.' Unnoticed by an engrossed Jady and the gang, Michael and his colleagues had arrived.

Hanif sighed and sat back in his expensive computer chair. He would rather have had cushions. He switched off his computer in the usual manner, by clicking on the button named 'start' and logging off. He needed to learn about Michael elsewhere. Jenna would be a good, as she was working for him, but Jenna might not co-operate. He would try Jady first. Jady would listen to reason, and then take it from there.

Anyway, Hanif considered, there was nothing more he could achieve at work. Home for a quick wash and change, then off to Lifeboats'. That was the way to proceed.

'Great progress, Jenna, at the Baths; I will tell you about it later. With your permission?' Michael bowed to the assembled company, lingering on Alison in a manner that Hanif, had he been present, would have considered a declaration of war. 'My group will sit at the next table. See you in a moment.'

Turning, Michael ambled towards the bar, as Marlene, Louise and Erich sat down in the wide armchairs around the adjacent table.

Reaching the top of the hill overlooking the Town Hall in the middle of Spawater, Harold stopped, turned and gazed down dotingly on his empire. The Town Hall and the Baths were Harold's fiefdom and it lightened his soul to see it from above, resplendent and proud. As he glanced beyond the Spawater Baths and up to the horizon, Harold noted Summer storm clouds, far away in the dim and distant, but unmistakably approaching his town.

Harold was not a romantic; Spring showers did not awaken nature and bring forth Summer flowers; they muddied up his driveway. Summer sunshine did not produce and illuminate the beauties of creation and the joy of living; it got in his eyes. Rolling Autumn mists did not part to reveal nature's store of hidden fruits and berries; they made his wife's washing damp. The snows of Winter were not to be crisply crunched through with a loved one on the way to a cheery pint pulled by a glowing, ruddy-faced landlord, a hearty welcome and a roaring fire; they were slippery and cold.

No, Harold was not romantic, but even he could see the symmetry between storm clouds on the horizon and what was occurring at the Spawater Town Hall. Those clouds are an omen, he thought, warily trying to guess how long they would take to arrive. Not long. Too soon, that's for sure.

The strain of metaphysical juxtaposition becoming wearisome, Harold returned to the issue at hand. What to do about the foreign impostor and his henchwoman - if that was the word - Jenna Whatshername. He would never forgive himself if anything happened on his watch. He was in charge of security and as such, outranked the Council Head. Outranked everyone, in fact; except of course, Mr Dauntliffe.

An unpleasant thought struck him; if anything went wrong with security, what would Mr Dauntliffe say? Mr Dauntliffe was the only person Harold would accept as a superior in security matters. Mr Dauntliffe had said he was proud of Harold. He'd said that Harold was a credit to homeland security. Harold could not let him down.

Mr Dauntliffe! Of course! Mr Dauntliffe had said that if Harold needed help at any time, he should contact him. That was the answer. First thing tomorrow, Harold would contact Mr Dauntliffe and state his concerns. Mr Dauntliffe would know what to do.

Harold straightened up, a weight removed from his shoulders like Atlas on his coffee break. The storm clouds were still approaching but Harold snapped his fingers at them. Kick up all the storm you want, challenged Harold silently, Mr Dauntliffe and I are ready for you.

'We are ready, Jenna; ready to go.'

Michael smiled confidently at a pleased Jenna over the top of his glass. These were the good times, he thought reflectively. The ideal sting; a Russian billionaire with a love of ancient history, a Roman monument virtually unguarded except by fallible technology and gullible humans who believed in machines more than the evidence of their own senses, a team of professionals to work with and a false identity to hide behind. What could be better? Shame he could hardly write his memoirs.

'Brilliant. I wish I could have seen Wood's face when he was ordered to cooperate fully with me. Wonder where he drinks? Maybe I could go there and point at him in front of his buddies, if he has any.'

'Now now, Jenna, no need to gloat; I am sure your pal Mr Wood is sufficiently upset without you making things worse. So, we start Monday morning. My colleague, Erich,' Michael glanced at Erich across the table, 'will make the initial soundings. You have met him before, of course.'

'Of course.'

Erich nodded, smiling. 'I look forward to seeing you on Monday, Jenna.'

Michael found himself once more regretting the subterfuge necessary to carry out the enterprise, and hoped Jenna would not feel too badly about him afterwards. Or Jady, or any of them; he had taken to them all. Still, there it was. Brutus had a similar experience with his friend Julius. Perhaps he should warn Jenna to beware the Ides of March.

'All right, Michael, I will be there first thing Monday. I have a dance class in the afternoon so it works out quite handy. Now,' Jenna reached over to the adjacent table housing Jady and the gang, rescued a bottle and poured out some more wine. 'Changing the subject entirely, Michael old chap, you said you found identity cards fascinating. Tell me more.'

'Could I have a word in private?'

'Of course, any word in particular?'

While Jenna and Michael were chatting at the table hosting Michael's group, Hanif arrived at Lifeboats' main saloon and made his way to the table adjacent, harbouring Jady and the gang. After the initial welcoming greetings, for form's sake, Hanif drew Jady aside to ask for a word concerning Michael.

Curious and puzzled in equal proportions, like a cat taking its first stab at a crossword and finding it cryptic, Jady agreed instantly.

‘Right, I will get a round in and you can help carry it back. I only need a moment. I need to ask you something.’

With an effort, Jady pushed back the heavy armchair he had been relaxing in and arose. Together they walked towards the bar.

‘Birds and bees?’

‘No. Something serious.’

‘Birds and bees aren’t serious?’

‘Stop clowning, Jady.’ He could be so infuriating at times, thought Hanif irritably. Jady tended to get flippant in direct proportion to the seriousness of the subject. Jady’s last words on his deathbed would likely be ‘Doctor, in front of you and these witnesses, I hereby revoke my last Will and Testament.’ Still, he needed Jady’s help so perseverance was the name of the game. They arrived at the bar and signalled Ron.

‘It concerns that Michael character. As you know, I am suspicious of him and worried about him and, er, Jenna. After all, he is employing Jenna and if he is a fraud it could cause Jenna problems.’

‘Problems, problems. Everybody has problems. You do not know what problems are until you have tried running this place.’

Ron was in midseason form, effortlessly wiping a glass with a cloth that could have been a candidate for the Turner Prize had it not taken to drink, glaring at Bullet for having the temerity to win on his fruit machine and discussing theology with Hanif and Jady at the same time. A true multitasker.

‘Hello, Ron,’ replied Hanif automatically. ‘Two bottles of House, please.’

‘Not started your celebrations yet, then?’

‘What celebrations?’

‘Oh that’s me,’ interjected Jady. ‘Our little project is starting on Monday. We may have a proper drink later if everyone is in the mood.’

'A mood to celebrate?' Ron looked at Jady as though he had proposed a march on Moscow, then uncorked a couple and placed them on a tray.

'That's all right, Ron. We will carry them.'

They picked a bottle each and walked slowly towards the far side of the room.

'Ok Han, what is the problem with Michael?'

Hanif paused. He knew Jady would laugh at his next sentence.

'You know I was suspicious of him? Well, I decided to look him up on the national database.'

Jady stopped walking. He found it difficult to walk, carry wine, grin and burst out laughing at the same time. As a male multitasker, Ron reigned supreme.

'You looked him up on the national database?'

'No.'

In anticipation of later champagne, Jady had gone easy on the wine. Sometimes the gods are kind.

'You speak in riddles, sir. Did you or did you not, bearing in mind that you have spent countless hours in this very establishment telling me and everybody else that the planned national database is a marvellous thing; posing no threat to civil liberties, and utterly safe; that it could not be tampered with or used by unauthorised people for unscrupulous ends such as spying on people who they are jealous of, did you or did you not, I submit m'lud, look up Michael on the national database?'

With his spare hand, Jady flicked imaginary braces like Rumpole on a role.

'I tried but I failed. That is why I need your help.'

Hanif turned and faced his friend. 'Tell me Jady, please. What is Michael's surname?'

Identity Cards
Chapter Twelve

'Of course,' insisted Joanna to Alison, Jady, Joanna and Hanif, 'the threatened national database is worse than the identity cards.'

'Do you really think so? I would have thought one was as bad as the other,' replied Jady.

The evening was wearing on, as was the conversation. At least Arnie thought so. Drinks were flowing and the conversation flowed with them. A passing hippy would have found it all very Zen. Arnie didn't.

'Chief, fancy a game of Pool?' he tried hopefully.

'I've told you, Millado, I don't want anyone seeing you do your tricks. You have a secret identity to protect. You didn't see Bruce Wayne doing wheelies in the Batmobile on his day off, did you?'

'Bruce who?'

'Never mind. It is just that you have to be careful, that's all.'

'But I need to practice. I have to keep my eye in.'

Jady considered. Yes, Arnie was right. Out of the mouths of babes...

'Fair enough, let's have a game. But no trick shots if there is anybody watching.'

'Suits me, chief,' enthused Arnie. I must try this 'I need practice' gag more often, he reflected happily.

Making their excuses, the pair picked up their drinks and set sail Poolward ho.

'Do you really think ID cards and the national database are that wicked?' asked Hanif earnestly. He welcomed the chance to be alone with Joanna and Alison. It gave him the opportunity to mend fences. 'I mean, I know we have our differences but surely the government knows what it is doing. This is not Hitler's Germany; it is Britain in the twenty-first century.'

‘What’s that got to do with anything?’ snapped Joanna. ‘Do you know something, Hanif? I am sick to death of people saying that things must be different because this is the twenty-first century. What the hell has that got to do with anything? It is just a man-made number, a contrived, artificial way of letting people know when to have their birthdays and what to carve on their tombstones.’

‘The tombstone writers were very put out by the twenty-first century,’ interrupted Alison.

‘Sorry?’ said Joanna and Hanif in unison, agreeing, it seemed, for the first time this century.

‘Yes. Apparently the tombstone carvers carve in advance and they had carved too many tombstones saying ‘Born 19 gap, died 19 gap.’ Not enough people died in 1999 and they couldn’t change the tombstones to ‘died 20 gap’ because you can’t change a ‘19’ to a ‘20’. Not in stone or marble at least.’

‘Thanks, Ali. So Hanif, to continue. What is the real truth behind identity cards?’ Joanna raised a hand, forestalling Hanif’s knee-jerk response. ‘Don’t say it is about terrorism or immigration; they are just excuses. What is it about numbering everyone that makes governments so keen on this control freak nonsense anyway?’

Hanif was relaxed. Jady had given him Michael’s surname in return for Hanif’s promise to cheer up Joanna. Sitting opposite her and beside Alison, it seemed an easy promise to keep. And once he had the goods on Michael, Alison would realise where her true friends were. Taking a sip and looking encouragingly at Alison who was busy cleaning imaginary stains from her wine glass, Hanif replied.

‘As I see it, it is not so much the words ‘twenty-first century’, but the event that has defined it so far. I mean, of course, September the Eleventh.’

Had Joanna been a horse, she would have reared up and disproved the theory that horses can’t kick with both front feet at the same time. Instead, she raised her hackles and grew two sizes. Hanif knew why.

‘No, don’t get me wrong, Joey, I know you are fed up of everyone using that date as an excuse for everything under the Sun, but the fact remains that it happened and compulsory identification cards and, yes, a national database, are the twenty-first century’s response to it.’

‘Plus a few wars, plus spitting on democracy by defying the wishes of the people and the United Nations, plus breaking the Geneva Convention by torturing innocent and guilty people alike, thus stirring up half the world against us to suit our political leaders’ vanities.’

Joanna took a breath. Round Two.

‘The eleventh of September 2001; that inglorious day when a bunch of deluded fanatics employed by a psychopathic and egocentric oil billionaire crashed a pair of hijacked planes into a building thereby murdering nearly three thousand innocent people. Instead of seeing it as the criminal provocation it was, and treating it as a police matter, two of the world’s stupidest leaders used it as an excuse to murder many more thousands of innocents elsewhere, thus rendering the world safe for terrorists. The West played right into the fascist murderers’ hands.’

Hanif suddenly had the suspicion that carrying out his promise to Jady might be a bigger challenge than he first thought. Napoleon, noticing the signpost saying ‘Moscow 2000 miles’, and reading the weather report, might have rubbed his chin and agreed. Hanif had to admit Joanna had it strong. Months of frustration, of fruitless campaigning in Spawater to an indifferent public, added to a few drinks had produced a volatile mix that would not be tolerated on any post nine-eleven aircraft.

Fortunately, Lifeboats’ thought it was a ship.

‘Identity cards are a desperate throw of the dice by a society that is not comfortable in itself and is inward looking and frightened. A confident society would neither want nor tolerate such an imposition on personal freedom. Your government, I am afraid to say, has frightened the British people so much that they will cry out for the man with the ball and chain in the mistaken belief that freedom equates with danger and therefore lack of freedom must mean safety.' Michael reached for his drink; wine and water.

Jenna was impressed; this was a slightly different take on the subject.

'You mean the government has frightened us so that we will run to them for safety?'

'More or less; not deliberately though. With the greatest of respect for the British government,' Michael smiled knowingly, 'with due respect for all governments, they are not always comprised of the greatest brains. I do not suggest that your government sought deliberately to frighten people into surrendering their rights; I suggest that many of its ministers are frightened themselves. Combine fear with a natural tendency for governments to seek greater control over the governed - in the people's own interest, of course,' Michael couldn't resist a smirk, 'and conditions are right for the real establishment to set the agenda.'

'What do you mean?'

'There used to be a British comedy showing that the civil service ran the country but let the politicians believe that they did. The reality is far more serious. The unelected establishment, who run this country and every other, always wish to control the people. The attack on New York was a godsend for the ruling elite. It gave them the excuse to persuade the politicians to take greater control over the people in the name of security.'

Michael paused, then summed up. He was enjoying this. 'Frighten the politicians, get them to frighten the people, and the elite will rule happily ever after.'

Marlene jumped in. 'Luckily for you British, and all of us in the long run, the national database and biometric identity cards will not work.'

'You have met Marlene, of course?'

'Yes. Hi, Marlene. Why won't they work?'

'It is rather technical. I would not want to bore you.'

'Try me. Better yet, if it is technical, let's involve Hanif. Excuse me. Hi, Han, hun,' Jenna cried over to the adjacent table, 'can I borrow you for a minute? I need your help on some technical matters. And bring a bottle.'

'With you in a moment,' replied Hanif. Joanna had just asked Alison her opinion on the situation and Hanif wanted to be up to speed.

'We should have forgiven them,' stated Alison quietly.

'Forgiven who?'

'The terrorists who died in the attack and the people who set them up; we should say to the Arab world that we understand their pain and frustration over the way we in the West have treated them for years. We should ask them to forgive us for all those who have suffered and died at our hands.'

Hanif could hardly believe his ears. He thought the world of Alison because of her sweet nature and was never happier or more complete than when in her company, but couldn't in all honesty regard her as a stateswoman. Cinderella might well go into politics, agitating for twenty-four hour Palace Balls and late night pumpkin transport; Snow White has always been a keen opponent of apartheid and champion of hygienic food standards, particularly apples; Rapunzel is a supporter of low rise dwellings and subsidies to the ladder making and hairdressing industries, but Alison? Hardly.

'Forgive them? Forgive the hijackers? They deliberately murdered thousands of innocent people!'

'Yes, but as Joanna says, they were deluded. They thought they were acting for the best.'

'You mean it is all right to carry out barbaric acts if you are deluded enough to think they are for the best?'

'No, Hanif, it is not all right. But it is too late for those poor souls in the twin towers and the airplanes. We now need to prevent the terrorist organisations getting bigger and more powerful. If we forgave the hijackers for the New York attack, saying we understand why and will join their brothers and sisters in seeking justice for all in the Middle East, the hard-line terrorist leaders would find it tricky to raise recruits.' Alison took a breath for emphasis and continued speaking, her hair falling into her wine glass. Her audience remained attentive.

'Having wronged us by the nine-eleven attack, they could not attack us again if we forgave them for it. The people the hardliners want to attract would see attacking people who forgive them as morally wrong. By starting mad wars the West has acted as a recruiting agent for the terrorists, which is exactly what they were after when they attacked the twin towers. They understand the West far better than the West understands them and they knew the West would overreact and seek revenge. The Western governments played right into the terrorists' hands.'

'So the terrorists are quite willing to sacrifice their own brothers and sisters to gain support for their cause? Pretty nasty people, aren't they? Surely we must resist them?'

'Pretty nasty indeed, Hanif, just as the Western governments sacrifice their own people for their own cause, tit for tat. We can only stop the cycle of violence by refusing to retaliate. Then decent people the world over will stop their leaders, democratic or religious, from killing ordinary people just because they were born into a different culture by an accident of birth. You cannot find peace through war, you cannot fight terrorism with intimidation and you cannot win hearts and minds with bullets and bombs.'

Alison paused, frowned at her wine glass and retrieved her hair. 'I do wish Ron would clean these glasses better. Oh well.' She raised the spotless glass and sipped placidly.

Joanna knew Alison well enough not to be surprised at her occasional high flown flights of Utopian fancy and was not entirely sure if she agreed, but it sounded first-class; do a Nelson Mandela and prevent bloodshed. Shame our leader was no Nelson Mandela.

'You would make an interesting politician, Ali; a soft answer turneth away wrath, as the proverb says. Good for you.'

Hanif had heard enough; he could not quieten the unpleasant niggling feeling that Alison was telling the unvarnished truth, the truth that neither the Western nor terrorist rulers could ever admit. Remove the rulers from both sides and the world would live in peace. The rulers on both sides had too much to lose and too much in common, being two sides of the same coin. Aloud he replied calmly,

'Perhaps you are right, Ali. To be honest, I am fed up of hearing about it. Can we change the subject?'

'Hannybabes, don't forget the bottle, will you?' spoke a voice from behind him.

Perfect timing. 'Coming, Jenna.' Turning to the others, he said with relief, 'Excuse me just a moment, will you? Duty calls.'

Hanif picked up a bottle and went to visit the neighbours.

'So, Millado, are you looking forward to next week?'

'Next week is fine, I don't have to do anything next week; it is later on when it all kicks off that I am worried about.'

Jady and Arnie were Pooling away gently in the empty Pool room, neither concentrating much on the game in front of them, more the Great Game ahead. Jady's chief concern was to bolster Arnie's confidence and prevent him making a mess of things by panicking in character, as it were. He was not too concerned though, having faith in Arnie's ability to take instructions from him.

'Fair enough, Millado, but I shouldn't worry even then, if I were you; Alison's people have told you how to behave when not on duty. All you do is look enigmatic and say naught.'

'Look what?'

Jady laughed humorously. What did they teach them in school these days? How to play Pool?

'Look mysterious, like you know something they don't.'

'Well, that's true enough,' laughed Arnie, but without the humour. 'I know what a con the whole thing is.'

'Don't say that, even in jest.' Jady's humour fell like the mercury in a polar bear's freezer when raw winter started chucking its weight about. He looked around at the thankfully still empty room and continued sotto voce.

'It is nothing of the sort. As you know, there will be a Pool competition, held at the Town Hall, beginning in two weeks time and lasting one month. Every citizen of Spawater is welcome. To ensure it is all above board and Spawater fashion, independent referees will be hired to oversee all matches. It is a free and fair competition open to all, regardless of age, gender or species, and may the best competitor win.'

'And who is the best competitor?'

'You are.'

'Cheers, Han. This is Marlene, Erich and Louise. You have met Michael before, I take it?'

Actually, Hanif had met them all before, just not been introduced.

'Yes. Pleased to meet you, I'm sure.'

Hanif was pleased indeed. This was his chance to find out what Michael, and possibly his friends, were really up to. After a few drinks discretion often went West with the wagons, as Hanif well knew. Jady had taken advantage of that fact on many occasions.

'So,' continued Jenna in her role as Master of Ceremonies, 'we were discussing ID cards and all that, and Marlene reckons they won't work.' Jenna turned to Marlene. 'I do hope you are right, of course, but what makes you think so?'

'Well,' Marlene replied, 'and I warn you it is all very technical. This is why biometric details held on a national database will not work.'

Arnie rested his cue on the Pool table, wishing he could crawl underneath. Daniel felt the same when his agent informed him the arena was booked and the lions were limbering up.

'Look, chief, thank you for your confidence in me and all that, but I am not as good a Pool player as you think I am. I am the best in this club, which is not very difficult as half my challengers are drunk, but if you throw open a competition to the whole of Spawater and offer an enormous prize, you are going to get serious players. Hustlers who play for money as well as the odd semi-professional, or maybe even real professionals for all I know. I am a very good pub player, not a pro. I won't stand a chance.'

Jady sighed. There was no telling some people, no wonder Bilco lost his hair.

'Listen, Millado, we have been through all this before. You are the best trick shot player I have ever seen. You must easily be the best trick shot player in town. True?'

'Oh yes, chief, I am great at trick shots. The trouble is that trick shots do not win serious Pool games. The reason you hardly ever see Pool on television is that the top games are so boring. No tricks; just grind your opponent down. The first player to make a mistake loses, and good hustlers do not make many mistakes.'

'Ah, but you do not have to beat every hustler in Spawater. As I have explained, the competition is seeded. This means that all you need to do is show off your trick shots to the crowd to get them on your side and leave the hustlers to knock each other out of the tournament.'

'Yes, but sooner or later I will have to play a hustler. How else can I win it?'

Jady grinned. He could see Arnie's point. Jady was glad he had not met anyone like himself when he was Arnie's age. Then again, Jady as a teenager was already like himself. His mum always said Jady would wind up rich or in prison. Possibly both.

'Don't worry, Millado, you just concentrate on what you do best and leave the rest to me.'

Identity Cards
Chapter Thirteen

Like children gathered around mother to hear the latest fairytale hot off the Toytown press, Jenna and Hanif pulled up chairs beside Marlene at the port side of the table, drinks in hand appropriately, to hear her story. Michael, Louise and Erich hove to starboard, immersed in idle chat; Michael keeping half a weather ear on duty just in case.

'As I see it,' began Marlene, omitting 'Once upon a time' and getting straight to the heart of the matter, 'governments and large scale projects do not mix. Think of all the large scale projects your various governments' over the years have been involved in and tell me one that has been an unqualified success.'

'True enough,' answered Hanif, his patriotic pride slightly stung by this attack on the country, made worse by its accuracy. 'But all large projects encounter problems, teething troubles if you like. There are bound to be hitches but these can be overcome in time.'

'Time and money, to be more exact, Hanif. Ok, the channel tunnel project was late and over budget, to put it politely. The Millennium Dome,' Marlene picked up her glass and continued, 'speaks for itself. Do you remember the 'TSR2'? A fighter plane designed and scrapped in the 1960's; the flying elephant called 'Concorde' that you English couldn't even spell right.'

'Concorde was a triumph of technology,' retorted Hanif heatedly.

'Maybe, but it was a financial disaster and an environmental catastrophe, and where is it now? The taxpayers who funded it could not, by and large, afford to buy a ticket for it. How clever.' Marlene took a drink and sneered.

'This is all very interesting,' interrupted an uninterested Jenna, 'but we all know that governments are rubbish at big projects. I learnt at a meeting recently that government IT projects have a 34% success rate. Public sector IT projects are always a disaster; look at the passport office, the emergency services response unit or the defunct Child Support Agency and you will see that.'

'True. And when it comes to government sponsored IT catastrophes, the national database scheme will be the granddaddy of them all.'

'The mother of all cock-ups,' sniggered Jenna. She was beginning to like Marlene.

'So you both keep saying,' commented Hanif, wondering if this was a plant. 'But the government is so determined to set it up that, allowing for hitches, they will just pay up the extra money and muddle through.'

'Ah,' said Marlene knowingly, 'with a smaller scheme that might be possible, but not with a national database. Here is why. In order for the government to implement its national database scheme, it will have to hire private companies to build it. The government itself knows nothing about technology. It has no choice but to place itself in the hands of advisors and technicians who have very different agendas to their own.'

'What agendas?' challenged Hanif.

'Making money, mainly, and the way to do that is to skimp on the materials used to construct the database. Make it as cheaply as possible.'

'Naturally, but how do you mean, cheap materials?' asked Jenna curiously.

'First of all, how do computers work?'

'Badly.'

Marlene laughed at Jenna's cynical reply. 'Yes, true enough. What I meant was, what is the technology behind computers? Apart from their internal clock, what makes them tick?'

There were several possible answers to this, as Hanif well knew.

'It depends on what level you are talking.'

'True. Ok, I will put it this way. Modern computer technology was made possible by the invention of the silicon chip. Agreed?'

Hanif and Jenna nodded.

'You were right about one thing, Marlene,' laughed Michael, leaning over and passing her a fresh glass, 'your conversation is boring.' He turned away and rejoined the casual chat with Louise and Erich. He did not need Marlene to convince him that the fledgling national database had more holes than a Transylvanian blood donor.

'Never mind him,' observed Marlene scornfully to the others, pleasing Hanif. 'Now, where were we?'

'You were saying,' answered Jenna, 'that we should blame the silicon chip.'

'Oh yes.'

'You are losing me,' Hanif interrupted. 'Why are you talking about silicon chips?' He leaned forward deliberately. 'I should point out that I am quite a senior computer specialist and I can not see any problem with implementing a national database so far.' He paused, honesty getting the better of him. 'At least, not from the point of the government knowing nothing about the technical details concerning silicon chips. They will just hire expertise, so what is the problem?'

Marlene paused and looked intently at Hanif, as the Sorcerer had eyed the Apprentice when telling him not to meddle with things beyond his ken.

'In order to obtain a government contract,' she continued, 'the software companies have to win the tender for the business. This means, corruption aside, the cheapest bid compatible with the competence to carry out the contract. To undercut the rival bids it is necessary to buy the cheapest hardware, including circuit boards and silicon chips. These are the thinnest; the ones with the fewest layers of insulation.'

'Is that a serious problem?' asked Jenna, no expert.

'It is if you want your database to last. You see, the problem with cheap silicon chips is that they wear out. They overheat because they are too small and have too many demands placed on them. A national database will be absurdly brittle, being accessed continually and altered as often as people's circumstances change. Multiply that by an entire country and you have a system which will malfunction from day one.'

Hanif was intrigued and a little alarmed. 'Explain the technical rationale for your thinking.'

'Modern, cheap silicon chips are too small and thin. You see, Hanif, as an expert you will understand that regular chips supposedly have, for example, 90 nanometre processes. However, the latest chips are built using one nanometre-scale semiconductor processes, one billionth of a metre. The heat produced by the electrical current passing through such circuitry will erode their essential metal connections or oxide insulation layers and cause transistors to break down. At this point we strike.'

'You strike?'

Michael looked round sharply at Marlene. Had he heard right? Hastily, Marlene corrected herself. 'I mean unscrupulous hackers strike.' She laughed. 'The whole system will be as inherently unstable as a house built with playing cards.'

'Are you saying,' put in Jenna, 'that the national database will be easy to hack in to? The government are forever bragging that biometric technology, whatever that is, will make hacking impossible.'

Not even Hanif could pass that one.

'Not totally impossible, Jen, nothing is foolproof; it is just impossible for the average person and very difficult indeed for experts without hugely expensive equipment.'

'Well anyway,' Jenna persevered, 'you mean that the database can be attacked because the chips are too thin?'

'Yes. Also, apart from fake chips, unscrupulous chip companies skimp on the insulation layers to save money.' Marlene looked serious. 'Chip technology is unstable. Hackers with sophisticated equipment, as you say, Hanif, could take control of them. Even without hackers, the circuit boards will erode and malfunction.' She shook her head gently. 'The whole thing will be an appalling mess.'

'I have always been led to believe that silicon circuits should last for hundreds of years,' protested Hanif. He was worried, could all this be true?

'Yes, the circuit boards made in the nineteen seventies, when computers filled entire rooms. Thick, cumbersome and slow, perhaps, but those old ones are reliable. Chips were fifty times as thick then as they are now. Government ministers do not realise this. They can't keep up with technological change and so are helpless in the hands of technocrats. By putting everyone's details on to one huge database they are playing, not with fire but with sandcastles.' She laughed again. 'Good news for the baddies, of course.'

'If it is so obvious, why doesn't someone do something?'

'Who? Governments don't understand or listen and the Civil Service wouldn't enlighten them even if it could, while industry does nothing unprofitable until it has to. Everybody keeps their heads in the silicon sand until disaster strikes, and then private companies make a fortune from the taxpayers in sorting it all out.'

'Ah ha,' claimed Hanif exultantly, 'so private companies will sort it out in the end.'

'Usually, but not this time; the only solution will be to scrap the whole thing, set up a Hutton enquiry to exonerate everyone concerned and pretend it never happened. That's if the government is lucky.'

'And if it is unlucky?' prompted Jenna hopefully.

'The national database will concentrate every scrap of information normally held by separate agencies such as the Police, Health Service medical records, local councils, Tax Revenue and Customs, plus Inland Revenue, educational establishments, passport and driving licence offices and goodness knows what else in one place. All this information could vanish in a puff of smoke. If financial data such as people's bank and mortgage details, credit ratings and debts are included also, as the government would like but the banks are too sensible to agree to, then the country will be plunged into turmoil far, far worse than anything the greatest terrorist attack could hope to achieve.' She reached out for her glass and continued.

'This country runs on information; it calls itself an information rich society. The government intends to concentrate all this information in one place and allow it to be wiped out at a stroke.'

Jenna clapped her hands and laughed aloud, attracting looks from all around Lifeboats' until the inmates realised it was her. Jenna often laughed aloud; she had hyena blood on her paternal grandfather's pet's side.

'Not to say the National Grid, telecommunications, the internet, traffic lights, CCTV cameras - it will all be integrated for surveillance purposes - and anything controlled by chips,' added Marlene.

'You mean to say,' crowed Jenna, 'that the entire financial, mortgage and criminal records of everybody in the whole country could be wiped out at a stroke? Why that's fantastic! That would make the national database the best thing that has ever happened to this country after the snooze button. We will be a born again country! Brilliant! What do you think, Hannybabe?'

Hanif never knew when Jenna meant what she said and when she didn't. In this case she probably did, he thought morosely. Jenna's upbringing in the orphanage had bred a hatred of institutions, regulations and bureaucracy. She found anarchists too hierarchical.

'I think it is a bit fanciful, to be honest,' he replied. 'It sounds a bit far-fetched to me.'

'Tell me, Hanif,' said Marlene quietly, 'you know about computer systems; do you believe that determined terrorists could break into the national database?'

Hanif did not like to consider this; his wishes clashed with his experience. 'Not easily.'

'In other words, yes. So then, Hanif, what do you think of trapdoors?'

'Oh come on, they will be discovered if anyone tries to make any.'

'What are trapdoors?' Jenna enquired of Marlene, enjoying Hanif's discomfort. She was a great friend of Hanif's and would not stand for him coming to any harm, but he had strayed from the path and was wrong about ID cards and wrong to trust control freak governments. Anyone who helped Hanif back to the path of righteousness was all right with her. Jenna was descended from Bo Peep on her maternal grandmother's side and wanted Hanif home, wagging his tail behind him.

'A trapdoor is a piece of computer code, like a virus, that unscrupulous programmers place inside computer programs so that they can get into them later from a remote workstation. Typically, it will lay dormant unless the programmer gets annoyed with his or her employers, then the disgruntled programmer will enter the program via the trapdoor and raise Cain. It is quite common, and with all due respect to you, Hanif, clever programmers can conceal their tracks. How much do you suppose terrorists, the Mafia, drug Barons or hostile governments, would pay for the key to a trapdoor into the British national database? Come to that, how much would the Americans pay? Enough for a hardworking programmer to retire in luxury on?' She poured out some more wine.

Hanif was aghast at such cynicism. An honest man himself - spying on love rats excepted of course - he was appalled at how low some people would stoop. At the same time, he could hardly deny it. Top database designers could put trapdoors into a database which would be invisible without the protocols to reveal them; it was the sort of thing Hanif kept from his company's clients when advising on security matters so as to prevent panic and despair.

But he did not give up that easily.

'The system is already up and running in prototype form. So far it has not encountered any serious problems.'

'Of course not,' Marlene mocked and took another drink, 'there is not enough traffic for the circuit boards and chips to burn out yet, and no point in hacking into it yet either. Wait until it is up and running nationwide. The only question is; will the system collapse permanently due to technical faults before the hackers get in, or, if the system limps on, which group of criminals, terrorists or hostile governments will break in first and will they bring it down or simply milk the system for all its data? Then again, will terrorists just blow the whole thing up the old fashioned way first? Are you a betting man, Hanif? Which is your money on?'

Marlene and Jenna knocked back the remaining wine in their glasses in an unofficial toast. They were both having a great evening.

It was too much for poor Hanif. Marlene's direct style made the collapse seem inevitable, and his own extensive knowledge of computer systems, including databases, could not contradict anything she said. How different from his discussions with Mr Dauntliffe! Perhaps he should contact Mr Dauntliffe and raise these points with him. Yes! Hanif stopped, considered his last thought and smiled. Of course he must see Mr Dauntliffe; in fact, as his company was being hired by Mr Dauntliffe, he had a duty to do so. All Marlene's points were his problem, not Hanif's.

Passing the buck is a joyous sensation, second only to removing tight shoes. As the weight of the buck is transferred elsewhere the previous carrier can breathe in and relax. Hanif would contact Mr Dauntliffe as soon as possible, pass him the buck and let him deal with it. He relaxed and took a much needed gargle of liquid livener. What is this life, thought Hanif, if, full of care, we have no time to sit and drink.

He felt much, much better.

Unaware of Hanif's sudden Zen moment, Jenna poured Marlene and herself more wine and piped up, hoping to add fuel to Hanif's pyre, 'At the meeting I attended with Joanna, they said the national database would be in breech of the Data Protection Act. Is that true, guys?'

Producing the matches, Marlene responded. 'The database will be in breech of all the government's eight principles enshrined in its own Data Protection Act, which says that all electronically held data must be secure, fairly and lawfully processed; processed for limited purposes; adequate, relevant and not excessive; accurate,' and here Marlene could not suppress a giggle; 'not kept longer than necessary; processed in line with human rights and not transferred to other countries without adequate protection.'

'Other countries?' interrupted Jenna, mystified.

'The database will be so hugely expensive that the urge to outsource it to India or somewhere will be irresistible to a hungry Chancellor with books to balance.'

'Or better yet,' added Jenna, 'the Chancellor could just tell the government to drop the whole thing.'

'Politically unacceptable,' countered Marlene. 'That would require the government to admit that its infatuation with technology was a disastrous mistake. No government could make such an admission. That is why schools spend more money on computers than on schoolbooks, music lessons, nutritious meals and playing fields put together. Everyone knows this is educational insanity but governments won't admit it. Once the database is set up it will require a different government to abolish it, and then only after it brings the country to its knees. After all, governments love to control their people and all the main political parties will support the database until it collapses under its own contradictions or is sabotaged, whichever comes first.'

'You certainly know your stuff,' enthused an impressed Jenna. 'You should have been at our meeting, they would have loved you.'

Had Hanif fallen into a vat of caffeine he could hardly have perked up so instantly. Jenna's remark about Marlene knowing her stuff shook him to the core. Of course! He had been so busy defending the national database against her criticisms that he hadn't wondered why on Earth Marlene, a supposed historical architect or something, knew so much about it. Whoever first coined the phrase about not seeing the wood for the trees certainly knew what they were talking about. Now that he had decided to let Mr Dauntliffe take the strain his brain was able to function once more. TSR2 indeed! Why would this foreign so-called architect know so much about an obscure 1960's failed British aircraft project, the British Data Protection Act and the rest? And she was one of Michael's crew. Well, thought Hanif with a smug satisfaction that would have had Sherlock kicking Dr Watson the length of Baker Street, if she is a fake, then Michael is too. Elementary.

'I must admit, you are pretty convincing. Tell me, Marlene,' said Hanif, a bit too casually, 'is there anything else?'

'Health and Safety, of course. They want to ban everything, dangerous or not.'

'Tell Ron about it,' Jenna agreed tittering. 'They are inspecting his kitchen, the most dangerous place in town.'

Hanif had decided on his tactic. Clearly Marlene was slightly the worse for wear. She was matching Jenna glass for glass, something attempted only by the brave or the foolish. Encourage her to talk and she might let something slip.

'And,' continued Marlene, enjoying the wine and being the centre of attention, 'when in doubt there are always the European Union regulations.'

'Brilliant,' chimed Jenna. 'The Brussels bureaucrats, God bless 'em. So they have stuck their noses in, have they?'

'The European 'Restriction of Hazardous Substances' directive bans substances such as lead in solder from circuit boards. Non-lead soldering requires a higher temperature and slows the manufacturing process. It behaves differently to traditional solder and has a shorter life span; dealing with this also increases production costs. Any tendering company that factors in this increased expenditure will lose out to cheaper tenders. If the government ignores the directive it risks being fined by the European Union and its database will encounter compatibility problems with any future pan-European database. If it doesn't if will increase costs and risks enormously.'

‘Anything else?’ Hanif was fishing now, more certain than ever that Marlene and her friends were not what they seemed. But this did not go unnoticed.

‘I think you have had enough, Marlene, don’t you?’ Had Michael been a fish he would have given lessons to other denizens of the deep in angler management. Had they gone to fish school with Michael, Jaws and Moby Dick would still be releasing films. Hanif’s last remark made it plain to him that Hanif was suspicious and was pumping a glowing Marlene for incriminating information. Time to go.

‘I’m fine,’ replied Marlene. She was enjoying herself and did not want the evening to end. Michael glanced at the others and they took the hint.

‘Yes,’ said Louise, ‘we really should be off now, we have a busy week coming up.’

‘True,’ agreed Erich, ‘I am bushed. Let’s call it a day.’

Hanif realised that he would learn nothing further this evening and was happy enough to pass a reluctant Marlene her coat and join in the routine farewells. Joanna and Alison waved from the adjoining table and Jenna looked forward to seeing Erich and Marlene on Monday morning.

Jenna and Hanif rejoined a much cheered up Joanna, and Alison.

‘I have just heard the government’s control freak database rubbish being comprehensively trashed,’ laughed Jenna to her friends.

‘Tell us about it,’ Joanna beamed. Wine, plus talking trivia with Alison, a European champion, had enabled Joanna to pack up her troubles in her old kit bag and smile, smile, smile.

‘I certainly will; at least the bits I understood.’ Jenna smirked at Hanif. ‘Still want a national database then?’

‘We shall see, Jenna, we shall see,’ he replied absently. Hanif had other, happier things on his mind, like getting the goods on the love rat.

Outside, awaiting the taxi, Michael was thinking too.

‘Why was that guy so interested in databases, Marlene?’ he said, as they waited for the taxi.

‘Hanif? He says he is a computer expert.’

‘Really?’ This could be awkward, Michael reflected. ‘We shall have to find out more about this Hanif. He is too nosy for my liking.’

‘We cannot risk interference from inquisitive computer experts,’ said a concerned Louise. ‘You fool, Marlene, showing off in public.’

‘Never mind that now. Erich, you and Marlene will see Jenna at the Baths on Monday. She is Hanif’s friend. See if you can find out what he is all about.’

‘Good idea,’ agreed Louise. ‘If he is trouble we may have to take care of him.’

‘Indeed we may.’

Identity Cards
Chapter Fourteen

Monday morning in Spawater. Things had changed a bit since Roman days. The traffic was slower and the pollution it generated did not help the roses. They had traffic lights now, and traffic calmers to pacify the people stuck at the traffic lights.

The road signs were no longer in Latin but in a dialect exclusive to the Highways committee. Advertising billboards, where the Romans had promoted gladiator matches, chariot racing and economy galley holidays to anywhere in the known world and sometimes back again, where youths drank themselves senseless on cheap wine, now advertised rugby football matches, motor racing and economy package holidays to all the known world, regrettably back again, where youths still drank themselves senseless on cheap wine.

On this particular Monday morning in Spawater there was one added difference. There was a competition. A competition to be held at the Spawater Town Hall; a Pool competition, open to anyone and everyone who hailed from Spawater. If Julius and the boys had came, saw and played Pool, the Romans might still be in town.

Alison's people had been busy. This was Day One of Jady's project, which involved taking full advantage of the introduction of compulsory identity cards. Jady, along with Alison's promotions company, was going to make serious amounts of money out of the government's folly or perish in the attempt.

Money had been invested in promotion. Throughout the night, teams hired for the purpose had put up advertisements for the Pool tournament on billboards, advertising hoardings and walls. Flyposters and taggers were surreptitiously hired to supply street cred; advertising space was rented on buses, inside and out, taxis and shop windows, pubs, clubs and colleges. Finally also, of course, the local radio and newspapers. Jady rued the demise of the local television station, Channel Fog, but, he reflected serenely, Verruca Salt notwithstanding, you can't have everything.

The motive for the kerfuffle was to proclaim a challenge; a challenge to the entire population of Spawater. The proclamation read as follows:

'I, the Masked Pimpernel, do hereby challenge the good people of Spawater to a game of Pool. It will cost nothing to pick up the cudgels on behalf of the town and accept my challenge. Should you beat me in fair and honest contest, I shall give you ten thousand pounds.'

The proclamation was accompanied by a huge picture of the Pimpernel, complete with voice-disguising scarlet and gold facemask, scarlet and gold cape, scarlet tights and tunic with 'MP' embossed in gold braid, gold pants worn on the outside and height-enhancing golden boots. The whole outfit was padded to give the chimera of muscles so developed they would frighten Popeye.

The adverts went on to explain the details. The challenge would take place in the main hall of the Town Hall where several Pool tables would be provided, with overspill rounds in local pubs and clubs. Anyone who lived in Spawater could enter the knockout tournament, the winner of which would get to play the Masked Pimpernel for the ten thousand pound prize. The Masked Pimpernel would demonstrate his ability - Jady had toyed with disguising the Pimpernel's gender but gave it up - at each round in the Town Hall by executing trick shots on his roped-off private Pool table. The Masked Pimpernel, the text continued, did not believe in identity cards and would therefore keep his identity a secret. The Masked Pimpernel believed in privacy and freedom, not submission and slavery, and so did the Masked Pimpernel's sponsors.

'Dare you,' the blurb concluded, 'take up the challenge of the Masked Pimpernel? If so, telephone this number and you will be entered into the tournament. Come one come all, for the honour of Spawater. See you there.'

Dates, times, provisions for challenged contestants, provisions for spectators and the press, and diverse sundry matters were explained in the small print.

'Do you think people will notice?' said a lulled Jady to Joanna over the breakfast table. The brisk aroma of coffee percolated throughout the kitchen, complementing the sunshine and symbolising 'start the week' time in Joanna and Jady's household. Had they a cockerel, it would have crowed.

Joanna switched off the radio, preferring Jady's chat to the local radio presenter.

'Was that really Arnie's voice on the commercial?'

'That was the Masked Pimpernel's voice,' chided Jady jokily, casually munching his fruit breakfast, 'spoken through the voice filter for added authority. Does it work?'

'It certainly does. Why, young er, the Masked Pimpernel, whosoever he may be, sounded almost menacing; not like anyone we know at all.'

Jady laughed. The onset of a nefarious endeavour was always Jady's favourite time. He had worked hard to set this up and intended to enjoy it.

'More coffee, my love?' Jady kissed Joanna on the cheek and squeezed her opposite shoulder lovingly. Skulduggery always brought out the best in him; had Jehovah's Witnesses called, Jady could have persuaded them that although they should not take the Bible as Gospel, there was a God in Heaven and all was for the best in the best of all possible worlds.

Arms akimbo and back gently arched, Joanna stretched slowly into a happy yawn. This was security, a loving arm around the shoulder with a gentle squeeze on the end. This meant she was cherished and treasured and nothing bad was going to happen to her. Were she in danger, people would rush to her aid. How much more secure than a piece of biometric implanted plastic connected to a database owned by brave politicians who cowered behind a wall in case the Big Bad Terrorists got them!

'Mmmm... More coffee please, I'll huff and puff and blow your wall down.'

'Sorry?'

'That's all right,' sniggled Joanna contentedly, kissing Jady's elbow with affection. She sneaked a quick glance into Jady's soul; a bit knocked about, slightly worn and patchy, with furniture any old how and a blind spot in the corner. Not good enough for the Pope, and the Archbishop of Canterbury would probably prescribe some hefty grease applied to that selfsame elbow and a scouring brush, but it was snug, safe and warm. It would do.

'Well, Joey,' announced Jady, rising and grappling with the percolator, 'today's the beginning of Operation Pimpernel. If all goes as well as the gods portend we will make a few pounds and embarrass the government at the same time. Two for the price of none.'

'Yes. And yes.'

'Yes what?'

'Yes, I do think people will notice. Ali's people will have their work cut out processing all the entrants.'

Jady passed Joanna her coffee with a steady hand.

'Good, let them earn their money. The more the merrier.'

The less the merrier would have suited Harold Wood. Less foreign architects, less meddling Council chiefs and definitely less Jenna Whatshernames. That would suit requirements, as less bees would suit Winnie the Pooh. And on top of that there was this so-called snooker tournament. Madness.

One of the principle banes of Harold Wood's bane-sodden life was that the Spawater Council would not let him run the Town Hall and its environs in peace. Left to his own devices the whole area would be off limits to the general public; hooligans and disrespectful yahoos the lot of them. Sadly, due to some terrible oversight in the democratic process, the public were allowed to hire rooms and facilities for their own sinister purposes. That Jenna woman regularly hired rooms for her exercise and dancing classes, as though exercise and dancing ever did anybody any good.

Interrupting Harold's thoughts, the voice of conscience, as represented by Mrs Wood, called from the depths. Well, he conceded, his official grimace temporarily replaced by the wistful smile last seen on Dorothy wishing she was back in Kansas and not lumbered with singing lions and scarecrows, dancing had its place. He and Mrs Wood could shake a leg with the best of them on their biennial holiday cruise, but that was to proper music, not the crash bang wallop that passed for it these days. As for exercise, a hard day's work was all the exercise anyone required. That's what these people needed, he thought, a hard day's work.

And now the Hall was to be the centre of attention for all the snooker-playing riff raff in Spawater. Harold would have his work cut out and no extra pay or even a thank you. An advertising and brandbuilding promotions company, whatever that was, had combined with a local business, 'Jady Enterprises' no less, and block-booked the main hall and bar for any number of nights and invited everyone in Spawater to turn up! Goodness knows, Harold had done everything he could to obstruct and delay, but eventually the Council Leader and the Treasurer had ordered his full cooperation, just as with the architects. If was almost as if that Jady character had a hold on them in some way. It was all too much, and on the day the foreign architects were due, of all days.

The security implications were horrendous. What if some of the snooker players were terrorists? Spawater Council was being completely irresponsible, allowing all and sundry from Spawater into his Hall. It was this kind of short-sightedness that had caused the fall of Rome.

Harold sighed the sigh of a sensible and compassionate man, brought low by the recklessness of others. One thing was certain, thought Harold with a determination Wile E Coyote found obsessive, no-one, but no-one, would enter his Town Hall without producing their identity card and taking a biometric eye scan. And that went double for the so-called Masked Pimpernel. Harold rubbed his neck and loosened his tie. After all, he thought nervously, if anyone got past his security, what would Mr Dauntliffe say?

'Dauntliffe here, what can I do for you?'

'Hello, Mr Dauntliffe,' replied Hanif, 'Hanif Singh here, from Spawater. I am phoning to ask you when you are coming down to Spawater next?'

'Why, is there a problem?'

'No, not at all, Mr Dauntliffe, nothing of the kind. No, it is merely a progress check and one or two minor points I would like to go over with you. I would appreciate your advice on presenting certain issues to the public.'

'How do you mean?'

Hanif's problem was one that faces technical people all the time when trying to deal with top management. It was how to ask them for help and advice whilst appearing to be completely on top of the job. Napoleon's generals were forever coming unstuck by asking the boss how to stay warm on a Moscow bound horse.

Try flattery, thought Hanif; Mr Dauntliffe didn't get where he is today by having a low opinion of himself.

'Well sir, in the course of my work I have encountered certain criticisms of the national database that I believe you should know about. Admittedly, they are of a technical nature, and I appreciate that you are above such considerations, being primarily concerned with implementation. Nonetheless, you should be aware of them. The technical details you can safely leave to the technocrats.'

'People like you, you mean?'

This wasn't going so well. 'People like me, of course. Now, as you know, I am here to implement identification cards in Spawater as a test run before you take it nationwide. As such, I have only a passing involvement with the national database itself. Nevertheless, as a keen supporter of what you are trying to achieve...' Hanif looked around to make sure that his secretary, Susan, was not in his office. She did not suffer flannel at the best of times and if she heard him giving Mr Dauntliffe the wash and brush up to this extent he would never live it down, '...I believe you should be aware of any possible weaknesses in your project. You will be able to put my mind at ease and this will help me persuade others to join in with wholehearted support.'

Mr Dauntliffe was impressed. He had taken a liking to young Singh, Hanif, from the start.

Mr Dauntliffe had encountered serious opposition to the whole database and ID card project when first he mooted it. The public would not accept such an assault on their freedom and the politicians would not dare take such a radical step, said the establishment. Fortunately, the fright that the nine eleven attack gave the politicians enabled him to whisper in the establishment's collective ear that now was the time they could get away with it. It was a simple matter for the establishment to convince a pusillanimous parliament that it was all their own idea.

Now what mattered was the implementation, and Hanif Singh, enthusiastic and, crucially, technically competent in a way that the establishment would consider beneath them - not to say beyond them - might well be inducted into the *real* conspiracy in a non-managerial, technical capacity. Hanif Singh could be his technical advisor.

'Well, Mr Singh, Hanif,' said Mr Dauntliffe in his friendly talk-to-the-minions voice, 'I will be in your neck of the woods quite soon as I have received a call for assistance from the Spawater Town Hall. Two birds with one stone, eh? Just as soon as I can get away. Is that to your satisfaction?'

He called me Hanif, thought Hanif curiously. He was not sure whether to be pleased or not. What would his secretary say? Susan would not approve, that was certain. 'Susan, book three tickets; I am going on a walking tour with Ming the Merciless and Lord Voldemort.' 'Ok, just as long as you are not getting friendly with that Mr Dauntliffe.' In fact, thought Hanif unhappily, nobody he knew would be pleased that he was on good terms with such a person but Mr

Dauntliffe was, unfortunately, his company's number one client.

'That will be fine.'

'Very good, I will be in touch.'

Hanif replaced the receiver. Speaking of two birds, he reflected, that is the buck passed, now to check the national database for information on Michael Lehmann, the historical architect whose German assistant was a British law and database expert. This time, Hanif would find out the truth and when he did, Alison and everyone else would know about it.

'Who on Earth is the Masked Pimpernel?'

Detective Sergeant Mathews knew better than to swear in front of Inspector Brewe, especially as he had a suspicion that she knew already and that he was supposed to know too. He was agreeably surprised to discover that he was wrong on both counts.

A sunny, summer Monday morning, the start of another hard working week, and the people of Spawater were busy discussing the identity of the Masked Pimpernel and the challenge of the Pool competition. Most people rather liked a break from the routine of discussing football, Hegelian philosophy or reality television according to taste, but most people were not Inspector Josephine Brewe, the world's most ambitious police officer.

Inspector Brewe had learnt the hard way that catching criminals was not the route to achieving high rank in the modern police service. No, catching criminals meant wasting time on paperwork and in the courts; time that could be better spent boning up on Health and Safety regulations and passing police exams. What Inspector Brewe wanted on the streets was a quiet life, and in her short incarceration in Spawater she had had precious little of that. What she did not want were mysteries, and the Masked Pimpernel was a mystery par excellence.

'I don't know, Sergeant Mathews, but I intend to find out. Ring the number on the advert and make enquiries will you? Report back to my office when you have something. I have got to see the Chief Inspector about matters arising.'

Making a mental note that she was not the one 'finding out', he was, and beginning to develop a secret respect for the Masked Pimpernel as someone who might annoy his high and mighty boss, Sergeant Mathews obeyed.

Thirty minutes later they rendezvoused as arranged.

'Ma'am, you are not going to believe who is behind this.'

Inspector Brewe looked up from her desk. The Sun was shining but she wasn't. If Sherlock's Hound of the Baskervilles had padded by she would have borrowed him and his howl from the great sleuth so as to supply atmosphere. The Inspector had just been given the worst possible news she could get short of being put back on the beat: her nemesis had returned.

'I'm afraid to say, Sergeant, that I know exactly who is behind this. I might have known. That's what the Chief wanted to see me about. He wants to know what is going on at the Town Hall and told me - us - to find out. He says we are the experts in Town Hall trouble.'

'The Pool competition is being arranged by two local businesses.'

'No, Sergeant; one local business and one local menace; Jady Enterprises.'

With difficulty, Sergeant Mathews suppressed a guffaw. Jady had been her downfall at the Town Hall the previous year and he knew the Inspector wanted revenge.

'Yes, Ma'am. What do you suppose he is up to this time?'

Inspector Brewe stood up. 'I don't know, Sergeant, but I intend to find out.'

Identity Cards
Chapter Fifteen

'Here we are then; Spawater Baths in all their glory. Or should I say, Spawater Baths, sadly eroded by the ages and going down the plughole unless you can save them.'

Thus Jenna's welcome to Marlene and Erich on what Spawater historians would forever acknowledge as Pimpernel Monday. They met in the café opposite, along with Arnie; the architects laden with mysterious equipment in industrial looking bags, Jenna toting a rucksack. Over coffee, she brought them up to speed.

'First of all, you know Arnie? He is my assistant and so you will see him around the place. He's quite harmless.'

Arnie smiled in greeting. Jady's idea of seconding him to Jenna gave Arnie a reason to be in and around the Baths as occasion demanded without attracting attention; much less obtrusive, Jady averred, than a wooden horse. Moving on, Jenna continued.

'I telephoned the Council Head first thing and he has instructed his chief busybody, one Harold Wood, worm to his friends like me, to leave us to get on with things. Knowing old woodworm, I expect him to stick his king-size oar in as much as possible.'

'Sorry, Jenna, could you clarify that?' Erich spoke fluent English but this did not run to the version intermittently practised by Jenna. One of her summer delights was giving directions to tourists who failed to show proper respect.

'I mean,' clarified Jenna over her cup, 'that you can carry out your examinations and tests and the staff are obliged not to hinder you. However, I believe that the manager, one Mr Wood, will cause you and me problems if he can.'

'Why should he wish to cause us problems?' asked a perplexed Marlene. 'We are here to help.'

Erich stole a quick glance at her and grinned slightly as Jenna replied.

'Mr Wood thinks he is in charge and does not like anyone here who is not under his control. He is what we call a control freak; an insecure person who fears everybody, and trusts nobody but himself to get anything important right. This means he consequently gets most important things wrong. Like the government deluding themselves they can fight crime and terrorism with their identity cards.'

Marlene and Erich stole another glance. Over the weekend they and their colleagues had had a full and frank exchange of views, akin to the one between Wyatt Earp, Doc Holliday and the Clanton Gang at the OK Corral, concerning Marlene's propensity to get drunk in public and talk too much. An unrepentant Marlene and a confident Michael thought it did not matter, whereas Louise and Erich thought it might endanger the project, and consequently their liberty. Finally, they decided to question Jenna, discreetly, to find out if she, or in particular, Hanif, was suspicious, and take it from there.

'Speaking of identity cards,' said Erich, trying to sound nonchalant but actually sounding as though he was sickening for something, 'that was some conversation you and your friend - was it Hanif? - had in The Lifeboat Club the other day. Hanif seemed well informed about ID cards, I thought?'

'Oh yes,' replied Jenna, 'he would. His company is in charge of implementing them in the Spawater trial. It has made him rather unpopular, I may tell you, but we still love him. Now,' Jenna drained her cup, 'shall we get on?'

Had glance theft been a crime in the brave new world of governmental databases and compulsory ID cards, Marlene and Erich would have been on the way to the slammer as they stole yet another. Jenna was beginning to think they were in love.

Michael was not so smitten, and it was not Spring, but this morning his fancy lightly turned to thoughts of love as recommended by the poet. Today, as his colleagues started measuring up the Spawater Baths for the removal people, he was constantly thinking of the current object of his desire.

'A penny for them.'

Michael turned to Louise and laughed. 'I was hoping for rather more than that. Any sign yet?'

Louise turned to her screen and pressed a few buttons. 'No, not yet, but the British government's database system is not as efficient as it should be. Not with it being designed on the cheap and staffed by minimum wagers. It should up be any time now.'

Phase one of Michael's project was complete. He had successfully managed to bamboozle the custodians of the Spawater Baths into allowing his team free access. His team had free rein to work out how best to remove the Baths from their current home prior to transporting them to Eastern Russia. This meant that he was in line for stage one of his payment. All he needed now was the code.

Louise emitted a muffled scream, like a considerate ghost. 'Here it is. It has just appeared.'

Even a professional technician, database engineer and criminal such as Louise found it difficult to hide her excitement at the appearance of the coded number on her screen.

'That's it? Excellent. Print it out and read it out so we can both take it down.'

Louise complied, reading out the complicated, impossible to guess code number while Michael repeated it back to her and wrote it down.

'Now to see if it works.' Louise switched screens and entered the number, very carefully, into the high security banking website. A stage wait.

'This is it.' Michael reverted back to the childish excitement he felt when he'd forged his first bus pass. How simple that was; just a black and white photocopy of a friend's pass with the name covered, then after a rummage through his mother's old lipstick case to find the correct shade, it was coloured in and sealed in a scent-proof plastic case. At the minor public school Michael had attended, a pupil with a bus pass smelling of lipstick would have attracted the sort of attention best avoided in an apprentice delinquent.

Time flies when you are having fun; it crawls like a tortoise on its day off when you are waiting to see if a bank accepts your transfer of funds in a false name.

'It works!' Louise shot her arms in the air, nearly catching Michael on the ear. Remembering that she was a professional, with computer blood in her veins and plastic plasma, Louise composed herself, printed the acceptance page, logged off carefully and switched off the machine.

'Mission accomplished.' She smiled, rising from her seat, yawning and stretching out to replenish her oxygen supply. Michael grabbed the back of her seat for support, grinning like Bill the Burglar given a community order. The tension in the room dissipated like mist in a breeze, the Sun shone through.

'The money has been successfully transferred to our account.'

'May I see your ID, please?'

'Shove it, Sam, you know who we are, now let us in.' Jenna decided to start as she meant to go on. She was having no nonsense from the Baths' staff; if they were going to be obstructive they needed to find out who was boss from day one.

'I am sorry, Jenna. Of course we know who you are but the rules clearly state that no-one is allowed in unless they produce an Identification Card or a tourist ID for scanning. We don't make the rules; we just have to enforce them.'

Jenna was not having this. Up with this I will not put, she reflected, echoing Churchill in one of his bilious moods. Turning to her colleagues and rolling her eyes, Jenna launched her attack.

'You want to make something of it? Let me tell you, Sam, that it is my job to ensure that my associates here,' she indicated Marlene and Erich, 'are allowed to carry out their important work unhindered by anyone. That means you and your moronic boss. The Council themselves have authorised us to inspect the Baths, as if you didn't know. Here is a copy of our letter of authorisation.'

Jenna thrust the copy under Sam's nose.

'I want you to be quite clear about this. We will be coming and going at various times of day and we do not expect to have to waste time arguing with jobsworths every time.'

'And night,' interrupted Erich. 'We will sometimes be working at night, when it is quiet.' And the quieter the better, he thought. Marlene grimaced.

'And night,' added Jenna. 'So you can let us through, Sam, there's a good lad. And you can tell your boss peckerhead that if he doesn't like it he can come and see me. Or would you rather I phoned the Council Head?'

'I will have to report this to Mr Wood,' said Sam defensively.

'That's fine, good for you, Sam. That covers you against any comeback. Now, hold on to something, we're a-coming through,' announced Jenna, swinging her rucksack over her shoulder. 'Mind you, something tells me your Mr Wood is going to have a busy day.'

With that, Jenna pushed past Sam and his colleagues, followed by an impressed Erich and Marlene. They were impressed both with Jenna and with Michael's perspicacity. What a good idea, thought Erich, to hire this Jenna. All attention would be centred on her, leaving his group to get on with the real job. Arnie, bringing up the rear, thought it about par.

'Hold on,' said Sam, doggedly. He was down but not yet out. 'What about your bags? We have to search them for bombs.'

'Sod off, Sam.'

Sam had only mentioned the bags for form's sake, he had no real hope that Jenna would stand for a bag search, and he was right. He was not concerned with losing face in front of his staff, as they all knew Jenna too well. In went the towel.

They walked through the foyer with their baggage.

'That was most remarkable,' said Erich to Jenna as they went into the bowels of the Baths. 'In my country if you spoke to officials like that the police would be on their way.'

'Don't worry,' Jenna replied, 'I am sure we will bump into the police sooner or later.'

In fact the police, as represented by Inspector Brewe and Sergeant Mathews, were already there.

'Just routine, you understand,' said Inspector Brewe to the Council Head. 'It concerns the Pool competition to be held largely in the Town Hall. We like to know what is going on in Spawater at any time, for security reasons, so we would be grateful if you could let us know the position.'

'Well, officer,'

'Inspector.'

'Well, Inspector, I think you will find that there is nothing for you to concern yourself with. As Head of Spawater Council, I am, of course, aware of the security implications of all the activities that take place here in the Town Hall. It is our job, among other things, to make the amenities here available for functions, and I would be failing in my duty, and failing the people of Spawater, if I allowed anything untoward to occur. Please feel reassured, officer, Inspector, that all is well.'

Inspector Brewe was not at all reassured. Anything concerning her old adversary, Jady, was about as reassuring as Neville Chamberlain at a peace conference.

'Thank you for that, sir,' she replied, ungratefully, 'but I wonder if you could tell me what precisely is the role of Jady Enterprises in this? It is run by a Jay Dein and we are curious about his interest in the Pool competition.'

Inspector Brewe had picked a bad day to badger the Council Head. Even Badger himself would not have appreciated being badgered on this day of all days. This was the day that Mr Lehmann's people, the architects, started their survey of the Spawater Baths.

Mr Lehmann had left the Head in no doubt as to the seriousness of the position. Should the Baths be suffering from severe erosion they might have to be temporarily dug up and removed for repair. If that happened he would have no end of trouble with the national media and the various heritage organisations. True, Mr Lehmann had given him good advice, informing him of the position with the European Union and the new members, but all the same, the protected status of the Baths was under threat and so, therefore, was his career.

And now he was being quizzed about a Pool competition! And by the very Inspector whose botched handling of security at a previous function had led to a riot!

He had been properly consulted about the competition by its main organisers, company directors who happened to be prominent Spawater citizens. They ran a respectable marketing business and were reputable employers locally based. It happened that they had put work his way in the past and might well, they had implied, do so in the future. He was not going to bother them with questions about their business partners.

The Council Head looked irritably at the two police officers. He was an important man and did not need to suffer such fools, gladly or otherwise. Nor would he.

'I am perfectly satisfied with the arrangements for the Pool tournament, thank you, officer. In the unlikely event that I encounter any problems I will let you know. Now, if you will excuse me..?'

'Right, Arnie, you know what you have to do. I have checked the staff changing rooms, the male ones, and if you go into the cubicle at the far end you will see that there is access to the ventilation shaft. I've loosened it so you can slide it open and get in. Remember to close it from the inside. Here is your outfit, in this bag. I want you to place it in the shaft. Later on, when the place is busy and noisy, I want you to follow your map and find your way to the back rooms of the main hall in the Town Hall itself. Have fun.'

'How did you find out about the male staff changing rooms?'

'Others have toiled while you slept, young Arnie. Now, are you ready?'

Arnie did not think he would ever be ready for the type of situations Jady and his friends conjured up, but que sera, sera. With a voice like a duck on the first day of the hunting season, Arnie replied,

'As ready as I'll ever be.'

'Ready?'

With the confidence of knowledge times experience, Marlene replied, 'Of course. You start testing the stone and I will take the soil samples.'

Marlene and Erich were not who they claimed to be, and certainly not who or what their identity cards and records on the fledgling national database stated they were, but they were certainly experts in their chosen fields. Marlene would check the soil to see how much resistance it would put up against an excavator, while Erich worked out just how much pressure the Baths could stand when removed from their foundations, without incurring too much damage. All the Baths would need to be tested so they could be removed in one go and with minimal fuss.

Macbeth and Jeeves looked down from their celestial abodes, Macbeth having done his time, and agreed that Marlene and Erich knew a thing or two about clandestine operations. 'If the Baths were moved,' Macbeth advised, 'when the Baths were moved,' Jeeves added, 'then,' they insisted in unison, ''t'were well the Baths were moved quickly.'

Identity Cards
Chapter Sixteen

'We need to move quickly on this one, Sergeant. Whatever that Jady character is up to, you can be sure it is going to happen in the next month or so, using the Pool contest as a cover. And who is this 'Masked Pimpernel'? What has he got to do with Jady? Why does he keep his identity secret? Who are his sponsors? There is something seriously suspicious about this whole thing, Sergeant, and I don't like it one little bit. This is a mystery and if there is one thing I do not like on my patch, it is a mystery.'

Then you shouldn't have become a copper, thought Detective Sergeant Mathews scathingly. Aloud, he questioned his superior as far as he dared.

'What makes you think it is illegal, Ma'am? Couldn't Jady Enterprises have teamed up with that advertising company to promote a Pool competition to make an honest profit?'

Inspector Brewe glared at him. They both knew the reason for her attitude. Not so many months ago, Jady had made a pudding of her over a stolen computer, a riot and a whole series of non-crimes. Jady had clearly been up to his neck and beyond in skulduggery but nothing was ever proven. In fact, there was no evidence of any crime at all; a fact that convinced the Inspector beyond doubt that something seriously illegal had occurred and Jady had skilfully covered his tracks. Well he was not going to get away with it this time. Inspector Brewe had vowed to nail Jady and this was her big chance.

'An honest profit you say?' Inspector Brewe reddened in the face. Had she been a contestant she would have risked disqualification for impersonating a ball. 'Show me where this honest profit is to be made,' she continued. 'Jady, or more likely his advertising friends, have spent a fortune arranging a competition with a ten thousand pound prize. They have hired the main assembly room and bar of the

Town Hall for several nights and farmed out knockout round matches to every pub, club and shady snooker den and Pool room in Spawater. They have advertised it all over town, including newspapers and local radio. They have hired proper Pool judges, referees and general organisers to ensure so-called fair play. And it is all for free. Gratis. Everybody in town is invited to enter this expensive competition for nothing.'

She raised her voice in a sarcastic sneer.

'Come on then, Sergeant, as you seem to think it is all prim and proper. Tell me how you would make an honest profit out of this lowlife extravaganza.'

Sergeant Mathews gaped like a goldfish refused admission to a funfair. Lost for words, but inwardly seething at being obliged to take such abuse from a fast track upstart, especially in earshot of a Town Hall receptionist, he quietly muttered his mea culpa.

'You are right, Inspector, sorry.'

'Good.' She looked towards the office at the end of the reception room where they were awaiting an audience with Mr Wood. Inspector Brewe did not intend to take the Council Head's dismissal as final. She knew that Jady was up to something and she would not rest until she had discovered exactly what, and arrested him for it.

'Now, how much longer will he be? We need to talk to him.'

Right on cue, like the Masked Pimpernel himself, the receptionist's buzzer buzzed.

'Mr. Wood will see you now.'

'How are things going so far?' asked Jenna, looking down at Erich busying himself at the base of a stone archway, and playing the good employee for a change. As a rule, Jenna prided herself on having no-one to call 'boss', apart from her cat, but on this occasion she was prepared to make an exception. Helping Michael and his colleagues, she knew, was one in the eye for Mr Harold Woodworm and the prying surveillance cancer endangering the country, which made it a pleasure. Anything that stymied the control freak little Hitlers and delayed a supine parliament sleepwalking its way to the midnight knock was fine by her. Also, it had the incredibly fortuitous side-effect of facilitating Jady's Masked Pimpernel scheme. She was on a retainer for that project too, she reflected happily, making her twice employed at the same time. Add that to her regular dancing and aerobics classes' income and Jenna's door wolf might just as well take a summer vacation.

Erich raised his eyes from the base of the structure he had been examining.

'Oh fine, Jenna. The Baths staff are leaving us alone to get on with our work. In fact, they seem almost anxious to keep out of our way.' He looked up at Jenna quizzically. 'Your help is much appreciated.'

'Any progress in your work yet, or is it too early to say?'

'I am afraid it is much too early for that,' Erich laughed dismissively. The last thing he needed was to have to supply regular progress reports to Jenna. The only reports that mattered were the ones to Michael establishing when they could lift the loot and what equipment would be needed to hoist it onto sufficient numbers of trucks to steal the lot in one night. Foundations excepted; Spawater could keep them as a romantic Roman ruin, Pompeii for beginners.

'We will need to carry out our work in its entirety before making a judgement,' Erich continued. 'The good thing is that thanks to you, we are able to work in peace and avoid interruptions. Interruptions we wish to avoid.' No truer words, thought Erich soberly, smiling like a penitent crocodile.

'Speaking of interruptions,' interrupted Jenna, 'don't be surprised if there is a rather noisy one. Let me tell you about it.'

'Tell me about it,' said Mr Wood, managing to be standoffish whilst remaining seated.

Inspector Brewe and her disloyal assistant shuffled awkwardly. They were in the presence of the Spawater Town Hall security chief, as Mr Wood saw it, or meeting that annoying jobsworth, as they saw it, and were enjoying it rather as they might enjoy cross-questioning by Rumpole with a Chateau Thames Embankment inspired hangover. Mr Wood was neither a big nor a forgiving person, inclined to let bygones be bygones with a hearty clap on the shoulder and say no more about it. Mrs Wood purchased his suits from the small and petty department. Harold nursed grudges the way gardeners nursed begonias; tenderly and with loving attention, and they blossomed accordingly. He allowed his reluctant guests to remain standing. The prodigal son's father would not have liked him.

'Well, Mr Wood,' said the Inspector with a diffidence she did not feel, 'we are concerned about the forthcoming Pool competition in the main assembly hall and we wondered if you could give us any information about it. Any help would be much appreciated.'

This was the first good news Harold had had since Mrs Wood cancelled her plans to join Jenna's aerobics classes out of spousal loyalty. Harold was having a rotten day. The public and press had plagued him since the early hours, asking about that dammed competition. Naturally, he had taken his public landline off the hook, his normal response to interference from the public, but there was still his private line. Not trusting the switchboard, for security reasons, Harold had installed a private direct line for important calls. Today he was waiting for his most important call ever, from Mr Dauntliffe no less, on his private line, only to discover that his secure number had been leaked. The press and local based websites had published it so he had to field annoying interference from the general public nuisances. He couldn't ignore any call in case it was the important one.

And it had to happen on this day of all days; the day when the foreign so-called architects arrived to nose about around his Baths.

He had warned the Inspector about them in good time and she had not been interested. His assistant, Sam, had already confirmed Jenna Whatshername behaving as expected and feared, throwing all his well-planned security measures to the wind like Rhett and Scarlet. To cap it all, the Inspector was back, begging favours. Well, thought Harold malevolently, generosity has its price and he intended to enjoy exacting it. Shylock would have liked him. 'Mr Prodigal,' said Shylock happily, 'what do you think of my protégée?' 'I fear he is a man after your own heart,' said Mr Prodigal sadly. 'And his kilogram of flesh,' added Shylock, who liked to keep up with modern trends, 'but I am sure you will forgive him.' 'Forgive Mr Wood?' roared Mr Prodigal, outraged. 'Do you know the price of free range fatted calves these days?'

'The last time we spoke, officer,' said Harold with enough relish to float a burger bar, 'you refused to take me seriously. When I had a complaint, you did not want to know. Now you need my help. Well, well.'

Inspector Brewe did not need to trouble Sherlock to have seen this one coming. Even Doctor Watson would have prescribed humble pie if progress were to be made. Just think of Jady in the dock, thought the Inspector grimly, and swallow the lumps with pretended good grace.

'On reflection, Mr Wood, I think we might have been a bit hasty the last time we met. You were right to bring the issue of the Baths to our attention and we should, perhaps, have taken it more seriously.' She leant her hands on the corner of Harold's desk and inclined towards him. 'Now, if there is anything we can do to put things right?'

Harold had not become successful in the public sector without understanding mutual backscratching.

'Where are my manners? Please sit down, Inspector, and you too, Detective Sergeant. Between us I am sure we can come to an understanding.'

'We understand,' said Erich confidently. Marlene nodded in agreement. 'You are doing a great job, Jenna, and I shall recommend that Michael increases your remuneration. You have prepared for every eventuality.'

'That's the spirit, Erich, credit where it is due, but cash is better.' As a self-employed individual, usually, Jenna could never understand other people's mumblingly embarrassed, 'oh, you shouldn't have's,' when offered cash and compliments. Jenna liked both and was happy to say so. She certainly deserved them, as Top Cat deserved recognition for keeping Officer Dibble in the long grass whenever his gang were up to flimflam. Jenna and Jady had gone to great lengths to ensure the success of the Pool competition, and Michael's associates were the lucky beneficiaries. It was Jenna's business, and her pleasure, to keep Harold Wood busy and bothered, thereby keeping him otherwise engaged.

Time had passed and the Baths were now open for the day. Tourists mainly, plus a few members of the public, were trickling in to gaze at one of the wonders of the ancient world. This was a nuisance from Marlene and Erich's point of view, as they were sure to ask questions and generally delay their work, but they were unavoidable and had been budgeted for from the outset. Being recognised and identified afterwards by the public did not bother them as their fake identity cards would be destroyed afterwards and their names would cease to exist. Meanwhile, the fledgling national database contained false data and could never be traced back to them.

The government would never admit that their identities were false; that would be the death of ID cards and the careers of those who introduced them. Erich forcibly suppressed a grin when he considered how the British government were being hoist by their own petard. In the unlikely event of Erich and his colleagues being arrested, the Government could hardly press charges and admit the truth publicly, because the truth was that this crime could only occur *because* of ID cards and the national database. If that leaked out, what would Brussels say? And how would the British electorate react to the knowledge that one of their national treasures had been stolen with the assistance of the very system that was supposed to fight crime? Paid for with money that could have been spent on *real* security measures, like providing opportunities and hope for young people? Britain would be the laughing stock of the world.

Erich looked up to the welcoming, all embracing deep blue sky and rejoiced that he was alive at this time. God bless biometrics! Thanks to them, people no longer believed their own instincts, experience and judgement, preferring to place their trust in a technology not one in ten thousand even begins to comprehend. Fools!

A sunny sky cheers everyone. Erich gave up his customary stoicism and grinned openly.

So did Jenna. Crowds suited her; their noise and general presence would conceal any bumps and scrapes Arnie might make on his lonely crawl through the arteries of the Baths and the Town Hall. He should be near his destination by now, she guessed. As if in reply, her phone chimed once, Arnie's call sign, showing both that Arnie was backstage in the Hall and that he had encountered no problems. Jenna immediately sent her pre-arranged confirmation that she was on her way. Arnie's mobile would vibrate, not ring, for obvious reasons. One chime and a quick vibrate in the Town Hall on prepaid anonymous mobiles. Let's see security work out that one, she reflected happily.

It was going to work! Jady's mad scheme, so unlikely, yet so simple. Jady was going to make a sack of money out of the Masked Pimpernel and the Pool tournament, shared with Arnie and herself, and it was all thanks to the introduction of identity cards! God bless 'em!

Jenna and Erich grinned at each other like drunken dervishes, both with their own cheerful thoughts. The Town Hall clock echoed around them. Lots to do, thought Jenna professionally, back to business.

'Well, if you will excuse me, Erich, I have to check up on my assistant, young Arnie. Remember, if you need me, just bleep, and if you need urgent assistance, utter the magic word and help will be on its way.'

Mr Dauntliffe too was on his way, but with considerably less satisfaction. Until very recently he had been congratulating himself on the smooth implementation of identity cards into Spawater and the relatively low amount of hostile publicity - apart from the usual suspects - that this had attracted. Mr Dauntliffe did not consider himself a dreamer, by any means; he was a practical man of management, but he allowed himself the luxury of a brief reverie into the recent past.

Fuelled by scare stories planted in the media suggesting that the country was under threat as never before from unspecified but nevertheless ruthless and terrifying enemies, the country was being led into a false sense of insecurity to the point where even otherwise intelligent people regarded the imposition of compulsory identification cards inevitable and at worst, a necessary evil. Likewise the national database. The Civil Service assured politicians that such a database would be invaluable in all sorts of indeterminate ways. Benefit fraud, immigration, crime, education, health and all manner of areas would be run more efficiently if only all the information about people was stored in the same place. 'A police State?' querulous MPs were told, 'In Great Britain? The country that stood alone against Hitler? Preposterous! Her Majesty would never stand for it, trust us.'

A true cynic himself - Stalin and Monty Burns found good in folk where Mr Dauntliffe saw only treason - it never ceased to amaze him that supposedly cynical politicians could be so gullible. Of course, it had long been Mr Dauntliffe's experience that the less people knew about technology, the more faith they had in its infallibility, like small children believing their parents know everything.

Not that Mr Dauntliffe knew about technology; he trusted it too, as much as the naive politicians he held in such contempt; he just did not trust people. People could not be trusted to know what was good for them. In this modern, global age of technology people simply did not have the knowledge or wisdom to manage their own affairs as they had in the past. No, people needed to be controlled for their own good. The technicians could handle the technical side; that was their job. Under guidance and instruction a system of control would be imposed, beginning with identity cards and ending with a properly ordered society, and for society's own good, he and his associates, the educated elite, would rule.

Mr Dauntliffe shook himself back to the present and looked at his watch. Time was important to him as a yardstick by which to measure his progress. This was the twenty-first century, he reminded himself, and the haphazard ways of the past where people came and went as they pleased could no longer be afforded.

All very satisfying thought Mr Dauntliffe; things were progressing discreetly and satisfactorily, and nothing must be allowed to spoil it.

But something had. Potentially at any rate. Two small and seemingly insignificant things, whether by coincidence or otherwise, concerning the Spawater Town Hall. First, the caretaker or whatever he was, that man Wood, bleating about German architects invading the Baths. The Council Head, on being questioned about them, was most uncooperative, suspiciously so. Then, and more seriously, this absurd talk of a Pool competition held by someone called the Masked Pimpernel, a mysterious figure who would not reveal his secret identity, like a comic book superhero. That capable man running things locally, Hanif Singh, had pooh-poohed worries about the Pool competition but Mr Dauntliffe was not convinced. Even Singh himself had telephoned seeking advice.

Straws in the wind, perhaps, but as a suspicious man to his very bones he was leaving nothing to chance.

Mr Dauntliffe wanted answers and he would only find them in Spawater.

Identity Cards
Chapter Seventeen

'Am I good or am I good!'

It does not take much to turn a hesitant teenager into a brash young irritant, thought Jenna as she escorted him out from backstage into the busy throng of the Town Hall proper. Weeks of nervous obstructions were steamrollered by success; in this case, Arnie successfully traversing the arteries of the Town Hall and arriving at the back of the stage as arranged.

'You are good indeed, young Arnie, and I am much impressed. Not that I had any doubt of course, I knew you could do it, we all did.'

Jenna didn't mind buttering Arnie up like a Devon scone, she knew the ancient wisdom concerning teenagers; one day they feel so happy, next day they feel so sad. Arnie was the lynchpin of the operation and as such had to be kept as happy as a teenager in love.

'So how was it? Any problems?'

'No. It was a doddle. I just followed the map the chief gave me; first left, straight to the end and turn left. When I reached the next corner I phoned you with the signal. Once you were there to guide me in it was simple.' Arnie smirked like Biggles returning from another bash at Erich Von Stalhein.

'Great stuff, Arnie. And you will have no trouble finding the right exit on your own in future?'

'No worries, no hurries.'

The rehearsal had gone according to plan. Jenna met Arnie at the exit point backstage as arranged, having guided him in carefully by the sound of her mobile. Arnie would know the route in future and would be able to appear in his Masked Pimpernel outfit when given the all-clear by Jady or one of the team. His outfit was concealed in the tunnel where he would change from his street clothes. Inconvenient, of course, as anyone who has dressed in confined spaces will know, but the maintenance tunnels were designed to accommodate Council repair workers, so were roomy enough for a teenager on a financial promise.

'Now, young Arnie, let's be getting back to the Baths. You can squeeze through the staff turnstile with me, you lucky dog, so as not to register your fake ID card in the security barrier. Security, my iris. You can't leave by the Town Hall exit as you didn't come in that way, of course, even Peckerhead might notice that. Then home for you so you can catch up on your study of classical Homeric mythology in the original Greek, or perhaps a well-earned killer computer game. We will meet up tonight in Lifeboats' with Jady and Alison for debriefing and de drinking. You deserve it.'

'This way to the Baths; when we get there I will show you what is happening and you can start your enquiries.'

Harold was making progress at last. In return for telling Inspector Brewe and Detective Sergeant Mathews everything he knew about the forthcoming Pool event, which was no more than they knew already, Harold had obliged them to take an interest in his 'foreign so-called architects'. They were feeling slightly cheated by this arrangement as they had learnt nothing from Harold and were going through the motions with no great enthusiasm.

'Let's get this straight then, Mr Wood,' said the Inspector. 'These people are here to carry out maintenance work of some sort, or an inspection of the Baths. This has been given the green light by the Council Head who has seen their identity cards and relevant database authority, but you are not satisfied. You wish us to talk to them to see what we can dig up.'

Sergeant Mathews tittered.

'Something funny, Sergeant?'

'Dig up. Architects. Get it?'

'Very droll. Now lead on, Mr Wood, will you?'

'All right, Arnie, and thanks for your help. See you tonight.'

Jenna escorted Arnie off the premises in her customary flamboyant and open way. This was not only because it was her usual style, but also to give the Baths staff the benefit of knowing that Arnie was her assistant and would be coming and going on a regular basis. Off-duty superheroes like to be invisible - apart from the Invisible Man, of course - and the best way to make Arnie invisible was for him to be seen around the place so often that he became part of the fixtures. Jady didn't think the alternative Plan B, the wooden horse, would work a second time. Not with Romans, anyway.

A falsetto from Jenna's mobile gate-crashed her thoughts like a dream-busting alarm clock; Erich and Marlene's signal.

'Jenna here.'

'Pimp,' sounded a quiet automated voice.

Like the rats and children when the Pied Piper sounded his summons, Jenna jumped to it.

'There they are,' said Harold to the two police officers. 'Ask them what they are doing.'

There is something intrinsically awkward about approaching people in white coats kneeling beside historic stone structures with a large open attaché case full of impressive specialist equipment and a clipboard. Such people look authoritative and in total command. Like sleeping dogs dreaming of their feral forbears, they are best left to lie. Erich looked up and smiled quizzically as the officers approached; Marlene reached for her bag.

'Excuse me, I am Police Inspector Josephine Brewe and I wonder if I could take up a minute of your time to ask you the nature of your work here?'

Erich rose and addressed the officer cheerfully.

'Certainly, Police Inspector; my name is Professor Erich Holtz and this is my colleague, Doctor Marlene Loffler.' Marlene smiled pleasantly, spoiling Sergeant Mathews's concentration. 'We are here to carry out structural examinations of your splendid Spawater Baths. How may we be of assistance?'

This is what Inspector Brewe had expected and feared. Clearly this was pukka, and best left alone. Still, she reasoned, a deal is a deal, and with Harold glowering at her like Lord Nelson expecting every police inspector to do her duty, she sailed on regardless.

'Could you show me your identity cards, please? Just routine, you know. After all, we can't be too careful. We will have to run them through the database.'

This sang to Harold's heart, his proudest moment. Even better than the Dancing Silver he and Mrs Wood had won on their last cruise. It would have been Gold had the funnels not blown at the crucial moment, spinning a startled Mrs Wood into a double helix when a single tap and shuffle was all that was required. Stowing this unhappy thought, Harold jolted his mind back to the present. This, he knew, is what the war against terrorism is all about; police and Town Hall working in harmony. This was full cooperation between the two security organisations keeping terrorists and foreign architects at bay, just as in 1940, and no unexpected loud noises to spoil things at the death.

'Come not between the dragon and his wrath,' said Shakespeare, a man who should know, Elizabethan England being stuffed to the roof beams with wrathful dragons. Come not between Jenna and hers either, his descendants may have added, assuming Francis Bacon had descendants too.

Jenna's wrath was currently directed at the encroaching, suspicious, all pervading control freak surveillance that was turning her once free and glad confident country into a prison without bars, as represented and personified by Harold Wood. Jenna's wrath was not one of those pleasant, forgiving and rational wraths with 'on the one hand this, on the other hand that' reasoning, but the real Crackerjack with all the trimmings. Jenna wanted to fix Harold Wood's wagon and this was her chance.

As the officers of the law approached Marlene and Erich at a moment when they would have preferred peace and solitude, Marlene reached into her bag and pressed the pre-arranged signal on her mobile. This sent a distress call to Jenna, who acted accordingly.

Marching determinedly through the main corridor of the Town Hall up to the nearest internal identity card recognition machine, Jenna removed a card from her bag and swiped it through the reader.

When Harold ordered the new security measures for Spawater Town Hall and the adjoining Baths, he had not scrimped. The plethora of security and alarm companies he'd hired had been astonished by the demands Harold put upon them. Some of the more ambitious security personnel marked down the Town Hall as a possible target for later private investigation, reasoning that such a surfeit of security denoted artefacts of serious value being housed there. Others simply installed the surveillance and alarm equipment whilst blessing the paranoid government that encouraged them, and the taxpayers for their bankroll.

For the alarm signalling an intruder alert Harold wanted the biggest, brightest and best. 'I want everyone in the municipal buildings to be in no doubt that there is an intruder about,' he'd informed all employees. 'When the alarm sounds, I want everyone to evacuate the buildings immediately. No exceptions, no arguments, just leave the buildings immediately and assemble at the assembly points previously arranged. Ignore anyone who tries to countermand this instruction, even me. That is because an impostor might impersonate me in order to spread confusion and doubt.'

Most of the Town Hall staff considered the real Harold more than capable of doing the impostor's job for him but wisely kept such treasonable thoughts to themselves.

All this meant, of course, that when Jenna deliberately set off the intruder alarm, it had the desired affect.

As the Inspector leaned forward and proffered her hand to receive Erich's identity card the intruder alarm sounded, if such a satanic hellblast could be humanised by the epitaph 'sound'.

Inspector Brewe was a strictly professional officer who stuck rigidly to the letter and spirit of the rulebook. The rulebook specifically forbade officers to blaspheme in the course of their duties and would have frowned at Inspector Brewe doing so in front of the public. Where the rulebook made its bloomer was in underestimating the natural human reaction to the loudest, ear-splitting banshee wail heard in Spawater since the garrison received its orders to invade Scotland and be sharp about it.

Harold's anti-intruder alarm was there to be noticed and in that capacity it did not disappoint. The stratosphere-pitched shriek assaulted the senses and cracked the thin veneer of civilisation that separates humanity from raw savagery. The niceties of nurture forgotten, nature took over with a vengeance Krakatoa could only envy. Erich performed a reverse head-over-heels not bettered since his school days, Marlene dropped her bag and yipped like a Pekinese in a kaleidoscope and Harold took off vertically, felt the weight of his responsibilities and landed again, his mind a double helix of confusion. Inspector Brewe made the rulebook consider its options and Sergeant Mathews held his head in his hands like the morning after the Distillery's Hogmanay do.

The Inspector recovered first.

'What the hell is that?' she yelled at the top of her voice at poor Harold, as if he didn't have enough noise to contend with.

Harold recovered his wits quickly, having few to collect, and shouted back, 'It's the alarm.'

'No kidding?' ad-libbed Sergeant Mathews sarcastically.

'It means there are intruders about,' continued Harold at full volume, ignoring the comment.

'How do you switch it off?' hollered the Inspector. The noise was paralysing all thought and action. Had real intruders been present and armed with earplugs, they would have had free run of the place.

After what seemed to the sufferers a lifetime but was in fact about thirty seconds, the banshee wail ceased, echoing through the ether like a departing soul with the wrong ticket.

For a moment all was calm. A sense of relief bonded them all, a shared hellish experience that would forever be a part of them and bond them in adversity like survivors of a shipwreck. Then, inevitably, the storm broke.

Harold had prepared his staff well. 'On hearing the alarm,' he had drilled into them, 'you get out of the building and don't stop to ask the way,' or words to that effect. This the staff did with an alacrity that would have gladdened the heart of any time and motions expert. Pandemonium reigned as the entire staff of the Spawater Baths and the Town Hall decamped as per orders. Visitors to both buildings, natives and tourists, soon picked up the idea. Time to go and none of this 'women and children first' pre-feminist sentimental claptrap; it was everyone for themselves and Devil take the hindmost. Captain Flint would be proud of them.

All this activity added nothing to the sense of calm Inspector Brewe was trying to instil in an overexcited Harold.

'There are intruders in the building, there are intruders in the building,' Harold parroted, as crowds of staff, tourists and natives herded towards the exits. A crowd built up at the main entrance as people had to swipe their identity cards to get through, one by one. Others gave up and sought the fire escapes; people were rushing to and fro like a demented human pinball machine from Hades.

'Had we better leave, Inspector?' asked Erich earnestly, ignoring the quivering Harold.

'Yes, I suppose so,' she replied, deadpan. 'You won't get much work done in this atmosphere.'

Marlene and Erich calmly collected their things and ambled over to the exit. They did not need their cards as the mob had broken through the turnstiles.

'What about the intruders?' bleated Harold.

'How was that alarm set off?' demanded the Inspector.

Facing the voice of authority, Harold simmered down.

'The alarm means that someone has swiped a fake identity card through an internal verifier,' he replied. 'This means there are intruders in the building. We have got to catch them before they plant a bomb.'

The two police officers exchanged that knowing 'we are in the presence of madness' expression normally employed when loonies enter the police station and confess to being Jack the Ripper. Clearly the only intruders around were themselves, intruding on Harold Wood's private fantasies. Inspector Brewe was about to make a suggestion along the lines of having the rulebook look up its own rulebook in fright when the banshee wail returned to its manic throne and ruptured their senses once more.

'It repeats every sixty seconds,' yelled Harold through cupped hands in response to the unspoken question.

'Switch – it – off,' stated Inspector Brewe at point blank range and with frozen calm, 'or – I – will – arrest – you –for – aural – assault!'

Erich and Marlene were delighted as they left the building amidst the mayhem. The main objective for the day was achieved; they had established themselves as the experts examining the Baths and were unlikely to be disturbed by staff or police officers in the future. Erich smiled as he recalled Jenna's words...

'Remember to inform Michael and Louise; send the emergency call of the Masked Pimpernel and there will be panic all around as Peckerhead's security alarms go crazyape. It is only little me causing a diversion with former employees' cancelled staff identity cards.'

Identity Cards
Chapter Eighteen

'Tell me Jady, is there ever a time when you are not celebrating? Rainy Monday mornings perhaps? When you get your credit card bills? When the government has another bright idea? Surely you have some miserable days like the rest of us? You can't celebrate all the time?'

'Life is for celebrating, Ron, just ask my pal Seneca the Younger. The great gift of life has been bestowed upon us and it is our duty to appreciate every moment. Rainy Mondays are pennies from Heaven, credit card bills are an affirmation of life, a record of our activities. Besides, we can always run them up and move house. If we all overspend together we will trash the system and get to keep our iPods. Government bright ideas are there to be opposed, especially this control freak ID card nonsense. It will collapse about the government's ears and serve it right. So, me old shipmate, let champagne reign like the rain in Spain, not on the plain but on the exceptional. That means us.'

Ron sighed the sigh of a frustrated Jeremiah. It was no use trying to dampen down a rampant Jady; sooner persuade a juiced-up Tigger to come quietly. Like Ken Dodd, Jady had been blessed with more than his share of happiness and Ron could guess who balanced the equation with the corresponding curse.

'Champagne it is then, for a change. You realise that means I have to go down into the cellar? With my back.'

'I'll get them for you.'

'Never mind, I'll get them. And you can tell your young pal Seneca that life is a serious business.' Ron turned around in a slow, dignified and morose manner, like a venerable sea-lion on a non-fish diet. Jady could be so annoying in this mood, thought Ron for the umpteenth time, denying him even the satisfaction of martyrdom. Cheerfulness can be so infuriating.

Monday evening, and Jady and Joanna were in Lifeboats' to celebrate the success of the next stage of the scheme. The gang were due any moment now, with Jenna and Arnie the heroes of the hour. Joanna set up camp in the discreet corner of the club that was rapidly becoming their headquarters, and presently a bubbly Jady arrived with the celebration juice.

Comfortably ensconced in two of the solid green leather armchairs around the even solider oaken ship's table, with other chairs waiting to be press-ganged into service when the others arrived, Jady turned to Joanna and squeezed her arm affectionately.

'Well, Joey my petal, here we are. Stage two of the plan is accomplished; Arnie has free access to the assembly rooms and knows how to get in and out of them unnoticed. As the local news confirms, Jenna's sabotage tactics were a total success. The government's loony ID card scheme is going to make us a fortune.'

Joanna smiled in response.

'Congratulations, Jady, you have done a great job. Fancy someone actually benefiting from identity cards. Apart from the identity card companies, of course, you must be the only non-bureaucrat or government creep to actually make something from them.'

'Everyone a winner,' agreed Jady laughingly. 'Actually, we benefit three ways. We make a pile of cash, we discredit ID cards and we have a good laugh at the bureaucrats in the Town Hall and the government. Success every which way you look.'

'Do you think this will discredit ID cards so much that the government will be forced to drop them?'

Jady considered this, staring into his drink and wondering for the millionth time where the bubbles came from.

'Well, no, not if they are determined to go ahead. They will just call it teething troubles, a blip that they have learnt from so that it could never happen again. Still, Jo, it is a step in the right direction and should help your Campaign Against

ID Cards people get new members. Remember, all bad identity card publicity is good publicity. The more foolish the government looks over the cards the more opposition to them will grow.'

This was nothing new to Joanna. They had discussed it at length and always concluded that on its own, embarrassing the government's ID card scheme would not be enough to scuttle it. Something more was needed. Something that not only showed how stupidly impractical and counter-productive the whole thing was, but also convinced people that identity cards and the national database were wrong in principle as well.

People needed to realise that the whole presumption of labelling the population and keeping tags on them as though they were guilty just by existing was a fundamental assault on freedom the like of which had never been seen on this planet before. Totalitarian states had tried, of course, to enslave their people, and had succeeded to the extent of the technology available to them, but totalitarian states could not watch and thereby control all the people all the time. The technology simply was not there. Eventually the contradictions of those societies outweighed the power of their secret police and the people overcame them. No longer. Totalitarianism was coming to freedom-loving Britain, and it was coming to stay.

'Are you ok, Jo?' Jady saw Joanna looking like George Orwell's little sister and was naturally concerned. 'You seem miles away. Is there anything wrong?'

Joanna smiled at her Jady again and cheered up. Human ingenuity would beat the machine. It must! Surely things could not be that bad. Surely people would realise in time and wake up to the threat. Surely there were millions of decent people in the country who simply would not stand for it.

'Sorry, Jady my love. I was just wondering how on Earth we can stop ID cards and the national database. What you are doing with Alison and the others is brilliant but as you just said, it won't stop the government going ahead. There must be something else we can do.'

'What about the Campaign to stop ID cards? What are they doing?'

'Getting organised, getting new members, spreading the word. We are not giving up, that's for sure. We will never give up.'

'If I can help in any way...'

'I know, Jady. There must be something else; I just need to think of it.'

'What were you thinking of? What were you playing at? Do you realise the trouble you have caused, and how much worse it could have been? You could have started a riot. People could have been killed. What do you have to say for yourself?'

Sitting on a wooden chair in the Police Station, with Inspector Brewe and Sergeant Mathews standing over him as per the best detective films, missing only the swinging bare light bulb, poor Harold was having a miserable time of it. Invited to reflect on recent events, he was obliged to concede that he had omitted to warn Inspector Brewe and Detective Sergeant Mathews that the Town Hall anti-intruder alarm was connected to the police station and the emergency services. As a high priority building this meant that all normal police activity was suspended as the police descended on the Town Hall en masse. Sirens whoo-whooped from every road approaching the Hall as all the police cars in town announced their presence in that unmistakable fashion guaranteed to frighten all within earshot, like modern day doodlebugs. As the public, tourists and staff rushed out, the police rushed in. Some rushed into each other, giving the ambulance people plenty to do when they arrived several minutes later, having been delayed by the traffic snarl-ups caused by the fire engines. Villains all over town could scarcely believe their luck.

A dogged Harold insisted loudly above the chaotic clamour that there were intruders about and the building must be searched for unauthorised personnel. Meanwhile, as the ambulance workers treated people injured in the melee, police and Council staff returning to see what was going on mingled with Harold's security team, while firefighters rolled out hoses and demanded, quite literally, 'Where's the fire?' Unsuspecting new tourists turned up to see the Baths, while people with business at the Town Hall mixed with the media; local newspaper reporters, radio and television crews, all watched from above by police, television and army helicopters.

No intruders were found.

'No intruders were found.'

At the conclusion of the local broadcast news Michael closed the television window on the computer and grinned at his team.

'Employing Jenna was a stroke of genius, though I say so myself; that Harold Wood character will not be able to show his face anywhere near you again. As for summoning the police, if he tries that he is likely to be wearing the handcuffs himself.'

The four conspirators had reasons to be cheerful. Day one had exceeded even Michael's optimistic predictions. Marlene and Erich reported back to Michael and Louise on great progress at the Baths and Michael and Louise produced their healthy interim bank statement.

Robin Hood looked down on them from his heavenly tree-house. 'See how merrie they are, Maid Marion; and I thought our lot were the merrie ones.'

'Merrie? Living in Sherwood Forest dressed as elves? Those robbers down on Earth are merrie because they have sheets and pillows and roofs and home comforts, plus, they get to keep all the swag. Now why didn't *you* think of that?'

Michael summed up

'Ecochtrust is firmly established as the specialist historical architecture organisation, with our experts examining the Baths, in the eyes of the Council Head, the Baths staff, the public and the police. Meanwhile our interim payment from our esteemed employer has transferred successfully to our joint account, to be accessed by our four signatures. We are on our way, boys and girls, on our way to victory and the spoils.'

Marlene and Erich exchanged glances.

'Tell him, Marlene. It is your responsibility.'

'Tell me what? Is there a problem?'

'Well, Michael, we asked Jenna what that fellow in The Lifeboat Club, Hanif, does for a living. He told me at the time that it was something to do with computers. It turns out that he is the local agent responsible for implementing the trial Identification Card scheme in Spawater. He might be able to check out our identities on the real national database.'

'Did you see it? It was all over the local news reports. What a result.'

Jenna held forth to the gang in Lifeboats', reliving the day's activities over Jady's champagne. In attendance were Alison, Arnie, Hanif, and of course, Joanna and Jady. Not over-burdened with humble conceit - Uriah Heep beat her to the Dickens job - Jenna gave credit where it was due.

'It is all thanks to that splendid intellectual powerhouse of a man, Mr Harold Peckerhead Wood. Without his unselfish and unstinting dedication to saving Spawater from militant terrorist architects, the Masked Pimpernel would not have got within sniffing distance of the Town Hall. We should invite our Harold, for that's how I now think of him, for a drink to show our appreciation.'

'Seriously though,' asked a curious Hanif, 'what exactly did you do? The whole of the town centre was blocked for hours and people are going ape. How did you do it?'

'Now now, Han,' Jenna laughed, 'how do I know I can trust you? You work for the evil empire and if I reveal my secrets, you might send the New Stasi round at midnight.'

Hanif was accustomed to this type of talk from Jenna and did not take it too seriously.

'C'mon, Jen, I won't use it against you. I am just curious, that's all.'

Jenna poked out her tongue.

'It is simple, Hanif,' joined in Joanna. Despite current differences, Joanna was not going to allow their friendship to suffer any more than could be helped; besides, she was seeking ways to oppose ID cards and by discussing things with Hanif, Joanna hoped she might find inspiration. After all, Shakespeare often chewed the fat with Bacon.

'Jenna's new friend Harold has annoyed plenty of Town Hall staff with his jobsworth mentality. Some have left and become disgruntled ex-employees in time-honoured fashion. Jady and Jenna know all the security routines thanks to them.'

'How did they set off the alarms?'

'Simple. Jady bought old, cancelled staff identity passes and gave them to Jenna. Naturally they were cancelled when the employees left. Jenna swiped one through a machine, setting off alarms and causing diversions. That Harold bloke caught it coming and serves him right.' Joanna looked into Hanif's eyes and sniggered smugly. 'Now what do you think of compulsory identity cards, Han?'

Ignoring the jibe, Hanif turned to Jenna. 'Why did you want a diversion?'

'You know you are sworn to secrecy, don't you, Hanif?' Alison joined in the general debate. 'In some ways you are on the wrong side of the fence.'

The wrong side of the fence was the last place Hanif wanted to be vis-à-vis Alison.

'Of course, Ali, yes I know we disagree about identity cards but I am against red tape as much as you are. I am against greater bureaucracy and for greater security.'

This caused the best laugh most of them had had for weeks.

'Honestly, Hanif,' said Joanna, bubbling champagne over the side of her glass in amusement, 'if you believe that splitting the country from top to bottom by inflicting ID cards on us will improve security, then you should be in Parliament.'

'We will see. Let's just agree to differ. Anyway, I know why you wanted the diversion; it was to allow Arnie to get into the Town Hall, wasn't it?'

'This is your greater security in action, Han,' replied Joanna gloatingly, with champagne-fuelled confidence. 'Arnie was able to slip in because, and that is *because* not in spite of, the high-tech security.' She paused to raise her glass and give an 'I told you so' smirk, then continued.

'Old-fashioned tried and tested safeguards such as manned barriers and doormen with common sense, human judgement and experience, would have stopped him, but they have been dispensed with. People are dumbed-down and don't use their discretion any more. They are obliged to rely totally on technology. Disable the technology and there is no protection. Breeching security is a doddle. Cheers.'

'In all the bars in all the towns in all the world, you had to get drunk and talk too much in Hanif's.'

Michael was not amused. The best laid schemes o' mice and men gang aft a'gley, as Jady's old sparring partner Monty once discovered, and Michael was not going to have his schemes gang a'gley just because of a mouse mangler who couldn't mind his own business.

'It is not a problem, Michael,' comforted Louise, 'even if he hacks into the database he will find nothing to incriminate us. The database will confirm that we are who we say we are.'

'That's true,' agreed Erich. 'Let him waste his time. He can't hurt us.'

'It is not him hurting us that we must consider, more the opposite.'

'How do you mean?' asked Marlene, concerned.

Michael laughed. 'Don't worry. We are not going to put everything at risk by indulging in juvenile gangsterism; we are far too near to success to take any pointless chances. Besides, violence is for losers, ask our former chancellor.'

'Then what do you mean? If he cannot find out about us from the national database, why don't we just ignore him?'

'Because he is clearly an intelligent man. What if he digs further? What if he contacts various architecture and historical organisations throughout the world to check on our bona fides?'

Louise laughed scornfully. 'Every possible relevant organisation? Impossible. Bureaucratic nightmares aside, commercial confidentiality would stop him in his tracks if the sheer size of the task did not. He would have to be an obsessive. No, Michael, there is no problem.'

Michael considered. 'Yes, you are probably right.' He rubbed his chin to assist thought. 'All the same, I would be a good deal happier if friend Hanif had other things to occupy him.'

'What sort of things?'

'How would you like another trip to The Lifeboat Club?'

'Good news, Arnie; one of the cheeses will let you practice on his own Pool table, in his house. Nobody will see you there.'

'Will you be coming with me? I don't want to face your bosses on my own.'

'Of course,' Alison beamed, 'Jady will come too, won't you Jady?'

'Sometimes, Millado, when I can spare it. Mind you, there is nothing to worry about at the big cheese's house; they need you as much as you need them. Just lay off the free hospitality, that's all.'

Having let Jenna blow herself out like a jovial hurricane, the gang ensured that Arnie got the acclaim he deserved. Drinks all round, of course, so they could share in his heroism, then the platitudes.

'I must say, young Arnie, you have shown skill and devotion above and beyond the call of duty. Have a drink on Jady.'

‘Thank you, Jenna, but it wasn’t that dangerous, was it?’

Jady was well aware that the trouble with congratulating someone for their ongoing bravery is that they start wondering just how brave they are being and whether it is so smart to continue. Being brave should always be in the past tense. Nobody wants to be brave tomorrow.

‘Not dangerous, Millado, but it could have been a bit tricky. It should be a doddle from now on. The important thing is the Pool competition. You must practice your trick shots for the tournament.’

‘The tournament?’

A voice resonated from behind Jady’s car. Ron was doing his rounds and, hearing the talk about the Pool competition, took his cue.

‘So you are entering the tournament, young Arnie? I thought you would. You are certainly the best player in the club, everyone tells me. So you should be after all the chalk you have used in the Pool room. Don’t get your hopes up about winning, though; the whole thing is obviously too good to be true. It must be a fiddle.’

‘How can *I* enter?’ replied Arnie, mystified.

‘Of course he is,’ interrupted Jady before Arnie could say something they would all regret. Where would superheroes be without their secret identities? If Superman and the rest had to register their names and addresses with the national database, Supervillans would have overrun the world long ago. Batman and even Robin know what paranoid parliaments do not, that you cannot have personal security if you don’t have personal secrecy.

‘How can I?’

‘Don’t worry, Arnie,’ said Alison, patting him on the shoulder, ‘my company are organising the contest. I will show you how to enter it.’ She turned to Ron and raised her voice in what, for Alison, passed for annoyance. ‘And for the record, Mr clever-know-everything-Ron, it is not a fiddle. It is being run by my company in conjunction with Jady Enterprises and is free, fair, and open to all. It says so on the billboards. Why don't you enter it yourself? It is free and you could win ten thousand pounds.'

Ron looked at Jady incredulously. 'You mean this is what you and Arnie are involved in? That job you said you had for Arnie? This Pool tournament?'

'Millado advised me on the rules for a Pool tournament so I could make my case to Ali's employers; that's all Ron,' Jady replied nonchalantly, not wishing anyone to connect Arnie directly with the contest.

Ron laughed aloud for the third time that year; hyenas started examining their copyrights.

'Now I get it. You are going to arrange for Arnie to win the ten thousand pound prize and split the money! I might have known. Jady, you never cease to amaze me. But you, Alison? I am surprised at you. Allowing yourself to get talked into this by Jady. Honestly.'

Alison reacted first, luckily for Ron.

'Ten thousand split three ways? Don't be so silly. You think my company would be involved in something like that? What would be in it for us? And to rig a Pool competition for peanuts? Not even Jady would stoop that low.'

'Thanks.'

'Besides,' Alison continued, ignoring Jady, 'it would be impossible. Our switchboard has been jammed solid with entrants all day. The whole town is involved. Thousands of people will be watching. You know what they say, Ron; you can fool some of the people all the time but you can't fool all of them all the time.'

'That's it! That's the answer!' Joanna eureka'd like Archimedes when he forgot to switch on the cold tap. The others turned to her in concern. Joanna sported a grin to shatter diamonds.

'That's it. Thank you, Alison. You have done it again.' Joanna kissed Alison on the champagne glass.

'Done what?'

Alison's chance misquote about fooling the people had unlocked that part of the brain that held the solution to Joanna's identity card problem. If identity cards were an assault on the people, it was for the people to resist them. Simple; Archimedes would have been proud.

'I'll tell you later. Sorry to interrupt.'

'Anyway, Mr know-all Ron. The Pool competition is completely honest and I won't have you saying otherwise.'

A professional sceptic - Eeyore could only look on in admiration -Ron had one last shot.

'So who's putting up the money then? And why?'

Unusually, all the gang were silent.

Jady raised his flute and looked Ron in the eye, changing the subject.

'How are your Health and Safety inspectors getting on?'

'Don't ask.'

'Exactly. Cheers.'

Identity Cards
Chapter Nineteen

Eager expectancy electrified the town like a promise from Santa Claus. Excitement grew over the next few days leading up to the first rounds of the Great Spawater Pool contest. Social, class and age barriers broke down like the artificial veneers they were as the population discussed the audacious challenge of the Masked Pimpernel and who he might be. At bus stops, the station, shops, Post Office queues, pubs, clubs, restaurants, launderettes, wherever two or more people met, people asked the same questions. 'Have you entered? Who is the Masked Pimpernel? What is it all about? Who is paying for it?'

The weather felt quite neglected, being relegated to second conversational place. 'You will be sorry for ignoring me, you fair-weather friends,' thundered the weather. 'Just you wait, as soon as I can collect a few clouds together, start building Arks.'

Alison, Jady and Arnie were kept at it during this period and onwards, especially Alison, along with her work colleagues. Thousands of enquiries leading to as many entries had to be processed; her company's telephones glowing as red as the Batphone when the Penguin was in town.

Arnie divided his time between practicing trick shots at the senior cheese's house, accompanied by Alison or Jady, and convincing his mother that he was earning an honest living. Mrs Bennett had once before summoned the police because she'd mistakenly feared her son was involved in drugs, when in fact his real mind-altering experience was working for Jady. This caused some embarrassment at the time and a repeat was not required.

Jady had the gruelling task of investigating every establishment in town equipped with a Pool table and inveigling them into staging preliminary rounds of the tournament. There were, of course, far too many entrants for the Town Hall alone; pubs, clubs and snooker halls were press-ganged into service by an insistent Jady, who had shanghaiing blood in him alongside the Bilco Positive. The venues also included Lifeboats', of course, as its exclusion would look odd.

'All right, Jady,' expostulated an exasperated Ron, 'you win. You can have your infernal competition here if you must; at least I will be able to sell a few sandwiches to the contestants.'

'Sell them the sandwiches after the game, there's a good lad, skipper,' replied Jady, who new about Ron's hurried resignation from the Navy catering corps.

'Look, Jady, for the hundredth time there is nothing wrong with my food, ok?'

'Just as you like, Ron; now I must cast off; lots to do.'

Others were busy too. Curiosity creates commerce and the Masked Pimpernel and his challenge caused the people of Spawater to be very curious indeed. As the days progressed, a Masked Pimpernel industry blossomed like a desert orchid. Jady owned the conceptual intellectual copyright but generously waived it so that anyone could produce Masked Pimpernel paraphernalia, the better to promote the tournament. Tee shirts appeared first; silkscreen printers suddenly became as much in demand as vendors of lion repellent during the gladiator season as every entrepreneur in town sought to cash in on this unexpected bonanza. Alison's company recouped some of their investment by producing mugs, towels, tee shirts, and pens, and as much general tat as the market would stand. Markets themselves sprouted stalls dedicated to bootleg Masked Pimpernel and grand tournament souvenirs with a flourish to gladden the hearts of western decadence theorists.

Binge-drunken city centre teenagers forsook gracing the area in sports shirts and instead sported Masked Pimpernel tops with evermore ambitious slogans; some speculating on his secret identity, others claiming ownership, the bravest alleging that they had met him in various unsavoury and anatomically unlikely circumstances. Not since the Spawaterians lost their bid for the Roman Games by hiring Brutus to make an impression on Caesar had a sports tournament aroused such blanket excitement.

Everybody wanted to be involved in the tournament, either as contestants or spectators, and everybody wanted to know the Masked Pimpernel's secret identity.

'Who the hell is he?' barked Inspector Brewe rhetorically at Detective Sergeant Mathews. 'And who is paying for this tournament?'

'You know who is paying for it, Ma'am, that Spawater public relations company and Jady Enterprises.'

Inspector Brewe and her disloyal assistant had enjoyed their interrogation of Harold Wood over the Town Hall incident. Grilling a pompous act like Harold until done to a turn is always entertaining. Less fun was the interview the Inspector subsequently had with her Chief. The art of enjoying a good grilling lies in being the griller, not the grillee. After a last slow rotation to ensure all over crispness, the Chief, employing high-grade sarcasm as befitted his exalted position, intimated that as the officer responsible for peace and harmony at the Town Hall she was strongly advised not to have it drawn to national attention and derision in such a humiliating manner again in the near future. Not if she wanted a career future, at any rate. The Inspector had her orders; under no circumstances was the Town Hall to attract any outside attention for any reason at all. Which, considering that looming ahead like a titanic iceberg was the most spectacular contest in Spawater Town Hall's history since the Lion challenged Daniel to a rematch, was a bit thorny.

'I don't care what is going on at the Town Hall,' bellowed the Chief, stoking up the fires once more, 'I want that Pool contest to pass without incident and unnoticed by the rest of the country. I do not want the other police chiefs saying I cannot control my patch. And if I lose out on royal recognition for my years of selfless and dedicated public service with no thought of reward, I will bust you so low you will be saluting traffic wardens. Do I make myself clear?'

It was a chastened if not contrite Inspector Brewe who slunk away from the Chief's office like a wolf on probation. If she were ever to occupy such high office herself it was essential that his wish for an uneventful Pool contest was granted. How could she ensure such a thing? Where was her Fairy Godmother when she was needed? As a girl, the Inspector had dreamt of a Fairy Godmother bringing her happiness ever after; though bumping off her two ugly sisters was taking it a bit far. Now she no longer believed in fairies and it seemed that her Fairy Godmother, like Tinkerbelle, was no longer around to send her to the Promotions Ball.

'Typical,' tutted her Fairy Godmother. 'No-one believes in us anymore, do they, Tink?'

'Help, I am stuck in a jar,' replied a muffled Tinkerbelle.

'Ok Tink, I believe in you.'

Released from her glass house, Tinkerbelle returned the favour. 'If you want your Human Goddaughter to believe in you...'

'Yes?'

'Then tell her what she most wants to hear.'

'You know something, Tink? That's Magic.'

In the twinkling of an eye, Inspector Brewe's Fairy Godmother revealed the cause of her problems. She whispered one word in Inspector Brewe's ear.

'Jady.'

'Jady?'

'Mmmmph?'

'You know I have been unhappy about how you, Alison and the others are showing up this ID card and database scheme for the dangerous nonsense it is while I have done practically nothing?'

Jady placed his glass of wine on the wide, aged leather arm of his armchair.

'Not how I would have phrased it, but yes?'

'Well how about this for an idea?'

Joanna and Jady were at home, relaxing over a film. What with Jady's hectic schedule and Joanna's day job, this was their first proper evening together since celebrating Arnie's Town Hall burgling success in Lifeboats'. Joanna had made some enquiries and decided that her Alison-inspired idea was, like their banister, a runner.

'You want maximum publicity for your Pool contest, right?'

'Right...'

'And I want maximum publicity for the Campaign Against Identity Cards, right?'

'Right again...'

'So how about I get the Campaign to stage a demonstration outside the Town Hall on the night of the Pool tournament final?'

Jady smiled happily, removed his glass to the table for safety and leaned towards the armchair where Joanna roosted. She looked at him expectantly.

'Why that's a great idea, Jo, two birds with one stone.' He looked up at the ceiling, musing thoughtfully. 'They were all wrong about you, Joey. They all said you were south of an amoeba, intellectually, and that you could not come up with an idea in a joke shop. Well they were wrong; probably it's my influence, but I have to hand it to you, you have come up with an excellent idea. Use the Spawater Town Hall tournament to make as much noise, fuss and publicity as possible. Go for it.'

Jady had overplayed his hand. Joanna knew him far too well to fall for the old oil. On the rare occasions that they fell out, Jady would lean against the bar in Lifeboats' and rail pathetically to Ron that his partner understood him.

'You knew, didn't you?' She laughed at the realisation. 'You had thought of using the Campaign as a publicity stunt all along, hadn't you? You want maximum fuss too for your own wicked financial reasons. You were just waiting to see if I thought of it myself. If I hadn't come up with the idea soon you would have suggested it to me, casual like, in the hope that I would run away with it.'

Joanna marvelled at the boyish expression of horror-struck innocence spreading across Jady's poker dial like galloping acne. She had seen that expression many times and it always preceded a forced confession.

'You hound,' Joanna continued, giggling through the release of tension. To think that she had initially been worried that Jady might resent her plans as getting in the way! 'Own up. You knew, didn't you? Own up.'

She bounded out of her armchair, grabbed Jady's glass from its placemat and ran behind his back. Putting her free arm around his neck she whispered in his ear.

'Own up. Own up, my love, or your neck will get a free wash.' She allowed a splash to trickle down the back of Jady's neck.

Jady was a great subscriber to the theory that if you are being tortured for the secret plans you might just as well confess immediately. After all, you are bound to crack sooner or later, so why suffer? He would have been a sad disappointment to the Spanish Inquisition.

'C'mon, Jady, own up or your neck gets it in the neck.'

Joanna had reckoned without the legendary Jady luck. As Harry Flashman could tell you, fortune doesn't only favour the brave.

Just before Jady's spirit, like his glass, sprung a leak, the doorbell rang. Had Joanna been a dratter, like Dick Dastardly, she would have dratted, probably a double, possibly a triple. Instead, feeling a twinge of annoyance as she contemplated how often they were disturbed just when they were at their lovingest, Joanna stopped pouring and started pouting, swapping the wine for a whine.

'If you say saved by the bell, I will kill you.'

'I suppose saved by the doorbell is out of the question?' replied Jady sweetly.

'Yes,' Joanna snorted mock-sternly. 'Remember our places; I haven't finished with you yet.'

The doorbell rang once again, sounding as though it meant business. Joanna shrugged good-humouredly.

'Ok, I'll get it; you stay there and invent some excuses.'

Jady's wine glass in hand for insurance, Joanna lazily traversed the large, over-furnished living room, passed past the huge vase set beside the flat's entrance, gainfully employed as an umbrella-holder so as not to upset the elephants, ambled out into the hallway shared with the upstairs neighbours and arrived at the street door. Two official looking silhouettes stood without.

'Good evening.'

'Is it? I am not so sure. You know, of course, what this is about. Come in.'

Mr Dauntliffe waved his associate into his city apartment and onto an armchair, skipped the customary preliminaries and, like Rumpole, got straight down to cases. Mr Pettifogg, a non-executive director of a private multinational security conglomerate, currently a Senior Governmental Liaison officer advising the government of the advisability of compulsory identification cards and national database - or junior lobbyist, as Mr Dauntliffe considered him - sat down unceremoniously.

Mr Dauntliffe opened the batting.

'How did the government react to the recent unpleasantness in Spawater Town Hall?'

'How do you think? They were not at all happy. This is precisely the sort of thing the government wishes to avoid. So does my company. As you are aware, we wish to implement identity cards in Spawater as smoothly and quietly as possible. This unpleasantness, as you call it, not only showed up identity cards but also the ideas of a central database. I understand the Town Hall database rejected a staff identity card because it had been cancelled. Had this happened to the completed national database goodness alone knows what would happen. It would be a disaster.'

Mr Dauntliffe put aside his resentment at being talked to like this by his inferior; time enough to deal with jack-in-office incivility later. Reassuring the government was the object of this meeting and that came first. Business was Mr Dauntliffe's pleasure, mirroring Mae West but agreeing with her that goodness had nothing to do with it.

'It only happened because of an overzealous local manager. He had a private security company install the database system at such a sensitive level that the slightest aberration from the norm produced panic stations. I am going to Spawater shortly to have a word with the people there to ensure that it does not happen again.'

Mr Pettifog did not often enjoy interviews with Mr Dauntliffe; usually experiencing the same emotional turmoil as Bertie Wooster when ensconced with his headmaster over hot biscuits, but this interview was an exception. The Town Hall incident had caused embarrassment at ministerial level and he had been empowered to unsure that it was not repeated. This gave him temporary leverage over his superior and he intended to take full advantage.

'That is all very well, Mr Dauntliffe, but it does not deal with the central issue. How many more overzealous local managers are there? We cannot afford any more incidents.'

'There will not be any more incidents, I will see to that. Now, as regards overzealous managers...'

Mr Dauntliffe eased back slowly into his creaky red leather armchair, crackling his knuckles in time with the cowhide.

'This incident could be turned to our advantage. It occurred because the Town Hall manager, a local nobody, had the power to set his own level of security. Obviously, cancelled identification cards should not set off alarms except in the most important areas, such as government buildings.'

'You think town hall buildings are less important than government ones? Remember, we want councillors on our side to assist with implementation.'

'Off the record, I do. Of course, we will keep the local councils on side until we have total database saturation.

After that they will be redundant as we centralise power. We cannot leave the decision making process in the hands of amateurs just because they are elected.'

'Keep that under wraps, for goodness sake.'

'I am not a fool, Pettifog. Now, what this incident demonstrates is that security is too important to be left in the hands of local, untrained operatives. When your final report and recommendation is presented to the Home Secretary and his minions it will stress the absolute necessity for centralising all security matters.'

Mr Pettifog was impressed despite himself. Where lesser minds might have conceded that security should be subsumed to the lowest possible level - in the recent case a doorkeeper with common sense could have sorted it out - Mr Dauntliffe used the incident as justification for going in the opposite direction. Overzealous local security arrangements had caused the problem and instead of becoming less zealous and utilising local initiative, security would be taken out of local hands entirely and centralised. In other words, given to them and their colleagues, regardless of cost, efficiency or sense.

'You excel yourself,' said Mr Pettifog and meant it. 'I see what you mean now. Every time something goes wrong at local level we blame the locals and transfer yet more power to ourselves.'

'You mean, transfer more security functions to central government,' sniggered Mr Dauntliffe in contempt. It is not easy to sneer and snigger at the same time but Mr Dauntliffe managed it in a way that would have had Dick Dastardly looking up his family tree.

Mr Pettifog frowned. 'What happens if anything goes wrong at central government level?'

'We conceal it. However, that is for the future. Until the national database is nationwide and everybody has accepted their identity cards there can be no more 'local mistakes'. The media have their eye on Spawater and have had a field day over this Town Hall incident. There must be no more incidents such as this.'

'What about this Pool competition and Masked Pimpernel character? The newspapers are watching even more closely than before. You must ensure that it causes no problems. Can you ban it?'

It was Mr Dauntliffe's turn to frown.

'If I could, I would. Of course, once we centralise and thereby control everything, particularly telephones, the internet, electronic media and the newspapers, we will be able to ban anything in the name of security and nobody will have sufficient knowledge or information to challenge us. Anyone who tries will be intercepted.' Mr Dauntliffe smiled at the thought. 'But for now,' he continued solemnly, 'banning it would be counterproductive. The anti surveillance organisations would claim we were overreacting and would win a moral victory. Those people are a growing nuisance and we do not want them playing the Police State card. No, blanket banning of private assemblies such as this one cannot occur until we control everything from the centre.'

He rose, signifying the end of the meeting.

'Yes, you are right,' agreed Mr Pettifog, rising in response. He had given up on being offered refreshments. 'Until then we must ensure that the contest in Spawater is uneventful. The quieter the better.'

'Absolutely,' replied Mr Dauntliffe, opening his door, 'you can tell your people there will be no trouble at the Spawater Town Hall Pool contest.'

'We want to talk to you about the Spawater Town Hall Pool contest.'

After uttering a loud call-to-arms announcement to Jady by way of warning, Joanna ushered Inspector Brewe and Detective Sergeant Mathews into their home.

In a fair impersonation of affability, Jady rose to greet them.

'Good evening, Inspector, and what can I do for you?' he announced in a pleased voice. He had always wanted to use that line; all he needed now was 'More tea, Vicar?' and 'Is there a Doctor in the house?' and he would have the set. Oscar Wilde would see the importance but Conan Doyle would have to look out for himself.

'Joanna,' announced Jady earnestly, 'allow me to introduce Chief Inspector Josephine Brewe and Detective Sergeant Mathews. These are the fine upholders of all that is finest who rescued me from the cellar last year.'

Jady waved to the officers. 'Won't you sit down? A drink? Or are you on duty?'

Faced with this reminder of Jady's supercilious manner, which was not quite mocking but not quite *not* mocking, the officers sat on the chaise longue.

'I notice you have a new computer, Jady,' said Sergeant Mathews conversationally whilst looking round like a good observant officer, 'have you finished turning your cellar into an office yet?'

'I am getting round to it. Good of you to remember,' laughed Jady. 'Those were the days.'

'It doesn't look very new though.'

Jady shrugged. The only thing new about the computer was the hard disk; the old one with the incriminating blackmail evidence had long been consigned to Alison's dustbin of history. At least, Jady hoped it had, but with Alison you could never be sure.

Inspector Brewe coughed the cough of someone who is not here for copper/lag reminiscences and wishes to bring the meeting to order.

'It is Inspector, not Chief Inspector, Mr Dein,' said Inspector Brewe tersely, rightly suspecting that Jady had promoted her deliberately to break her train of thought.

'Call me Jady. Everyone does.'

'Now,' she continued, ignoring the interruption, 'I won't take up much of your time. As I told your partner, this concerns the impending Pool tournament at the Town Hall.'

She leaned forward and looked Jady in the eye. He twinkled winningly.

'I am responsible for policing the Town Hall and I want this contest to run quietly. I know you are behind it and

I want your assurance that it will pass without incident. I also,' she leant back for effect, 'want to inform you of the consequences if it does not.'

Identity Cards
Chapter Twenty

Christmas comes to the spirited naughty children as well as the mealy-mouthed goody goodies. Ignoring fervent forebodings from the wise men, starlight faded and the sky duly transmogrified from black to shimmering red over the verdant hills of Spawater, evoking a celestial Pool table in the febrile imaginations of local shepherds and sheep, whilst heralding the advent of the great day. And it looked like rain.

Saturday would see the tournament's opening firework festivities outside the Town Hall, Master of Ceremonied by Alison, as chief representative for her Public Relations and Brand Promotions Company. Alison was a local Spawater celebrity having presided over last year's Town Hall riots, and telegenic to boot. Added to an almost sectionable unawareness that public speaking is supposed to be daunting, Alison was as comfortably cool behind the mike as Elvis on his South Pole tour.

Stage One completed; everything set. Thousands of Spawaterians of all shapes, sizes and genders were drawn randomly and selected to play each other in the first preliminary round.

This was the deal; the entrants would play their elimination matches in the various designated Pool emporiums throughout Spawater. There were to be wall-to-wall Pool games, supervised by independent outsiders to ensure fair play. Some lucky contestants were slated to play in the Town Hall main Assembly room on any of the fifteen Pool tables supplied by Alison's outfit in the presence of the Masked Pimpernel himself.

The preliminary rounds would take place over the following weeks until the numbers had been reduced to the final sixty-four. These finalists would play for the right to challenge the Masked Pimpernel in single, open Pool combat for the ten thousand pound prize.

As by far the best player in Lifeboats', and consequently its Pool pride and joy, Arnie was expected to enter and put up a good show. Bullet, the club's chief wager broker, opened a book on him and found many takers. Arnie therefore entered in his own name.

'I won't win, but I will give it a bloody good try, chief,' sparkled an excited Arnie days earlier over a small orange juice. Arnie was in training and on a strict, no lager diet. Wine yes, lager no. This wasn't darts.

Jady had been hoping against hope that it wouldn't come to this, but the hour had come to introduce Arnie to partial reality.

'I am afraid I have some bad news, Millado,' sighed a reluctant Jady sadly, like a village elder cancelling Christmas because they had roasted Rudolph. Jady was well aware of Arnie's pride in his ability and his general youthful enthusiasm for life and all its challenges, and had seen this one coming. He had been hoping that Arnie would realise without his prompting that it was impossible for him to be a serious entrant.

'I have to ask you to deliberately lose your first preliminary match.'

'What?'

'You must be knocked out of the contest.'

Arnie stared at Jady incredulously. He was no expert, but could have sworn that orange juice packed less punch than his usual tipple, though it would, perhaps, explain Gussie Fink-Nottle's newt habit.

'Sorry, chief, I thought you just said I must be knocked out of the contest.'

'I am afraid so, Millado. In the first round.'

'You mean throw the match?' Arnie was perplexed. 'But why?'

As a responsible member of the human race, Jady was naturally concerned that should Arnie play well and actually win through to the final, he would be up for the prize against the Masked Pimpernel himself. This, as Jady was only too well aware, would cause a fissure in the Space Time Continuum. Goodness knows what might happen.

'Because it would look rigged. People would assume we'd arranged it to keep the ten grand ourselves.'

Arnie's plumage drooped like a cockerel the day the clocks go back.

'I suppose so,' he mumbled. 'But,' with more animation, 'it is wrong to throw a game. I have never done it before. I don't like it, chief, it is wrong.'

Jady didn't like it either, but this was hardly the time for Arnie to develop a conscience. Especially when the success of the whole scheme depended on the Masked Pimpernel beating his challenger. Arnie did not know it yet, but the Masked Pimpernel had to win by hook or by crook, and hook was out of town.

Jady placed a father-like arm around Arnie's shoulder.

'Millado, my lad, there are times when we all have to do things we do not particularly like. I know you would put up a great show if you tried, but don't you see that it is impossible? You have such an individual style; if people saw you play and then the Masked Pimpernel do his trick shots they might put two and two together. And why do they never see you and the Masked Pimpernel at the same time? No, while we have a Ringer posing at the children's hospital donating Masked Pimpernel teddies for publicity shots next week - Alison's idea - you will, sadly, be being knocked out of the tournament in Lifeboats'.'

Jady looked Arnie sidelong in the eye.

'I know it is a terrible sacrifice to make, Millado, but you can do it.' Jady sniffed. 'You can do it for us all. I know you can, Millado, I have faith in you.'

Arnie sat up bolt upright. Throughout his childhood, while his loving mother worked all the hours to keep the family together, he did not have many role models and was not told by many adults that they had faith in him. Well, Jady was right to have faith in him; he would not let Jady down.

Arnie laughed aloud. 'And I just thought of something else, chief.'

'What's that?'

'If I got to the final, I would have to play against myself!'

Jady laughed alongside, withdrawing his arm and massaging his heart back up from his boots.

'Great Scott! Well thought of, Millado, you'll do!'

Game on.

'Good afternoon, Ladies, Gentlemen and people of Spawater, and welcome to the opening ceremony of the Great Spawater Pool Tournament.'

From the podium erected for the purpose on the Green opposite the Town Hall and Baths, Alison began the opening ceremony. Alongside her were a couple of her company's cheeses, the Council Head, the Mayor and a few assorted bigwigs. Directly behind the podium, carefully out of sight and awaiting his introduction, stood the Masked Pimpernel himself. Not the real one, of course. The trick was for Arnie and the Masked Pimpernel to appear in public at the same time.

As an employee of Jady Enterprises, Arnie was gainfully employed as a roadie supervising the sound system. This entailed standing on the stage before the ceremony began, in full view of the gathering Spawaterian throng, droning into the microphone, and 'testing 123 testing' in the authoritative yet casual manner reminiscent of hairybacked roadies worldwide. During Alison's peroration Arnie would stand at the edge of the stage ostensibly ready for any aural emergencies but actually visible at the same time as the Masked Pimpernel when he appeared.

After introduced the assorted cheeses and bigwigs to the multitude, Alison continued.

'I would like to thank the thousands of you who have entered the tournament in the finest traditions of our Roman ancestors, and remind you that we all have the Masked Pimpernel and his sponsors to thank for the opportunity to have some great fun and for one lucky, no skilful, Spawaterian to challenge the Masked Pimpernel himself for the one thousand pound prize.'

Some discontented mutterings from the crowd.

'Sorry, ten thousand pound prize.' Alison giggled. 'Well, what's a few grand between friends? Anyway, without further ado, I have the honour of presenting the man, or superman, responsible for the whole thing.'

Alison made the signal.

'Step forward, the Masked Pimpernel.'

From a discreet position near the back of the Green, Michael looked on approvingly. When the tournament and its use of the Town Hall and environs had first been brought to his attention, Michael had been perplexed. This was one of those 'plans gang aft a'gley' moments he did not need. On learning more about it, chiefly in Lifeboats', where he and his colleagues regularly repaired after a hard day's skulduggery, Michael realised that he could use it to his advantage.

Things were progressing well. Marlene and Erich were making sterling progress at the Baths, loosening the ancient Roman cement around the foundations. Louise had the local loop under control, monitoring all wired traffic between the Town Hall and the outside world, particularly the fledgling national database and all identification card authentication checks, and no suspicions had been raised. Hanif had not caused them problems and was left on hold.

Meanwhile, Michael's employer, the Russian art lover and Mafiosi chief, had arranged for some of his employees to collect the Baths in several trucks and convey the convoy to the coast where a ship was waiting with enough false export documents to transfer the Elgin Marbles back to Greece with the Tower of London thrown in for luck.

Michael's assignment would be completed when he transferred the Baths to the transport gang's trucks at the Spawater site. That was the nasty bit, thought Michael, shuddering. The Mafiosi gang collecting the goods were not nice people; Orcs and Nazgul shunned their company, and the sooner they vamoosed with the Baths on board the better he would feel.

Still, thought Michael, brightening, this tournament and the general confusion it generated would serve as excellent cover for the operation. After due discussion with the others it was decided; the Baths would be lifted on the evening of the Final.

The ghosts of Spawater's gladiators and lions quivered, dreaming they were back in action as a colossal roar greeted the Masked Pimpernel stepping out onto the podium and up to the dais. Like a mighty wave crashing onto a particularly crunchy beach, the roar crescendoed into an expectant silence.

'Friends, Spawaterians, countrymen,' announced the Ringer through his voice-disguising mouthpiece, 'I come to you in peace, friendship and the spirit of sporting harmony, to open the Great Spawater Pool Tournament. I come to you anonymously, as my work can only be done by protecting my secret identity.' He paused to assimilate Jady's words coming through his earpiece.

'I, and my sponsors, believe in freedom and justice for all, in the inalienable right of all humanity to go about their law abiding business whilst governments mind their own. We believe people must be free from the shackles of the totalitarian, mistrusting nanny State. The State must justify itself to us, not us to it. The State is our servant, not our master. By taking part in this tournament, as an entrant or spectator, you are striking a blow against the paranoid surveillance State, the one that hides behind the catch-all of 'security' when stealing our freedoms; the one which preposterously parrots the mantra 'If you have nothing to hide, you have nothing to fear,' while imprisoning people without trial and menacing us with the midnight knock. This great event is intended to cock a snook at control freak politicians everywhere, to show the government that by seeking to control us it is seeking to control the human spirit; to control humanity itself and freeze it in subservience to them, forever.'

He paused for more over-the-airwaves inspiration.

'Well, my sponsors and I have news for the Westminster bureaucrats and the parliamentary poseurs; we, the people, create governments and we, the people, can destroy them. By attempting to freeze human development by controlling the people you have exceeded your remit. You have gone too far and you will go no further. We will not suffer your identity cards and we will not suffer your database.'

The Masked Pimpernel paused again, this time for air. Even superheroes and their Ringers need the stuff occasionally.

'Too pompous, Jady,' whispered Alison though her walkie-talkie to Jady behind the scenes. 'Lighten it up a little before they get bored.'

Outside the world of promotions and brand building, Alison's thought processes defied logical analysis - Chico Marx was baffled for one - but inside, she was excellent at her job and unsurpassed at reading and manipulating an audience.

'Boy that-a girl,' puzzled Chico, scratching his halo to assist celestial thought. 'Hey boss, you know-a what? That crazy girl she when she at work she no so crazy, she-a clever as Confucius.'

'Confucius?' Groucho replied, gazing wistfully at his unlit cigar in no smoking Paradise, 'you certainly do. I haven't been so Confucius since I tried to make love to twins in the Hall of Mirrors.'

'..!' nodded Harpo with enthusiasm.

'That's easy for you to say.' Groucho wagged his cigar vigorously. 'Is there light after death?'

Jady was relaying his speech to the actor playing the Masked Pimpernel on-stage via microphone to earpiece whilst linked to Alison by walkie-talkie, an off-line, hard to trace short-wave radio, so she could gauge audience reaction and modify the speech where necessary.

'But enough about the boring old government and its pompous schemes,' lightened up the Masked Pimpernel.

'Now, the best way to annoy a pompous government is to laugh at it, so, on to the fun side...'

'What do you think of it so far?' asked Joanna of Jenna. They were at the front, assessing the show and trying to gauge public opinion about identity cards and the database. Naturally, people would enjoy the celebrations and launch of the contest, but would they go along with the greater significance? That, like civilisation, remained to be seen.

'Not bad, not bad. Jady has certainly got the point across that it is about government becoming too big for its boots, but I can't tell how it is going down with the people yet. Alison will know. Still,' she nodded cheerfully, 'not a bad start.'

'You think it will work?'

'Which 'it'? Jady's moneymaking scheme or your idea for the demonstration?'

Joanna considered. 'Well, both, actually. Jady thinks the demonstration will help publicise the tournament and vice versa, which in turn will help his scheme to work. He reckons it will add thousands to the price.'

Jenna laughed.

'I think they will both work. You have to hand it to your Jady, making money out of a riot. What an operator.'

'There will not be any riot,' retorted Joanna tetchily. 'The Campaign Against Identity Cards does not believe in violence. In fact, a violent demonstration would play into the hands of the government control freaks. They would announce that the riot was just the sort of thing that identity cards were set up to oppose, and that people against them were just troublemakers and criminal elements. No, Jenna, we have had this discussion before; riots are counterproductive and just drive respectable people away. Riots do not work.'

'Like the Poll Tax riot, you mean? Total flop?'

Joanna hated arguing with Jenna. It never seemed to get anywhere.

'The Poll Tax riots were the last straw for a discredited idea that was not going to work anyway. The whole concept was flawed. Also, the riot frightened an unpopular and incompetent government led by a megalomaniac leader who was losing touch with reality.'

'Go on...'

'Enough.' Joanna had to laugh at Jenna's fatuous grin. 'Yes, I admit there are comparisons, but unlike the Poll Tax, the national database is an attack on us all, the entire country, by a government that wants us under their control because they are scared and inadequate. Our campaign therefore is aimed at getting support from the whole country, and the whole country will not support rioters.' Joanna laughed again at Jenna's typical defiant reaction. 'So, missy, put your tongue back in your mouth and learn to behave. No riots.'

Jenna placed an affectionate arm around Joanna's shoulder. 'You said that last time and look what happened. Still, whatever you say.'

'Thank you. It is all arranged. On the evening of the Final, the Campaign Against National Identity Cards will hold a peaceful demonstration all around the Town Hall, the Green and the Baths.'

'Why the Baths?'

'Jady sees it as extra cover for the Masked Pimpernel; the more confusion, the better.'

The more confusion the better was not an opinion shared by Harold Wood. Poor Harold had had a miserable time of it. Scholars debate who had the rottenest break in history; some say Odysseus was born on the path leading to a black cat retirement home, others think Mona Lisa was a steadier in a cliffside ladder factory, whereas another school of thought maintains that Dick Dastardly would be the world's number one racing champion if only the racetracks were six inches shorter.

Desperately unlucky though these people were, they had one thing going for them; they were not up against gun-for-hire Jenna and her assertive associates.

Normally an employers' nightmare, Jenna had taken to her two assignments like James Bond to double Martinis, leaving Harold both shaken and stirred. Michael wanted an easy run at the Baths; Jady wanted no interference from Harold in his tournament. Both were paying Jenna and both got the result they wanted. Her job was made easier by two factors.

One: The Council Head believed implicitly in Michael's authority. He had fallen for the lunatic notion that biometric technology was better evolved than the human minds from which it sprang, and that identity cards were correspondingly more trustworthy than human senses. The Council Head's blind faith in Michael's authenticity outranked Harold's suspicions and Jenna took full advantage.

'The architects use sensitive electro-magnetic equipment,' stated Jenna to the Council Head. 'Your caretaker's surveillance toys are interfering with their delicate balance.'

'My assistant, Arnie Bennett,' argued Jenna, 'needs to come and go on architect business at my discretion. Your caretaker's goons are delaying him with pointless identity checks and thereby delaying the entire project.'

'We need peace and quiet to concentrate on our work. The public we can tolerate but we will brook no interference from your caretaker or his staff. We have a job to do and he has drains to clean.'

Two: The triumph of Health and Safety over risk and reward. Health and Safety legislation supplied the knockout.

'I wish to object,' objected Jenna to the Council Head, 'in the strongest possible terms, that the turnstiles beside the identity scanners are not wheelchair compatible. They must be widened at once.'

‘The iris scanners,’ complained Jenna, ‘are at the wrong height and could cause a pain in the neck.’ The Council Head knew how they felt.

‘The fire escapes are not integrated with the new security arrangements.’

‘The alarms discriminate against deaf people.’

‘Under European Health and Safety legislation...’

‘All right, all right, all right!’ There is only so much a mild-mannered Council Head can take.

For the duration of the architects’ work and the Pool Tournament, Jenna was given de facto authority to run the Town Hall and Baths admissions however she liked. Harold’s bureaucratic spirit, once so puffed up and defiant against the barbarian hordes of architects, tourists, staff, public, delivery drivers, Uncle Tom Terrorist and all, collapsed like a spurned soufflé in the face of the onslaught. When fifteen Pool tables arrived unheralded, toted by humanoids lower in the food chain than even roadies, accompanied by the local media swarm interviewing Alison’s team of publicists, Harold barely raised a whimper. Mr Dauntliffe had let him down, Harold rued, scared off by the recent publicity. The Council Head undermined his authority and that Jenna fiend smiled pleasantly at him to his face.

But...as Harold watched through the Town Hall windows the speeches marking the opening ceremony of the Tournament, contemplating the invasion of yahoos over the following weeks and the general lack of discipline this would entail, he smiled grimly. Mr Dauntliffe had not let him down, shame for even contemplating such a thing. No, Mr Dauntliffe had rung Harold and told him that the best policy was to let Anarchy reign temporarily. Make notes, Harold was told, note down everything that occurred, who did what, where and when, the better to ensure that such an event could never happen again. And the Council Head should look to his laurels; central government could overrule local democracy.

Mr Dauntliffe would meet Harold and act upon his findings. He would also witness the final of this so-called

'Tournament' himself and watch Harold's security system in action. If Harold could sabotage the final, in the name of security, so much the better. He, Mr Dauntliffe, was counting on him.

Like the rest of Spawater, Harold longed for the final. That and the completion of the architects work would be Jenna Whatshername's last hurrah. Then he, Harold Wood, would once more reign supreme over his Hall and his Baths.

Roll on, thought Harold, roll on the Final.

Identity Cards
Chapter Twenty-one

Crack. The Masked Pimpernel kicked off the Tournament with an astounding display of Pool table trickery. Cannons, jump shots, twin ricochets, alternating cushion kissing, every fifteen-ball permutation possible. The oohs and ahhs of the audience at the earlier firework display in the summer drizzle were as a starter before the main course. The Masked Pimpernel bedazzled them all; the lucky ticket holders watching from the gallery, the contestants awaiting the opening matches in the Town Hall and in every tournament venue in town, the supporters and media representatives in the adjoining Town Hall bar and the Green outside via the large screens erected for the purpose. The Masked Pimpernel ruled; the form-paralyzing nerves Arnie had displayed before curtain up dissolved like champagne froth as he bestrode the stage like a Pool-playing Begothe Titan.

It was the make-up that did it. At Alison's insistence Arnie's dial was coated with enough stage slap to upset the finer sensibilities of Dame Barbara Cartland. 'Don't overdo it, dahling,' condescended the Great Dame, 'nice and easy, like me.'

'Why must I have stage make-up when I am wearing a full face mask with visor?' protested an affronted Arnie when told to sit still for an hour.

'You'll see,' replied Alison, who had seen it all before. 'Hiding behind stage make-up will give you confidence.' She smiled winningly. 'Sub-consciously, you will feel you are protected and therefore have total confidence in front of audiences. It is all in the mind.'

Coming from Alison's mind, this was no great assurance, but to Arnie's surprise, it worked. Behind the make-up Arnie was as confident as the Goliath All Stars challenging David's Slingshots to a game of basketball.

Jenna easily dealt with Harold Wood's predicable, unimaginative insistence that the Masked Pimpernel, having appeared apparently out of thin air into the backstage dressing rooms, should take a biometric eye scan.

'Are you mad?'

'Everyone who enters the Town Hall must prove their identity,' chanted Harold automatically.

'As a Pool champion, the Masked Pimpernel needs, no, insists on, perfect eyesight. If the Town Hall scanner damaged his eyes he would sue for zillions. What would your boss say to that?'

Jenna tried not to laugh as she watched Harold desperately fighting his rear guard action. They could have used him at Dunkirk.

'Iris scanners are perfectly safe. Do you think the government would permit dangerous scanners? Of course not.'

Ignoring what the government might or might not do, and sticking to the résumé with masterful condescension, Jenna continued.

'It has obviously escaped your attention, but eye scanners use laser beams and lasers are delicate and can be dangerous. They might have been safe in laboratory conditions, but what makes you so sure they are safe now? Day to day wear and tear can easily screw up the lasers and ruin people's eyes. Do you want to be responsible? How stupid are you? Forcing people to risk their eyesight by staring at unsupervised laser beams? Are you an eye specialist? No! Then what the hell do you think you are playing at?' Jenna gained on the eloquence Swings what Harold lost on the dignity Roundabout. 'If you want to ruin people's eyes you should be locked up. You are a danger to yourself and others and it is about time your boss knew about it. Well?'

As Harold crumpled, Jenna softened; she was beginning to look upon Harold as Frodo looked upon Gollum. 'Maybe you need a holiday. Gardening leave or perhaps one of your booze cruises with the wife.'

Harold was stung. 'I do *not* go on booze cruises! My wife and I like to holiday on cruise ships. We like to dance.'

Jenna rubbed her elbow doubtfully. 'Sounds like a booze cruise to me. Still, I don't have the time to gossip with caretakers, there's work to be done.'

With that dismissal, Jenna, Alison and the Masked Pimpernel, surrounded by his Alison-supplied minders, wended their way. Harold looked on, angry but impotent, betrayed by everyone. Shakespeare's pal Malvolio knew the feeling.

The Tournament proper was launched simultaneously in the Town Hall and all the allotted Spawater bars and clubs. The Masked Pimpernel's prowess was beamed to them all to show the contestants the calibre of the champion they were aspiring to challenge for the prize. The national media were present in epidemic proportions to witness and report the official Masked Pimpernel opening ceremony speech. On Alison's advice, Jady toned it down a little from the introductory speech on the outside podium, but the population were nevertheless left in no doubt as to where the Masked Pimpernel stood.

'On privacy and the right of citizens to go about their affairs unharassed by the authorities, I and my sponsors oppose full square the surveillance, database and DNA State.

'Totalitarianism begins with daily harassment from the legions of jobsworths and bureaucrats just itching to demand identity cards from everyone under the guise of 'security', when in fact they wish simply to cover their own insecurities and to bully decent people with official sanction.

'This leads inevitably to the midnight knock, the cattlewagons and the gulag. But for now,' the Masked Pimpernel continued in lighter vein, repeating Jady's words and wondering what transporting cows had to do with it, 'we are here to stick it to the State and have a good time, so on with the tournament.'

On it went. Hearing the Masked Pimpernel's injunction to have a good time and get the show rolling,

Spawater obeyed with the enthusiasm of kittens ordered to chase catmint-flavoured mice. Celebration was the order of the day and identity cards were forgotten as the people awarded themselves the freedom of the whole town and the bureaucrats were obliged to give way to the most revolutionary force in existence; the people en masse set on having a good time.

The Masked Pimpernel, having established his Pool-playing credentials and How, disappeared through the air-conditioning tunnel aided by an exultant Jady, emerging as a mild-mannered assistant to Jenna at the Baths. The Baths were, of course, closed to the public at this time of the evening, but not closed to Jenna and her employees or employers; the historical architects examining the Baths with the Council Head's approval and Harold's confusion.

'We must have access to the Baths at all times,' Jenna insisted to the Council Head, officially backed by Michael's authority but in fact using authority of her own acquired by the simple expedient of acting as though she had it, 'in order to carry out work unhindered by the public or by your caretaker and his staff. We must have keys.'

'Mr Wood does not like being called a caretaker,' protested the Head feebly, 'he prefers to be addressed as the senior security executive.'

'Yeah, whatever. Anyway, Mr Lehmann and his staff need unhindered access, so I need a set of keys to override your senior security executive's alarms. We don't want them going off in the middle of the night, do we? Your caretaker caused enough trouble last time.'

The Council Head most certainly did not want a repeat of last time. Jenna got her keys. She met her assistant Arnie quietly as arranged, scraped off his stage slap in the changing rooms, locked up and escorted him unheralded to Joanna and Jady's home.

'Well, Ma'am, what do you think of it so far?'

Detective Sergeant Mathews and his superior officer were observing the festivities from the Town Hall peripherals. Town Hall events were not known for their riotous tendencies, last year's unpleasantness excepted, and this one was no exception.

'Pretty uneventful, I am happy to say, Sergeant,' replied Inspector Brewe without enthusiasm. 'But it is early days yet. There are several weeks of this nonsense to go, with a grand finale, and I shan't be happy until the whole thing is over and done.'

'What about the Masked Pimpernel?'

'Childish nonsense. It is simply a gimmick to attract attention.'

'It works though, Ma'am; it has certainly attracted the attention of the newspapers and television.'

And indeed it had. Inspector Brewe was obliged to concede that the Great Spawater Pool Tournament was the hit of the summer. Luckily so far, a hit without violence.

'Yes,' she replied. 'Media attention to a peaceful, silly tournament is all well and good, but if anything kicks off they will turn. They will not blame the organisers or the rioters, they will blame us.'

'Do you think there could be trouble then, Ma'am?' asked Sergeant Mathews hopefully.

Inspector Brewe looked along the foyer where they were ambling in regular police-with-things-under-control fashion and through into the Town Hall bar. People were animatedly recounting their exploits in the tournament and admiring the skills of the Masked Pimpernel. A friendly atmosphere with much laughter.

'Not tonight, or in the knockout rounds. No, if anything goes wrong, or if your new friend Jady pulls any stunts, the likeliest occasion will be the evening of the final. And if things do kick off, Sergeant,' the Inspector gazed fixedly at one of the huge screens showing replays of the Masked Pimpernel's trick shots, 'heads will roll.'

'Here he is, the hero of the hour! Come in, Arnie, you too, Jenna, and pour yourselves a large one.'

Depositing her umbrella in Jady's vase, Jenna acceded to Jady's suggestion and followed him kitchenwards. Joanna rose and raised her glass in a salute that would have had Caesar preening and giving the thumbs up. There were just the four of them; Alison, escorted by Hanif, would arrive as soon as Alison's duties permitted.

'Welcome aboard, Arnie,' greeted Joanna with an affectionate kiss, 'you did a magnificent job. We are all very proud of you.'

Less proud, but equally impressed, Mr Dauntliffe switched off his television. The News had been full of the Great Spawater Pool Tournament; it was late summer and the Silly Season was in full swing, Parliament was in recess and the nation was lacking in trivial amusements. The Masked Pimpernel filled the gap. 'Who can he be?' speculated the news and magazine programmes on the screen. 'And who are his sponsors?'

This last question had been exercising Mr Dauntliffe in no small manner. Clearly, money was being spent, ostensibly by the Spawater promotions agency but obviously on behalf of the Masked Pimpernel's mysterious sponsors. Who were they? What was in it for them? Mr Dauntliffe did not know but recognised a threat when he encountered one. Obviously, someone, or some organisation, was cashing in on Spawater's use of compulsory Identification Cards to glamorise the so-called Masked Pimpernel for their own ends. What ends? Financial? Political? Whatever the reason, the Masked Pimpernel was making the entire identity card scheme look foolish. People the length and breath of the country were laughing at it and its backers in the government. That a tournament could be held in the Town Hall at the centre of the pilot scheme without anyone knowing who was behind it, who were the sponsor or sponsors, what it was for, and who in the world was the Masked Pimpernel, reduced the whole idea to absurdity.

People were no longer afraid. It is impossible to be afraid and amused at the same time. Without fear people would not accept the limitations on their freedoms inevitable with a compulsory Identification Card scheme and a national database. People must be afraid. They must be made to fear the unknown so that the establishment, hiding behind the government, may rule.

Mr Dauntliffe frowned and sipped his tea ominously. The elixir oiled his brain, stimulating his prions. There was only one thing for it. He would have to see for himself.

Mr Dauntliffe placed his china cup and saucer down delicately on the placemat and reached for his telephone.

'Hello! Here we are, isn't it great!' Alison raved as only a dedicated Ham can after a successful show. 'I have had reports in from all the venues and it has been a roaring success all over town. The Masked Pimpernel has taken the place by storm.'

Indeed, the rainstorm currently putting the Spa in Spawater and reminding any tardy Romans why they went back to sunny Italy in the first place took second billing in the storm stakes to the one created by the Masked Pimpernel.

'And where is my hero? Where is the man of the moment? Come here, my little one and give me a cuddle.'

Arnie remained transfixed in the centre of the living room, clutching his wineglass for moral support and wishing the carpet was deeper. He could never work out how to respond to Alison's inanities. Undeterred, Alison jumped forward and embraced him in an auntie-like crush, much to the chagrin of Hanif, would didn't understand her either, but knew what he liked.

Alison and Hanif arrived at Jady's shortly after Jenna and the hero of the hour. They were there for a celebration and debriefing combination. Drinks all round, enough toasts to cause a wheat famine, and down to business.

'So, Ali,' said Joanna, as they gathered around Jady's huge table, the one that once was used to trap Jady in his own cellar, 'how were things when you left?'

'Fine. Everything is on autopilot. The stewards in all the venues are running things splendidly, everybody accepts their authority, no serious disputes, the local press are out in force, interviewing everyone in town and there is one question on everyone's lips.'

'Who is the Masked Pimpernel?'

'We all know that, silly boy Hanif. But they don't, and they would love to know. We had a slight problem with the television people.' Alison reached for her drink. 'They were trying to get close-ups of the Masked Pimpernel in the Hall to try to recognise his body shape and language, so we had to throw them out. That just made them even more curious, of course. I have recommended to the cheeses that in future we hire our own camera crews for the Hall and sell the footage after we have vetted it. Apart from that, it went without a hitch.'

'What about the police?'

'Good as gold. They snubbed that caretaker guy who Jenna keeps bullying; he was nearly in tears.'

Jady leaned forward. 'Are people asking who the sponsors are?'

'Oh yes,' Alison nodded, overspilling her glass for emphasis, 'that is question number two. Who is the, you know who, and who are his sponsors? The whole country would like to know the answers to those questions. I will go to the kitchen.'

As Alison departed to fetch a cloth, Hanif surfaced.

'Pardon my ignorance, but remind me, just who, exactly, are the sponsors?'

'Sorry, Han,' said a steely-eyed Joanna shaking her head, 'but people who work for the enemy cannot be trusted.'

'Oh come now, Jo, you know I won't say anything. I know we disagree over this ID card stuff, but there is no reason to take that attitude. We can still be friends.'

'Can we? Are you sure?'

Jenna, in the unlikely position of peacemaker, entered the fray. 'Shut up, shut up, or as you would say Jo, enough. By the way, why do you say enough?'

'Enough.'

'Anyway, this is a celebration and we have no time for old scores. Hanif, when the time comes and the people rise up for freedom, peace and justice, Joanna and I will take great pleasure in having you shot. Until then, you are our friend and ally and there will be no harsh words, understood?' Jenna downed her glass to settle it.

'Excuse me?' Arnie piped up. 'As my ex-boss just said, who, exactly, are my sponsors?'

Identity Cards
Chapter Twenty-two

'What? Are you serious?' Inspector Brewe stared at her sergeant with the expression patented by Captain Smith when informed that the iceberg was coming aboard on the lee side.

It was the final week of the contest and Inspector Brewe had been congratulating herself on how quiet things were on the Town Hall front. From day one onwards, Alison's company had run things with a precision the Swiss could only watch and envy. The knockout competition knocked out its competitors as arranged, leaving the remaining sixty-four due to play in the Town Hall on Saturday, the winner of which would challenge the Masked Pimpernel for the ten thousand pound prize.

The secret identity of the Masked Pimpernel along with that of his sponsors remained the most talked about mystery since the whereabouts of Elvis. The national press doorstepped the Town Hall to Harold's consternation, accosting staff and tourists alike, promising gold in return for information, but as the accostees knew nothing the gold remained in its bag.

From an undisclosed location, Elvis gave his opinion. 'There's a guy works down the chip shop swears he's the Masked Pimpernel, but he's a liar and I'm not sure about you.'

One early casualty of the preliminary knockout stages was Lifeboats' Pride, young Arnie. To Jady's relief, Arnie bit the bullet and threw his opening round match against an opponent he would normally have beaten in his sleep. Bookmaker Bullet was bitten too, in the pocket, and spent the rest of the evening feeding the fruit machine with sour grapes.

Minor casualties of competition aside, the contest flowed like the Danube in love, and Inspector Brewe was enjoying the quiet. Now this had to happen. A demonstration outside the Town Hall protesting about identity cards and the national database, and on the worst night possible. Could it really be true?

'I am afraid so, Ma'am, the National Campaign against Identity Cards is holding a demonstration this Saturday outside the Town Hall to coincide with the tournament final.'

A reputable organisation, the National Campaign against Identity Cards informed the police of its intention to peacefully demonstrate outside the Town Hall on the night of the Final for maximum publicity. As part of its tactics to lull the public into accepting compulsory identity cards and the national database with the minimum of fuss, the government had ordered police forces throughout the country to allow such protests.

'What attack on civil liberties?' the government would remonstrate to its critics, like a lowlife petty thief shrugging his shoulders and purring 'who, me guv?' when asked where he was on the evening of the nineteenth.

'See?' the government would say, 'we even allow protests against us.' Not for long, of course. People would be reluctant to demonstrate against rulers who could control every aspect of their lives and those of their families, but for now, demonstrations against identity cards were permitted.

Fat lot of good the government's tactics did Inspector Brewe. She slumped in her chair and reached for her coffee, wondering what in Heaven the gods had in mind when they created Monday mornings.

'So I am under triple red-light instructions to ensure a peaceful ending to that infernal competition in the Town Hall and the very bosses who issued me with those orders are allowing a demonstration right outside. Tell me Sergeant; what do you suppose will happen?'

'I don't know, Ma'am, do tell?'

The sergeant was enjoying this. He knew the Inspector saw Spawater as a stepping-stone to greater things and held regular plodders like him in contempt. Bad news was all she deserved, and largely all she got.

'The rowdier element that always turns up will try to storm the Hall. The contestants and fans will join in the fun and we will have another riot on our hands, that's what will happen. And guess who will get the blame?'

Not me, thought the sergeant complacently, hiding it with a non-committal expression any decent poker player would recognise straight off.

'Us, Ma'am?' he replied.

'Us, Ma'am, indeed,' repeated Inspector Brewe. 'Us, Ma'am, indeed.'

Caffeine is the fuel for those on a deadline and she knocked her coffee back like a gladiator when the five minutes to curtain up is sounded and the lions await.

'May I ask how you intend to cope with it, Ma'am?' pressed Sergeant Mathews stirringly.

'How? As always, there is only one way, Sergeant. Press for overtime for everybody and surround the place. Those demonstrators must be prevented from using the Pool competition for their own ends, for cheap publicity for their cause.'

Unlike many of her superiors, Inspector Brewe was not a supporter of identity cards and the national database. Some senior officers saw the database as a means to identify and thereby control the public, making their crime figures look better. The Inspector disagreed. An intelligent officer, she foresaw an upsurge in mugging of people forced to carry the cards and guessed that once the scheme went nationwide the big boys of crime would hack into the database for their own, criminal ends.

She did not trust the assurances of politicians and vested interests that the database was built on solid foundations. So was the housing market. Blackmail and money laundering would just be the beginning; political corruption at the centre would soon follow, and crime would explode and spread exponentially, like the splash and ripples from a brick thrown into a pond.

Nevertheless, Inspector Brewe believed in upholding the Law. The demonstration was legal and so, while not encouraged, would be tolerated. Lawbreaking, especially Town Hall trespass, would not.

'We will have to liaise with the organisers of the National Campaign against Identity Cards; tell them what they can and cannot do and where they can and cannot go.' She turned to her sergeant. 'Whose names are on the notification letter and what is their contact address?'

'Well, let's see...' Sergeant Mathews scrutinised the official police notification form and the accompanying headed letter from the Campaign.

'Well, Ma'am, the Campaign is based in London but has many provincial branches. We can liaise with London but finalise details with the local branch.'

'I see. And where is the local branch? Who runs it?'

The sergeant fingered his way down the page. 'Got it. It is run from a private address by one Joanna Wilkins.'

'Joanna Wilkins?' The Inspector put down her cold coffee. 'That name sounds familiar. Do you recognise it at all?'

'Yes, Ma'am, it rings a bell.' He looked again at the address. No. It couldn't be.

'But where from, Sergeant?' The Inspector persevered, toying with her cup. 'I am sure I have heard that name before somewhere. A rent-a-mob character, maybe?'

Feeling like Hitler the day after telling his generals to invade Prussia, only to discover too late that they had misheard, Sergeant Mathews shook his head.

'Not exactly, Ma'am.'

'You speak in riddles, Sergeant, tell me, who is it?'

The sergeant told her.

The Pool competition was running as smoothly as Pool competitions can run. Not so the path of friendship. Joanna and Hanif, having been great friends for years, had reached their Stalingrad.

Monday night in Lifeboats'; Joanna's carping like a demented stickleback about the database and the consequent ending of freedom and the advent of a totalitarian State had finally pushed Hanif over the brink.

'Listen, Joanna,' he announced with red-faced wrath as the others looked on, 'you and I have been friends for a long time, good friends, but I have had it up to here with your criticisms. If I have said it once I have said it a thousand times,' Hanif raised his voice for clarity, 'if you have nothing to hide, you have nothing to fear. I know it annoys you to have to inform the authorities every time you travel anywhere or move house. And you don't like the government recording you every time you withdraw money from a cash machine.

'Yes, I know it hurts your ego to have to line up with all the ordinary people, people you consider to be inferior, to have your fingerprints and biometric details taken. You object to the government recording your DNA on its national database and making it available to the police and others along with your medical records.

'Naturally you think it is not the government's business who you live with or who your friends are or how you spend your money, but if you thought a little less about yourself and a little more about the good of society you would realise that identity cards and the national database are here to protect us all. This is the twenty-first century and the age of individualism is dead. Live with it.'

Joanna responded with a loud silence.

Hanif shook his head sadly, picked up his jacket from across the armchair and walked away from the table, leaving Lifeboats' quietly by the back door like Samson when the insurance people called.

Jenna smiled whimsically.

'Either Hanif is embarrassed by his loss of control or he has gone to get his gun.'

Jady placed a supportive arm around Joanna's shoulder. Alison smiled encouragingly through her fringe.

'Don't be upset at Hanif's outburst; the poor boy is going through a bad time right now. He doesn't mean it. Here he is, involved in a project that in his heart of hearts he knows to be wrong, and when he turns to his friends for moral support, they hoot at him. No wonder he is upset, nobody understands him. Sooner or later Hanif will come around to our position and we will all live happily ever after.'

Jady smiled at Joanna knowingly.

Joanna reciprocated, realising once again why she loved him so much.

A friendship broken up because of identity cards, she contemplated bitterly. Her anger grew, not towards Hanif, but towards the parliament that voted for such madness. Introducing a scheme guaranteed to set people at loggerheads and calling it a security measure!

'Why don't we try to understand Hanif?' suggested Alison.

'Sorry?'

'Well,' she continued, 'poor Hanif hears all about how he is in league with the Devil, as Jen puts it,' Jenna grinned and raised her glass in recognition, 'but we never look at things from his point of view.' Only Alison could make this point without causing upset. Alison was a malice-free zone and as such got away with metaphorical murder on a regular basis.

'Go on...'

'So why don't you, Jo, phone Hanif and ask him to show you the database from his office? You don't have to agree with him but at least you would both be forced to have a civilised conversation. After all, Hanif can hardly shout at you in his own office, can he?'

'Never stopped me,' contributed Jenna, placing her glass on the oaken table.

Joanna considered. 'Yes, that's a great idea, Ali. Brilliant, and,' glaring at Jenna who had started an arm-wrestling contest with Jady, 'free of drunken distractions.'

'Will Hanif agree?' wondered Jenna, replacing Jady's arm. 'When you phone him he might give you a full and frank reply. I know I would.'

'How about if *I* telephone him?' asked Alison brightly. 'He is always polite to me.'

And so it was arranged.

'May I reiterate the position as I see it?'

'Certainly, and may I stress, once again, that these arrangements are highly confidential.'

Tuesday morning and Michael was in the office of the Council Head explaining why the Spawater Baths had to be temporarily moved.

The Council Head shuffled uncomfortably in his seat. The respected architect, Mr Lehmann, had come to him with serious news.

'Your experts have informed you that the Spawater Baths are on the verge of serious erosion due to the effects of acid rain?'

'Sadly, this is what I have been informed.'

'And it is imperative that they are coated with an insulating chemical before that erosion takes serious hold and causes them to disintegrate into crumbs?'

'I cannot stress the seriousness of the position. We have examined and caught them just in time.'

'So,' the Head continued, 'your experts insist that the Baths are removed, block by block, in order that they may be coated all over with insulating chemicals?'

'That is it precisely, sir, and may I say that you have grasped the seriousness and urgency of the situation with an alacrity that does you proud.' Lay it on with a trowel, thought Michael complacently; it never hurts.

The Council Head was flattered but nevertheless perplexed; testing the Baths for wear and tear was one thing, allowing them to be removed for refurbishment quite another.

'But why? Why can they not be treated here in situ?'

'As I stated, the insulating chemicals are highly toxic in their liquid state. They are perfectly safe when absorbed into the stone, of course, but a danger during the insulating process.'

'But can we not simply close the Baths to staff and public until they dry out?'

Michael smiled the smile of one who holds the trump.

'Alas, Health and Safety. If word got out that such activity was taking place in a tourist attraction, the Health and Safety people would be down on you like a July thunderstorm, to say nothing of the European Rights legislation committees. Also,' here Michael leaned forward conspiratorially, 'if the European Union Heritage people got wind of what we were doing there would be serious ramifications.' Michael chuckled inwardly as he considered how much the art of bamboozlement depended on telling the Goat the truth.

'They would try to stop us, claiming that the Baths were damaged beyond repair and any chemical restoration would invalidate them as a genuine Roman relic. All funds would be withdrawn and Spawater would lose its heritage prestige. No, the essence of this operation is that it is carried out in secret.' Again, no truer word, thought Michael severely. 'Now, I must have your cooperation in this serious matter.'

Michael looked the Council Head squarely in the eye, man to man, as he had been taught all those years ago at the old alma mater. Say what you like about elitist education, Michael always insisted, but for a lifetime's training in how to stoop lower, dig dirtier and con grander, you couldn't whack the English public school.

'Afterwards, we will ensure that you reap full credit as the man who saved the Baths from acid rain.' True enough, thought Michael, his Mafia employer would keep them indoors. 'Can I rely on you?'

The Council Head knew there was only one possible answer to the smiling gentleman currently proffering his right hand from the opposite side of the desk. Even without proof positive that he spoke with the authority of Ecochtrust, set up by the world's greatest authorities on historical artefacts, he could not have refused him. And he had proof positive; the Head had checked out Mr Lehmann's bona fides on the national database itself. The politicians had insisted time and time again that the national database was foolproof, and that was good enough for him. Besides, if by some freak occurrence the database had made a mistake, it would be down to the politicians who had staked their reputations on it, not the public who took politicians at their word. Imagine the chaos and resulting claims for compensation if the database gave out wrong information! It didn't bear thinking about.

With the happy realisation that if anything went wrong it would be no fault of his, the Council Head accepted Michael's proffered fin and pumped heartily.

'Very well, Mr Lehmann...'

'Call me Michael.'

'Very well, er, Michael, you know best. When do you wish to proceed?'

'This weekend.'

'This weekend?' The Head frowned. 'But this is the weekend of that Pool contest with the Masked Pimpernel. Not only that but I have just been informed that those anti identity card people will be staging a demonstration outside the Town Hall and Baths at the same time.' The Head shrugged dismissively, as a politician will when confronted with ordinary people bypassing the bureaucracy and going for direct action. 'Trying to gain publicity I suppose. There will be people everywhere. Surely a quieter weekend would be more suitable?'

Au contraire, rebutted Michael privately, absolute pandemonium is more suitable. Aloud, he replied.

'With all due respect,' Michael suppressed a grin; this con-artist lark wasn't all roses, 'not at all. For one, it is urgent; every day weakens the Baths and there is no time to waste. Two; this must be done discreetly, and the best way is to do it is under everybody's noses. After all, if there were anything smoky about it we would remove the Baths in the dead of night. Removing them in front of everyone shows that it is a routine operation. We hope to start and finish the business in about three hours on Saturday evening, right in the middle of the Pool contest. We would like you to inform the police that there will be extensive activity in and around the Baths that evening. No need to go into details,' Michael repeated his conspiratorial grin, 'we simply want them to leave us to it. Now,' he concluded, 'are we all set?'

'Oh yes, oh yes indeed.'

Michael stood up and proffered his hand once more.

'May I take this opportunity to thank you again for your splendid cooperation in this matter. Thanks to you, the people of Spawater need never worry about the Spawater Baths again.'

Identity Cards
Chapter Twenty-three

In his office the following day a desperately unhappy Hanif, realising that in jumping ship in such a manner the previous evening he had burnt his boats with Alison, decided to Hell with everything and gave his all to the identity card and database cause. He contacted Mr Dauntliffe and offered his full support in any way possible. An intrigued Mr Dauntliffe arranged to meet him on the evening of the Pool contest final.

'I shall be visiting the Town Hall that evening, er, Hanif, to speak to Mr Wood, the local operative. You know him. I wish to see the system in action during a crowded live event, and how the technology and staff cope with such activity.'

Hanif winced. The Town Hall had not exactly been an overwhelming success so far. Suitably edited, he mentioned this.

'Quite right, this is precisely why we began with a trial period. We have much to learn about the practical implementation of biometric security, as I believe you stated in an earlier call.' Mr Dauntliffe hesitated momentarily, and then cast his die. Mr Singh could be just the man he needed. 'Let's say I meet you in your office early Saturday evening, before the contest begins. We have much to discuss. Afterwards we can travel together to the Town Hall.'

Hanif agreed.

'I need hardly add, Mr Singh,' Mr Dauntliffe's voice darkened the atmosphere like approaching thunderclouds, 'that any discussion between us is highly confidential. We may only talk in private. Will there be staff in the building at that time? Is your office secure?'

'It most certainly is secure, Mr Dauntliffe. We are a security company; it would be a strange thing if we were less than totally intruder proof.'

'What about staff?'

'My secretary, Susan, will be there to allow me entrance to the building and to my office, but I will let her go when you arrive.'

'Why does your secretary have to allow you access? Can you not just let yourself in?'

Hanif relaxed. Security matters were his territory.

'For security reasons, Mr Dauntliffe. In my office I have access to many security secrets. What if I were kidnapped? If criminals obtained my identity card and keys to the building they could get into my office and perhaps force me to reveal confidential information, causing a major security leak. No, the keys and my identity card are never together outside the building. Susan is another matter as she knows no passwords or sensitive security details and could therefore be of no assistance to criminals after secrets.'

'Fine. Thank you, Hanif, the meeting is arranged. Tell no one.' He hung up the telephone without a goodbye. Civility pays nothing.

Mr Dauntliffe was delighted. Having studied the classics, he was totally ignorant concerning the technical nature of the scheme he was introducing and was well aware that the vested interests of the private biometric, DNA and high-tech security companies could lead them to bamboozle him with technical jargon to obtain their own ends. Hanif had said as much in their earlier conversation concerning the practical introduction of silicon chips and the rest. Taking this on board, he knew he needed the private support of a technician who could unravel the gobbledegook and keep him ahead of both the private vested interests and the government. Someone with technical expertise but no political ambitions. Singh was just the man.

Mr Dauntliffe felt the smug satisfaction of a spider that has just completed its stickiest web. If parliament thought the national database was for its own benefit, parliament would learn too late that it was in error. He contemplated parliament's arrogant naivety, bordering on negligence, in confusing itself with the State and believing they were one and the same. Mr Dauntliffe sneered.

Democratic government was tolerated by the State because it kept people quiet and prevented them governing themselves, thereby rendering the State redundant. The relationship between the State and the government resembled that of the crocodile and the weaverbird. The crocodile allowed the weaverbird into its mouth to pick out scraps of food from between its teeth, thus cleaning them. It was a symbiotic relationship, tolerated by the crocodile for its own convenience. A foolish weaverbird might believe that it controlled the beast, but should it ever start giving the crocodile unpleasant orders it would discover that it was in error. Similarly, should parliament try to order the State around it would find itself in the same position. The weaverbird and democratic parliaments were tolerated while they were of use. Outlive that usefulness and they would be consumed as quickly as the goose when it stopped laying golden eggs. When the database and related matters were truly completed and implemented, democratic parliament would have outlived its usefulness.

'Goodbye, Mr Dauntliffe,' intoned Hanif to the dead mouthpiece, 'until Saturday.'

Thoroughly miserable, Hanif slowly replaced the handset as if in a late-night triple cheese and brandy dream. Here he was, arranging to help a cause that he believed was good for society but that all his best friends opposed with their hearts and souls. Here he was betraying them.

At least, he reflected through his gloom, Judas had been paid.

Misery in Spawater was not confined to the private sector. Over at the Town Hall, Harold was tottering on his toes like the Titanic's chorus line at the news that the Spawater Baths were to be removed for refurbishment.

'But that is impossible,' wailed Harold, 'the Baths have been there for thousands of years.'

'Very nearly,' agreed the Council Head. 'The architect report that Mr Lehmann showed me suggests we are lucky they have lasted that long. If we want them to last another two thousand years we have to look after them, which means allowing the experts to get on with their job with no interference.'

He emphasised the final words. If there was one thing the Council Head respected about Harold, it was his ability to interfere in matters that did not concern him. 'I am telling you this, Mr Wood, to make you aware that a fleet of trucks with hoisting equipment and workmen will be arriving at the Baths on Saturday evening in order to carry out removals. Screens will be erected between the Baths and the Green so that the public is kept away. This includes the identity card demonstrators; we do not want them interfering. The police have been informed and will be keeping an eye on things. Do you understand?'

Harold understood the words of command, if not the reasoning behind them, but knew where his bread and butter came from. He would have made a great stand-in for Lassie. 'Go get help, Lassie old pal,' cried little Timmy anxiously, 'I have fallen down the disused mineshaft.' 'Wruf,' thought Lassie, 'there goes my tin opener. I had better get someone to pull him out... again.'

'But,' protested Harold doggedly, 'Saturday is the night of the Pool contest final. The place will be jam packed solid with contestants, spectators, the media and all sorts of other hooligans. How on earth do you expect me to maintain security under those conditions? A terrorist bomber could easily infiltrate under cover of the tournament or those troublemaking demonstrators. Now you want to allow a bunch of workmen into the Baths to remove them for refurbishment? Have they been vetted? How do you know there isn't a terrorist amongst them? It is just not good enough.'

The Head sighed, wondering if he could sack Harold for being a general pain. Ever since the government decided that there were more votes to be gained by frightening the public than in offering hope, the more gullible had been seeing terrorists in every shadow. It was like living in the 1950's American McCarthy era. Aloud, he retorted tetchily,

'The workmen are skilled operatives employed by Ecochtrust. They all have visitor's Identification Cards and are vouched for by Mr Lehmann. You have nothing to worry about and you will not interfere with them in any way or shape at all. Those are my orders. Satisfied?'

Harold wasn't, but knew better than to argue. Besides, Mr Dauntliffe would be in attendance on Saturday and would see for himself how things were. When he saw how a complacent Council Head who did not realise that terrorists strike where they are least expected, had tied Harold's hands, he would take action. Perhaps Mr Dauntliffe could get the Head fired. True, the Head was democratically elected, but could Britain afford soft democracy in the twenty-first century? Security came first, and freedom of the individual could not overrule security for all. Why, thought Harold, did his friends in the pub not believe him? Allowing people to come and go as they pleased, unrecorded by anyone, put society at risk. Freedom had to be put on hold until the war on terror was won.

'As you say, sir,' accepted Harold resignedly, not wishing to put his own job at risk. He was furious but consoled himself with the knowledge that Mr Dauntliffe was on the way. Soon it would be Mr Dauntliffe's turn to give orders; ones that Harold would be only too happy to obey.

'We have our orders, Sergeant, so let's have no complaints. It is up to us to get on with it.'

'Just as you say, Ma'am,' replied Sergeant Mathews stiffly, passing her coffee across the desk in a manner which suggested that were it not for the conventions of civilisation and the fact that she outranked him, he would have told her to get stuffed. Accepting the stimulant, Inspector Brewe softened; it was hardly Sergeant Mathew's fault. Life was hurling slings and arrows in her direction outrageously, as though she were a dartboard in the public bar of the David and Goliath Residential Retirement Home. Just keep a bulldog-steady hand on the tiller, she inwardly maintained, and her fortune, like the smoke around a bonfire, would come to her.

'I'm sorry, Sergeant, I did not mean to be so abrupt, it is just that everything seems to be happening at once. Let's not both get in a tizzy about this, let's just keep calm and go over the details once more.'

Both? thought the sergeant.

Replacing her old, cold coffee cup with a fresh, hot one - shares in the Spawater Coffee Beans Are Us Company were soaring - she went back over the details.

'As you know, the final of the Masked Pimpernel's Pool contest takes place on Saturday evening. Simultaneously there will be a demonstration outside the Town Hall and Baths by the National Campaign Against Identity Cards. Just in case that makes the centre of Spawater too quiet for a Saturday night, we are now told that there will be a major upheaval at the Baths. It seems that the external sections of the Baths, not the foundations of course, are to be temporarily removed for repairs. The Baths will be screened off from the rest of the area for this purpose. Why they could not move them some other time is beyond me. Apparently it has to be done immediately. It is our job to ensure that the people loading the Baths onto the trucks there for the purpose are not disturbed. We want them in and out as quickly and with as little trouble as possible.'

The Inspector took a workman-sized slug from her cup. She deserved it. 'Apart from that,' she smiled, wiping her smile with the back of her hand, 'it should be a quiet weekend.'

The buzzer buzzed.

'Call for you, Hanif, from Alison. Shall I tell her you are too busy to take the call?'

Oh joy. Alison calling! All was not lost, after all. Hanif's emotion-altering endorphins leapt into action at pit-stop speed, shifting his driving force from misery to exultation in the time it took to change a mood. As for telling

Susan he was too busy to take the call; that was as likely as the Seven Dwarfs throwing a sickie.

'No Susan, put her through,' Hanif replied, attempting to sound nonchalant but instead assuming the voice of a particularly delicate mouse that had dropped a giant's anvil on its tail. Hanif knew perfectly well that Susan knew perfectly well that he was spoony on Alison and would never be too busy to take a call from her; too busy for the Prime Minister certainly, Father Christmas perhaps, but Alison? Never. Susan's question had simply been mischievous. Susan thrived on Hanif's confusion as Santa thrives on sherry and mince pies.

'Hello, Hanif, this is Alison.'

'So everything is arranged. Everything is in position.'

Now that they were nearing the end of the operation, their earlier light-heartedness had evaporated and the seriousness of what they were about to do was uppermost in their minds.

'Yes,' replied Marlene briefly. 'We are all ready.'

The others nodded in confirmation. Michael took the floor again.

'Good. As you know, when we hand the goods over to the truckers, their operative will hand us the bank code and our part in the operation is over; it will simply be a matter of entering the code on-line to release our payment and transferring that payment to our joint account. We will then enter our own private codes to withdraw one quarter each.' Michael grinned, trying to lighten the mood. After all, this was what they had aimed for; this was what it was all about. 'Everybody happy?'

Marlene laughed. 'I fancy a drink.'

Michael grimaced. 'After the operation you can have all the drink you want. Until then I want you to take things easy.'

'Won't we be going to The Lifeboat Club on Friday?' countered Louise.

'Yes of course, but we will all,' and he stared pointedly at Marlene, no schoolteacher could have bettered the authoritative expression, 'drink in extreme moderation.'

'Why do we all have to go?' enquired Eric. 'I know you have to go, Michael, to square things with Jenna so that she keeps that interfering caretaker out of our hair, but are all of us required?'

Michael looked around at the all.

'Yes Eric. You see, it is not just about seeing Jenna, important though that is. I also wish to ensure that her friend Hanif is kept busy on Saturday, so he does not have time to spy on us.'

'Are you sure he will be there?'

'He is sure to be there on the night before the Pool final, and I have the perfect way to ensure he does not cause us any problems.'

'What is that?' asked Marlene.

Michael smiled and, looking over at Louise, laughed heartily. 'Poetic justice really. I am sure Hanif will see the funny side...eventually.' He gave Louise a look that screamed mischief and smiled winningly. 'I have a special job for you.'

'So that's that job over then. Everything is in place and it is just a matter of letting events take their course.'

'Yes, it has been a dream,' agreed Alison. 'Everything has gone according to plan, just as you said it would. I must admit, Jady, that when you first suggested the idea I knew it could work but I did not expect things to run so seamlessly.'

Jady and Alison were enjoying a debriefing coffee in a local emporium having just attended a meeting of Alison's big cheeses and potential sponsors for the Masked Pimpernel. Everything had gone as swimmingly as the Atlantis Olympic synchronised eel team.

'Yes,' replied a modest Jady, stirring his cup. 'The game is all over bar the cueing. It has been a stunning success so far. The finals are set to go on Saturday, the contestants are lined up, the Masked Pimpernel is ready to defeat the tournament winner and the sponsors are ready to take the credit.' He raised his cup in salute. 'And we, of course, are ready to take the cash from the sponsors. Everybody is happy, everybody wins.'

'What about the winner of the Pool tournament? Won't they lose out on the ten thousand pounds? If Arnie beats the winner, as you say he will, then the winner will not get the prize. The winner is the loser.' Alison's nose wrinkled at the perplexing scenario. Shakespeare's audiences often felt the same when wondering why Hamlet didn't just call in the Ghostbusters.

'Don't worry, Ali,' replied Jady with a nonchalance he did not feel, 'we'll see the winner goes home happy.'

Jady frowned. Unlike the cheeses, Alison was unaware of the final stage in the operation. When claiming that it was all over bar the cueing, Jady was getting slightly ahead of himself, as well he knew. Before victory was his, he had one last task, one small factor that could not be reconciled until the tournament was concluded and the winner was preparing to square up to the Masked Pimpernel for the grand ten grand finale.

On Saturday evening, the organisers, citizens of Spawater and the entire country would congratulate and pay due respects to the winner of the Grand Spawater Pool Tournament. This was the reincarnation of the old Spawaterian Roman Games, the spiritual inheritor of the hopes, aspirations and ideals of the once greatest empire ever known. Under the aegis of the mighty Masked Pimpernel, upholder of truth, honesty and freedom, and scourge of the paranoid control freaks, craven party-line peddlers and lying government lackeys, the true spirit of honest fair play and endeavour would be reborn.

As Jady conjured up the inspiring image of the tournament winner approaching the podium prior to laying down the gauntlet before the Masked Pimpernel for the ten thousand pound prize, one thought was paramount.

How could he ensure that Arnie won?

Identity Cards
Chapter Twenty-four

D-day minus one. Deliverance or damnation tomorrow. Friday night, and the various parties were marshalling their troops and their thoughts for the big day. Churchill, gazing down portentously from the celestial VIP smoking room - cigars only - whilst supplying Groucho with a light, raised a well-worn glass to Jady and Michael.

'Never,' he boomed, 'in the field of human endeavour, has so much knavery been possible by so few, due to so many...' Churchill blacked out his admiring smile and glowered bulldog-like at the Members of Parliament cowering behind ugly stone blocks, '...damn fools.'

Down in the land of the living, Joanna and Jady had invited Arnie over to their flat in order to keep him out of mischief. Arnie, displaying nerves fit to make the most self-effacing fawn bellow in annoyance, would have preferred Lifeboats', where the Dutch courage flowed aplenty, but Jady was concerned to keep his alcohol intake down whilst keeping his spirits up. Alison was in attendance early, prior to meeting Jenna at the Club. Over a glass of orange juice she entered her report.

'So, it is all systems go for tomorrow then. Are you looking forward to it, young fellah?'

Arnie shrugged pathetically, as teenagers do when they don't trust their emotions. Ignoring his non-committal shoulders, Alison prattled on.

'I certainly am. Afterwards we must go out and celebrate.' She winked, leaned over and tweaked Arnie's cheek; it was the Marilyn Monroe blood talking. 'We deserve it for giving Spawater the biggest night of its life. Agreed?'

Arnie did not agree. Shuffling uncomfortably in his oversize armchair in response to the cheek-tweaking and wink-blinking, he steeled his vocal cords into nervous response.

'What if I am found out? What if I am too nervous on the day? How do I know if I can go through with it?' He was talking himself into a panic. He looked around glassy-eyed at Joanna and a concerned Jady like the last lobster in the tank.

'I am scared I will let you down.'

Not half so scared as Jady. Everything hinged on an Arnie triumphant. Fortunately, Jady had a dauntless Alison in his camp; a bit like bringing on Samson as substitute.

'What's to worry about? You have done the hard stuff, my bonny lad, and now it is all plain sailing. Just turn up in the usual way, do a few trick shots to get the crowd going, relax while I oversee the tournament, congratulate the winner, then beat him for the prize money. Nothing to it.'

'Everything is in place; all is arranged. Now, does anyone have any questions or comments?'

Louise, Marlene and Erich looked at each other. There really was nothing to ask or add. Michael was a thorough general - Wellington would have liked him - and his associates were experts in their respective fields. In Louise's case that expertise stretched to a bit of light-fingered Fagin fun. She could pick a pocket or two.

'So you definitely want me to sort out Hanif. No question about it?'

'That's right,' Michael replied firmly. 'I know it seems a bit unnecessary but in my opinion Hanif is just the kind of fool who might blunder into the scheme and wreck it. Whenever we are in The Lifeboat Club he keeps looking at me and sneering.' Michael chuckled jovially; despite being wholly aware of the seriousness of his chosen profession, he could never stay poker-faced for long amongst friends. Amongst the targeted goats, yes; friends, no.

'Won't it just serve him right though. Hoist by his own petard.'

The Spawater Town Hall clock sounded its refrain. One hour nearer to the big day.

'All right troops, let's phone a cab.'

'Your cab's here.' Joanna, home in Chez Guevara, put down the receiver. 'So that's it until tomorrow. Give my love to Jenna.'

'And ours,' added Jady, speaking for himself and Arnie. Jady was delighted with Alison. Somehow, life was difficult to take seriously with Alison around. Like an anorexic Teletubby, she seemed to inhabit a different, kinder world.

'Bye bye,' she waved happily, 'see you tomorrow.'

'Bye bye.' Had he needed it, Jady would have been reassured.

She had certainly reassured and boosted Arnie, making him feel like the indestructible fictional character 'The Masked Pimpernel', for whom all things are possible and failure exists only in some far off dimension, like planet Earth.

Alison had also arranged, on Joanna's behalf, for Joanna to meet Hanif at his place of work the following afternoon, prior to the contest. The idea was that in order to make peace they would meet metaphorically halfway. Hanif would demonstrate to Joanna the workings of the fledgling database in an attempt to show her that it was not the Big Brother control freak threat she thought it was. In return, Hanif would give due consideration and respect to Joanna's fears and concerns and seek to alleviate them. Fat chance, thought Joanna, but anything to oblige Alison and besides, she did so want to be friends with Hanif again.

Not for the first time, Joanna cursed the short-term vote grasping idiocy of the politicians and the greedy, amoral lobbyists who fed their vanity, breaking up friendships and in so doing damaging society with their dangerous and counterproductive notions of security. They were a cancer on the human spirit, those health-and-safety-big-bad-terrorist-threat fearmongers, preaching that it was better to live on your knees than die on your feet. In their condescending hysteria, they could not see that the people on their knees died first and those who lived longest were the ones who stood tall. Joanna imagined their ancestors erecting railings around cemeteries to protect the dead. Doubtless they would like to place a fence around Mount Everest to prevent foolish folk climbing it. They might get hurt.

She was jerked out of her reverie by a Teletubby-like finale from Alison.

'Bye byee, see you all tomorrow then, and good luck.' Smiling, waving and blowing kisses beside the vase, Alison let herself out.

'All set for tomorrow then? I must admit, Michael, I have enjoyed having you and your team around. You certainly livened up things at the Town Hall. I shall miss you. Cheers.'

Jenna raised the first glass of the evening to Michael and his team of faux architects. It was unusual for Jenna to part from an employer in such good terms and it made her feel wistful, like Wendy bidding farewell to Peter Pan.

Michael, his veins tidal with the buccaneering blood of the ages and resembling a Cap'n Hook with the right priorities - 'Belay the lost boys and that cannibalistic croc, me hearties; where be that treasure?'- responded in kind.

'We will be back in couple of weeks, of course, for stage two, which is replacing the renovated Baths, but that will only take a week at most. After that I will miss you too, Jenna,' he replied sadly. 'We had some laughs together and you did a fantastic job. Without your help we would still be tied up in red tape and arguing with jobsworths.'

They were in Lifeboats' as usual, combining final details for tomorrow with farewell drinks tonight. Marlene, Louise and Erich were on strict orders to take things easy; Michael was on wine and water, needing at least half a clear head to ensure last minute details were attended to. Of course, half of Michael's head was more than enough to outwit the humans running the biometric security system set up at ruinous expense to fight crime and identity fraud. Once human beings surrendered their critical faculties to machines built by other human beings, fooling them was simple.

'Yes,' continued Michael, 'everything is in place. While the Pool tournament is keeping everybody busy, we will be handing over the Baths to our transport firm.' Michael shuddered as he considered his Mafiosi employer's hirelings. The sooner he was finished with them the better.

'Then stage one of our work here is completed. Stage two will begin in a couple of weeks when the Baths have been safeguarded from further erosion. Your fee will be transferred to your account tomorrow evening as agreed, bringing us up to date. Later on, I may be able to arrange a bonus payment, probably in cash.' He would too, as soon as the heat died down. He felt he owed it to Jenna, and would owe it even more when the world discovered that there would be no stage two. Jenna would be caught in the middle of the maelstrom, like Jason and his thieving Argonauts, except that it was Spawater that was being fleeced.

'Don't be shy,' replied Jenna, 'I accept money in all its forms. Even Euros,' she grimaced, 'in emergencies.'

'I don't accept Euros,' droned Ron, doing the table-wiping rounds and spreading staff and customers' germs equitably around the Club. 'They are not a real currency. They will collapse and end in ruins; you mark my words.'

Jenna was intrigued. 'You know Jady wants to be a Euro MEP, don't you, Ron? Or rather the back-seat driver behind one?'

Nothing surprised Ron where Jady was concerned. He placed his cloth on the previously clean table and pronounced judgement. 'So he likes the Common Market, does he?'

'If you mean the European Community, no. He hates it. That's why he wants to be the power behind a European Union MEP.'

Ron swapped his normal jaded expression for a baffled one, considered a moment, decided it was not worth it and switched back to jaded.

'I wish him luck; he will need it.' Ron picked up his cloth, a few million bacteria lighter, and set course to the adjacent table spreading sunshine and cleanliness in equal measure.

Michael looked over his shoulder at Ron's stern.

'There's another one I shall miss.' He smiled jovially. 'A true Brit; it is people like him who ensure that Britons never never shall be slaves.'

'Here's one you won't miss quite so much though, eh, Michael?' Jenna pointed out the familiar outline of Hanif steaming slowly but steadily towards them, like an oil tanker going to the dentist. 'Your greatest living critic, I understand.'

Hanif's approach shocked Michael back into business mode. Perhaps Jenna could enlighten him as to Hanif's hostility and so help his mission. He turned back towards a knowing Jenna.

'Why does Hanif seem to dislike me so much? He sneers sarcastically at everything I say.'

Jenna raised her glass thoughtfully. 'Well Michael, it is like this. Hanif has got the hots, or should I say hotz, for Alison and he believes you are muscling in on his territory. In his opinion, the last Austrian who had that idea got his comeuppance and so should you.'

Michael was thunderstruck. Not only that Hanif, a twenty-first century computer geek, could harbour the old anti German jackboot nonsense, but that he was inadvertently endangering Michael's assignment and with it their team's liberty, simply because he wrongly thought Michael was trying to deadleg Hanif's love life. Such nonsense could cause problems. He had better put Louise and Marlene on the case pronto.

'Foolish boy,' he replied nonchalantly. 'Alison is a sweet kid but not my type. If that is Hanif's only problem with me then tell him he has nothing to worry about.' If Jenna passed that message on then Hanif might cease to be a danger to shipping and Michael could relax. If only he had known earlier.

'Oh yes,' whispered Jenna, rising to bid Hanif welcome, 'he also thinks you and your colleagues are a bunch of frauds and he intends to expose you.'

'Fraud? Fraud? How can you say such a thing? Of course it isn't fraud. It is merely insurance against the wrong outcome.'

'This is serious, Jady, so don't lie to me. You are proposing to bribe the winner of the Pool tournament into throwing the match against poor Arnie just so you can sting the sponsors for a fortune.' Joanna tut-tutted in sham disappointment, like Sir Lancelot when the dragon cried off through laryngitis. Control freak governments could never conquer the people whilst imaginative rogues like Jady existed. There are more schemes in the minds of honest crooks than are dreamed of in Stalinist philosophy.

Joanna was amused but for the sake of Jady's soul, tried to hide it. 'Quite right, young lady,' proclaimed Queen Victoria from her heavenly palace. 'Do not let them know you are amused. If people knew how funny I found the charge of the Light Brigade and Roork's Drift, Britain would be a republic.'

They were sitting in the kitchen, officially making a light meal for themselves and an Arnie who was currently being distracted by a computer game bought by Jady for distracting-Arnie purposes. Arnie was staying over. Keeping his thoughts off the big day was the idea and it was working. To Jady's surprise, keeping Joanna's scruples from overflowing into his dormant conscience and waking it up was working too. Joanna's involvement with the National Campaign Against Identity Cards had hardened her; any non-violent attack on authority was now acceptable and would remain so until authority learnt not to get above itself. The State existed to serve the people, so when it tried to control them instead it became the enemy of the people and consequently a legitimate target. The identity card and database threat was turning normally law-abiding citizens into enemies of the State, and a liberating experience it was.

'Well,' Jady conceded inevitably, dicing fruit over the pizza base; his very own invention, 'I suppose it could be described as a bit near the knuckle, but it is a victimless crime. Arnie is happy, the winner will be looked after, the sponsors are happy, Alison's employers get their share and I get mine.' Jady was a mile too shrewd to say that Joanna would benefit also.

Joanna was going through a full and busy time. Meeting Hanif early tomorrow evening to hopefully make peace and repair their friendship - always an uncomfortable experience - later helping to organise a demonstration by the Campaign Against National Identity Cards and the national database outside the Town Hall, whilst keeping a weather eye out for Jady's entrepreneurial activities and their possible consequences. She did not need a fruit pizza to feel stuffed.

'Well good for you, darling,' she replied firmly. 'Go for it. Now, I wonder how I should deal with Hanif tomorrow?'

'So, young Hanif,' said Marlene, keeping it light and making to pour out the wine, 'how are things in the world of computer security?'

The plan was simple; Marlene would distract Hanif by engaging him in conversation about computer security while Louise sought her chance to carry out operation Nobble the Suspicious One. It was not difficult; computer technicians are rarely asked to discuss their digital doings. Anglers are grilled on their catches, trainspotters will be asked their favourite anecdotes and anyone wishing to explain the dream they had last night will never want for an audience. Not so computer geeks.

Settled into their regular far corner in Lifeboats', Hanif found himself quartered between Marlene and Louise at the furthermost table. Jenna, still awaiting Alison's arrival, chatted pleasantly around the adjacent table with Michael and Erich. Had the fireplace been roaring - not necessary in the warm late summer - it would have made for a perfect, innocent, yuletide vista of friends gathered in comfort over a glass against the chill of the night. God was in his heaven and all was well. Even Doctor Watson would have smelled a rat.

'You tell me,' replied a wary Hanif. 'You seem to know such a lot about it.'

'I only know what I am told, that's all. I get this information from my brother back home.' After the escapade where Marlene had aroused Hanif's suspicions by knowing far more about computer networks than the average bear, Michael and his colleagues had put the word out that Marlene's brother worked for his father-in-law's computer network company in Eastern Germany. Michael had to call in a few foreign favours to make the story stand against prying Hanifs, but he managed it and the story was that Marlene's brother kept her up to speed on security developments. It helped her, he said, in the architectural world to keep up with such matters. It was specious, and everyone except Hanif was convinced.

'Oh, do lighten up, Hanif, for goodness sake. I know it is your job to be suspicious, but can you not leave your suspicions at work? This is the time for relaxing, for fun. The trouble with you, young man, is that you work too hard. You need to relax more. Now, have some wine and let's drink a toast to being suspicious.'

Marlene poured a unit-busting serving of Lifeboats' best into Hanif's unresisting glass. Hanif mulled over the wine. Marlene had a point; ever since he had accepted the identity card and database job he had been as nervously suspicious as a horse invited to the opening of a glue factory. He had fallen out with Joanna and suspected people all around of not being who or what they purported to be. In order to become friends with Joanna again as well as for his own peace of mind, perhaps Marlene was right; he should lighten up a little.

'You are right, Marlene. I have left my work back in the office. This is the time for relaxation. What was that toast?' Hanif raised his glass and smiled, his face cracking like spring in the Antarctic.

'To suspicion.'

'To suspicion.'

They emptied their glasses together, a sure sign of trust. Doctor Watson would be filling three pipes for his master and polishing the larger of the magnifying glasses.

'Now,' continued Hanif, determined to be cheerful come what may, 'forget boring computers; what's going on in the world of architecture?'

'Good night all.'

'Good night, Arnie,' said Joanna sweetly, 'pleasant dreams.'

Arnie was having an early night. In Jady's view, the less time Arnie spent conscious before curtain up the better. Arnie was still young enough to take the hint that it was bedtime when responsible adults hinted it was so. That meant Joanna. Making a round of cocoa, something Joanna and Jady would not normally drink for a bet, had convinced Arnie that he would be outstaying his welcome unless he went to his room immediately. It would never have worked for his mum.

'Pleasant dreams? I hope so,' giggled Arnie nervously. 'I just hope I can sleep at all. Well anyway, goodnight all.'

'Good evening all.' Alison joined the others in the corner of Lifeboats'. To Hanif's mild chagrin she docked alongside Jenna at the far side of the other table, opposite Michael. Well, thought Hanif stubbornly, I will just ignore her and carry on here then.

'Hello, Han,' cried Alison freely across the tables and wobbling the glasses. 'Are you ok for tomorrow? Joanna is so looking forward to seeing you.'

An outflanked Hanif went for damage limitation. 'Hello, Ali,' he answered in similar volume. 'Yes, I am looking forward to seeing her. And seeing you, of course, at the Pool tournament.'

Marlene saw her opportunity. 'Hanif, go and talk to her, for heaven's sake, instead of shouting in front of the whole Club; our conversation can wait.'

Taking his cue, Hanif nodded discreetly. Pausing only to collect his glass, he arose and strolled Alisonwards. John Wayne could only admire his aplomb.

Marlene's cursory glance at Louise was not needed. Taking her cue, Louise sidled into Hanif's seat, on the back of which was Hanif's jacket. Using one hand, Louise picked up Hanif's wine bottle and filled her glass. 'Cheers,' she announced to anyone in range, resuming her seat and betraying slight irritation as she knocked her bag onto the floor. 'Clumsy me,' she tutted, as she reached below the table, fumbled around a bit and resurfaced. 'That's better.'

Louise raised her glass and gave thumbs up to the world. At the far end of the other table, Michael noted the signal and glanced at Hanif, animated between Alison and Jenna. Yes, that's better, he thought grimly; that's better indeed.

Identity Cards
Chapter Twenty-five

'Hello, Susan, Hanif here; could you let me in please?'

It was turning into a bad day for Hanif. Late Saturday afternoon found him outside his place of work trying to get inside his place of work.

'Good afternoon, Hanif,' crackled Susan his secretary's disembodied voice through the intercom. 'How do you mean, let you in?'

'I mean, could you let me in please,' replied her exasperated boss. 'I seem to have mislaid my ID card.'

Earlier, Hanif had risen from a late, tranquil Saturday lie-in, lazed into a comfortable bath, steamed into a not-in-training-or-on-a-diet breakfast and considered his day. It was not an easy one. First, an appointment with Joanna to try and rekindle their ebbing friendship, then a meeting with Mr Dauntliffe, doubtless to discuss matters Joanna would find obnoxious. Hanif felt like the piggy in the middle, idly wondering if there was a way to let the two protagonists fight it out amongst themselves with him at the ringside, offering sympathy and gum shields to both.

Such a lovely day on the outside, Mother Nature taking the perverse view that the dirtier the deeds due to be done, the sunnier the day they should have for it, Hanif left his car and walked through the pleasant, tree-lined streets and avenues to his place of work. Foregoing the pre-office coffee, he entered the foyer, bid the Saturday concierge good afternoon and approached the staff-only entrance to the lifts and stairway. It was then that he was forcibly reminded of the maxims that nothing is so bad that it cannot get worse, and that if a thing can go wrong, it will. Opening his wallet, he flicked to the back where, within its transparency, his credit-card sized identity card resided, and swiped it across the biometric reader. A loud beep, as unwelcome as it was unexpected, resonated throughout the foyer, bounced off a few walls and finished by raising the concierge's eyebrows. This was all he needed on a Saturday.

Two beeps later and Hanif was staring, aghast, at his empty transparency. His brain reeled like a Scottish line-dancer in a spin dryer. This could not be happening! Where had it gone? What was going on? Flicking futilely through the other plastic pages of his wallet, Hanif tried to come to terms with this new reality. Seconds earlier his problems were the manageable ones of dealing with Joanna and Mr Dauntliffe: Beauty and the Beast; now life had taken on a new and threatening hue. Samson felt the same after a trip to the barbers.

With the eyes of the concierge burning holes in his back, Hanif gave up ransacking his pockets and dialled the number of his secretary's intercom. Luckily Susan was at work today; Susan would let him in.

'Here it is, Millado, the big day, and the big announcement. This is what we have been working towards the whole time.'

Jady handed Arnie his breakfast bowl. It was the middle of the afternoon and Arnie surprised himself by how relaxed he felt and the length of time he had slept. Rip Van Winkle would have approved. A dreamless sleep in a strange bed - had he slept at home he would have had nightmares about the tournament - coupled with Alison's relentless cheerfulness and inability to take the whole thing seriously had left Arnie feeling a cross between confident and fatalistic. What will be, will be, and there is no point in worrying any more. Arnie picked at his breakfast; as a strong coffee with optional beans-on-toast type of breakfaster, he looked askance at Jady's offering of mixed fruit from the freezer thawed in orange juice and water. Still, when in Spawater...

'How do you mean, big announcement?' he replied nonchalantly, staining his shirt blackberry purple.

Jady looked down at him from the sink. Joanna had already left, driving to her tryst with Hanif, and Jady was ensuring Arnie was presented with a scene of domestic ennui by washing her breakfast things and generally being everyday until it was time to go. Jenna was calling for Arnie ostensibly to take him to work at the Baths, where, of course, he would enter the maintenance tunnels and emerge as the Masked Pimpernel in the Town Hall. The important thing for now was to baby-sit Arnie until the tournament was upon him. Coolly discussing the tournament in a placid, domestic setting, as though it was a routine day, would keep Arnie calm until he was collected.

'Today the Masked Pimpernel announces to the world the names of his sponsors. Once you have beaten your foolish challenger, you will tell the world who it is that believes in freedom and privacy as much as you do.'

'And who is that?'

'Oh, very funny, boss,' Susan replied humourlessly, 'but I am rather busy, you know. This is the weekend and I have things to do. I want to get out of here as soon as possible.'

'No really, Susan, I can't find my ID card. Open the door please.'

There was a stage wait, then a quieter reply.

'Seriously, Hanif, are you really asking me to let you in without your ID card?'

'Yes of course!' Hanif strove to keep his temper. Losing his identity card was bad enough without a protracted debate through a tinny intercom system. 'Hurry please, Susan, I am expecting clients and it will look bad if they see me like this.' That's putting it mildly, he thought anxiously. If Mr Dauntliffe arrived early he would see better security than he bargained for.

Another stage wait.

'Let me get this straight, Mr Singh,' followed a deadpan voice, 'if indeed you are Mr Singh. You want me, the secretary to a senior manager in a computer security company, to let you into a virtually empty building containing serious confidential information, without any security check. Is that the situation?'

A new and darker world opened up before Hanif. Five minutes ago he thought he had a difficult day ahead. Oh, how happy he had been, five minutes ago! If only he had realised at the time. When Paul McCartney penned 'Yesterday' he certainly knew what he was dreaming about. Hanif's waking moments were rapidly turning into the kind of dream Dante had after an evening on the cheese.

'Listen to me, Susan,' he pleaded, trying and failing to keep the desperation out of his voice. 'This is very serious indeed. I have two meetings in the next hour and I have mislaid my ID card. I have no idea how or where. It is vital that I get into my office for two reasons. One, to meet my clients; two, to get my passport from my desk so I can use that for temporary ID, and also to inform the central database that I have lost my card so I can get a replacement.'

'That's three.'

Hanif lost it.

'For the last bloody time, let me in! If you don't I will fire you on the spot, so help me! Let me in now!'

'So,' replied Susan, dignity personified, 'if I do not break the number one rule that you, my boss and senior manager, drill into all your staff from day one with constant reminders on a regular basis, you will fire me. And if I do break the number one rule, what then? Let me tell you, Mr Hanif Singh, if I do break the number one rule and let you in, you will fire me. Interesting choice, don't you think?'

Hanif was close to tears. Susan was right and they both knew it. He could not fire her for doing her job, no matter what trouble it caused him and the company. In saner moments, he would admire her for sticking to her guns. Now was not, however, the time or the place for sanity. Sanity had no place in the brave new world of the database State.

'I'm sorry, Susan,' whimpered a contrite Hanif, 'you are right, of course. Forgive me, I am just a bit agitated because I have lost my card. Now please, seriously, let me in. There will be no recriminations, I promise. In fact, you have behaved in exactly the right manner. I am pleased you did not give in to intimidation. In fact, you did such a good job that I am going to give you a pay rise. You deserve it. Now, if you can just let me in,' Hanif paused, breathed in slowly, and tried to make light of the situation, 'we can try and sort this nonsense out.'

The offer of a pay rise was a mistake.

'Your patronising sweet talk cuts no ice with me. Think you can bribe your way in here? Don't make me laugh.' Secure in the knowledge that she was doing the right and unsackable thing, Susan began enjoying herself.

'But the fate of our company hangs in the balance! You know who I am, let me in!'

'Rules is rules, I say, and if I made an exception for you I would have to make it for everyone and then where would we be?'

Hanif recoiled in despair. Those bloody ID cards! Joanna was right; ever since the government introduced them Spawater had been crawling with jumped-up jobsworths demanding ID cards all over the place. Everywhere people went, they were stopped by fixated flunkies demanding the production of little bits of plastic before they could go about their business. It was the wrong side of enough, flailed Hanif wretchedly. Only criminals liked them; stealing cards and selling them or holding them to ransom was a nice little earner. Better than working, thought Hanif bitterly.

Losing his ID card gave Hanif a new perspective. As one of those with a say in the implementation, Hanif had little time for the doom mongers who saw a national database as the harbinger of a nightmare State. Rather, he saw it as benevolent control; keeping an eye on the masses for their own good. Finding himself on the wrong side of the argument as well as the wrong side of the door, Hanif saw things from a new angle. Perhaps he had been wrong.

'Right, Millado, this is how it is.'

Jady pulled up a chair beside the fruit-munching Arnie and, reversing it so that its back leant against the table in fine, teenage-approved style, settled into position.

'Who are our sponsors? Who believes in freedom and privacy as much as the Masked Pimpernel?' Jady picked up an apple and rolled it around his hand in an imitation of a globe. 'The answer, Millado, is whoever pays us. Simple as that.'

'How do you mean?'

Jady looked thoughtfully at the apple. Up until now, he had protected Arnie from the knowledge of good and evil. Now was the time to let Arnie in on the truth, or part of it anyway.

'Millado, it's like this. When the government inflicted its crazy database nonsense on Spawater, I tried to think of ways to exploit it. Now, it was perfectly obvious from day one that the more the general public found out about the biometric ID card scheme - especially the national database part - the more opposed to it they would be. For practical reasons the scheme could never work and for reasons of principle it never should. The question was,' Jady reminisced, holding the apple aloft in contemplation, 'how to cash in before it collapsed under its own contradictions and expense.' A dreamy, far away look caused Jady's eyes to mist over as he contemplated those happy, conniving days. Arnie dropped his spoon, breaking the atmosphere and returning Jady to the present. He gazed at Arnie and grinned, like Max Biallistock contemplating Leo Bloom.

'Clearly, the ID card scheme would soon be so unpopular that anyone who symbolised resistance to it would be a hero. Or in your case, a superhero.' Jady put down the apple. The time for imagery was past. 'I was stuck for a while until I saw you playing Pool. You are good, Millado, very good. I realised you were good enough to impress the whole country. So all I had to do was make you into the symbol of resistance against the ID card scheme and sponsors would fall over themselves to be associated with you. Putting you into a superhero costume did that. I persuaded Alison's bosses to supply the organisation, credibility and cash to set up this tournament, for a percentage, and the rest is history.'

Fruit is usually easy to digest, but Arnie felt as though he was eating chalk.

'So you planned the whole thing in order to get money from sponsors?'

'Yes, of course. Alison's cheeses have arranged for the representatives of several cash-rich companies to watch tonight's tournament and bid to become your sponsors. Highest bids win. After you defeat the tournament's winner, Alison will invite you onto the stage to give a pro-freedom and privacy speech. I will tell you what to say through your earphones. Alison will then reveal your sponsors and you will welcome them to the fight against totalitarianism and government control freakery. You will applaud their short speeches saying much the same thing and Alison will wrap up the show.' Jady stood up, turned the chair around and sat back down. 'And that's it.'

'But what if I don't beat the tournament winner?'

This was the awkward bit. Arnie was not rich but he had an expensive conscience to maintain. Jady did not want it disturbed.

'You will, Millado, you will.'

'Hiya Han, how's it hanging?'

Might as well get off to a friendly start, thought Joanna, entering the foyer and spotting Hanif at the staff entrance. She was facing a conflict of interests; on the one hand she did not wish to lose an old friend through an honest difference of opinion, on the other she could never concede the principle that the State is there for the people, not the other way around. Hanif, she well knew, misunderstood, so this meeting was going to be an uneasy one, fraught with the tension inevitable when close friends fall out.

'Joanna, darling!' Hanif flung himself at Joanna, embracing her like a tipsy teenager. Where there are friends, there's hope. Colonel Custer could have used Joanna at Little Big Horn.

'Nice to see you too, Han,' replied a bemused Joanna. Keeping it friendly was one thing but this was ridiculous.

This was a Hanif she hadn't met before outside of a maudlin bottle or three. Noticing the look of not so quiet desperation on Hanif's normally reserved and in control face, she became concerned.

'Are you all right?'

Hanif was too far-gone for dignity. 'I'm locked out,' he replied pleadingly, disengaging and sagging pitifully.

This was mysterious. 'How do you mean, locked out?'

'I've lost my ID card and Susan won't let me in.'

'Pardon? What do you mean?'

'I mean,' croaked Hanif in pathetic resignation, 'I can't find my ID card so my secretary will not let me into my office.'

Joanna stared intently, seeing at last the woebegone Hanif in all his misery, Toad in a hole. Joanna did not have a heart of stone; realising the true import of Hanif's remarks, a twitch, maturing into a smile, ripening to a grin and flowering into a bodywide tension-releasing explosion of mirth shook Joanna like Krakatoa on its birthday.

'You mean,' she gasped, struggling to control her voice, 'that you have lost your ID card and can't get in?'

Identity Cards
Chapter Twenty-Six

'Hi ho, hi ho, it's off to swindle we go. Come on, Arnie my son, there's skulduggery to be done.'

Arnie turned to Jady in fright. 'Swindle? Who's being swindled? What skulduggery?'

Jady tch'ed Jenna irritably, bulls in china shops.

'She's just kidding, Millado. Don't frighten the lad, Jen,' he remonstrated, turning to Jenna. 'This is simply the final of the tournament and Millado will be there to take his bows.'

'Face the final curtain, you mean,' sniggered Jenna. Seeing Arnie's disconcertion she softened. 'Don't take any notice of me, young Arnie; I'm just taking the mickey out of your chief. Now, saddle up; this is our last day at the Baths as well so I really ought to be there.'

Jenna collected Arnie, Arnie collected his toothbrush and himself and, escorted by Jady, left the flat and headed carwards.

'All right, Millado,' said Jady in final farewell, 'see you at the contest and don't you worry, you are surrounded by friends and by this time tomorrow we will all be laughing about it.'

'That's right,' agreed Jenna, pointing Arnie towards her car, 'and as the champion, you will have the biggest laugh of all.'

'Hello, Susan? It's me, Joanna. Joanna Wilkins. I have an appointment with Hanif. May I come in, please?'

'Hold on, I'll check.'

Living with Jady, Joanna knew all about unwelcome surprises and what to do about them. Compared to imaginary burglars, attempted assault by upstairs neighbours, late night visits from police officers demanding good behaviour or else, being trapped in cellars and goodness knows what besides, losing an ID card hardly hit the radar. Having milked the situation dry - were Hanif a cow he could have sued under the European Bovine Rights Act - Joanna simmered down and decided to put poor Hanif out of his misery.

'Nil desperandum, Hanif old chum. I can get you into your office before you can say 'ID cards are the dictators' friend.' Just trust me.'

Hanif had no choice. Joanna, who had met Susan several times through Hanif, buzzed her intercom number and requested admission so that she could attend her meeting.

'All right, Joanna, do you have your identity card?'

'Of course. It is our duty as citizens to carry our Identification Cards at all times. It will soon be a criminal offence not to. I am surprised it isn't already.'

Susan chuckled. Joanna was no actor and her sarcasm seeped like radiation from a telephone mast. Hanif writhed in embarrassment. This was not his idea of being rescued; Joanna, and Susan for that matter, exacted their pound of flesh as though he were something on a slab.

'Is Hanif with you? He has lost his card, you know.'

'Yes and yes. Oh well, these things happen in a database State.' A thought struck her. 'Why don't you have one of those biometric eye scanners like they have in the Town Hall? After all, this is a state of the art security company. Then Hanif could just wink and he would be in. Unless he lost his eyes too, of course.'

'Biometric eye scanners?' Susan snorted scornfully. This made working on Saturday worthwhile. 'You are with Hanif, why don't you ask him?'

Hanif, hearing this banter and wondering what, at the end of the day, life was for, replied flatly.

'Because they are not reliable.'

'Pardon?'

'They cannot be trusted. They can be fooled by a picture of someone else's eyes, vaseline around the eyeballs, flash photography and all sorts of other ways.'

'Then why did you encourage them at the Town Hall?'

'That was Mr Dauntliffe's idea. The Mr Big behind the scheme. He said we have to try them out somewhere and private industry would not take the risk.'

It was all coming out now. A disillusioned Hanif had no fight left in him.

Joanna had plenty. 'I would like to meet your Mr Dauntliffe.'

Hanif sighed. 'Why not? He will be here in about an hour. If we are still here you will be able to see him firing me for a blundering incompetent who is locked out of his own office.'

'Do you want to come in?'

'Sorry Susan,' a distracted Joanna replied. 'Yes please.'

'Ok, swipe your card.'

Joanna turned. 'Come on, Hanif, we are going in together.' She swiped her ID card across the reader and the door opened to reveal a full-length turnstile. 'Here we go, Han, squeeze in with me.'

Using the system Jenna employed when smuggling Arnie through a similar barrier, Hanif and Joanna went through on the same rachet of the machine. Like Jenna, Joanna blessed the Health and Safety regulations that dealt with symptoms not causes, and ensured a continuing supply of fat people by demanding wider turnstiles, rather than encouraging a healthy way of life.

'There you are, Han,' said Joanna as they fetched up on the right side of the barrier, 'we're in.'

Harold Wood gave his biometric eye scanner a loving wipe with a Council issue tissue and considered the big night. Hundreds of people, contestants, film crews, spectators and various other riff-raff would be infesting his Hall, but all of them - Jenna Whatshername's rabble excepted - would produce their identity cards and submit to his biometric eye scanner first.

Recent unpleasantness with Jenna's crew notwithstanding, Harold felt great affection for the technology that would protect his Town Hall from the menace of the world. When this absurd and dangerous Pool tournament was over he would ensure that no such similar threat to the smooth and safe running of the Town Hall could ever happen again. On Mr Dauntliffe's orders, Harold was composing a report illustrating the perils of allowing ordinary citizens to hire Council property for unauthorised and anarchic contests. The Town Hall was for administration; for the safety, well-being and control of the people for their own good. Not for silly games. Mr Dauntliffe would back his recommendations and the Council Head would have to go along with them or be seen to be putting lives at risk. People could not have the freedom to organise their own amusements; such freedom was a security risk. After all, Harold knew, security was far more important than freedom.

'Damn and blast.'

Hanif was no swearer. When it came to cursing, Trappists outranted him every time. Even the most placid Trappist would have felt the urge to violently vibrate the vocals if confronted with Hanif's latest setback.

'What's the problem now, Han?'

Joanna and Hanif had finally made it to Hanif's office, passing an unrepentant and unsurprised Susan en-route. Tetchily ordering her to make coffees for them both, Hanif tried to fire up his computer.

'I can't access it.'

'Sorry?'

Hanif sighed the sigh of surrender. Had he been a camel his back would have broken.

'I can't get into my computer or the network because I do not have my ID card.'

Joanna clutched the desk for physical and moral support. Her soft heart came into play as she realised the depths of Hanif's despair and with an effort, suspended the mocking.

'Why do you need an ID card to boot up a computer?'

Hanif spat out the word. 'Security.'

That weasel word again. Joanna had had the word 'security' thrust at her by the database huggers as the ultimate excuse for each and every attack on liberty this century. It led to the absurd conclusion that the two could be traded; as though less freedom equalled more security and more freedom equalled less. Those who wanted to hide behind plastic ID cards, biometric databases, compulsory fingerprinting, DNA checks and spy-cameras seemed unaware that security and freedom march together, like hope and justice. You cannot have freedom without security and you cannot have security without freedom. Anyway, Joanna concluded coldly, Hanif's computer had plenty of security but was denying Hanif the freedom to use it. She suppressed her urge to give Hanif the 'told you so' gloat, remembering in time that Hanif was an old friend and needed sympathy. She would throw the brickbats later.

'Surely you have backup? Some kind of cover?'

'That's it!' For the first time in about a decade, or so it seemed to Hanif, hope returned to its throne. Long live hope. He pressed the buzzer.

'Susan? Could you come here now please?'

In her own time Susan appeared with the coffees.

'Susan, as you know,' Hanif kept his voice calm; he was not taking any chances, 'I have lost my ID card. That means I cannot access my computer. Luckily, you can. Could you access it, please?'

Susan placed the coffee tray firmly on Hanif's desk.

'You don't get it, do you, boss? Here you are, having broken into the building, asking me to help you hack into potentially the most important database in the world. You're lucky I don't phone the police.' She held up her hand, forestalling Hanif's outburst. 'You have trained me well, Hanif. Yes of course I know it's you. I know you have threatened to sack me. By rights you should sack yourself. However,' Susan paused while Hanif blew bubbles, and continued, 'this can easily be resolved; remember our contingency plan?'

'That's right!' Again Hanif's graph of life lurched upwards. 'My passport! Passports can double up as emergency ID until they are scrapped.'

'Exactly. Show me your passport and I will access your computer for you.'

'Where is your passport?' asked Joanna. 'At home? I can give you a lift if you like.'

Hanif whewed with relief. 'Even better. It is in my desk. I keep it here for business trips.'

He stepped behind his desk and reached for the drawer. Rattling it for a second, he paused, froze, eyes staring unseeingly and blood draining into his boots. Collapsing into his chair he sank his face into his hands. Any passing elephant would have directed him immediately to the secret graveyard with no questions asked.

'What's wrong?' cried two voices in unison.

Hanif inhaled slowly, raised his head and spoke sotto voce.

'I can't open my desk without my identity card.'

Locking her desk, Inspector Brewe rose and turned to her assistant.

'All right, Sergeant; we had better go and brief the troops.'

Detective Sergeant Mathews nodded. This was a big day for Spawater and it was the job of the police to ensure it passed peacefully.

'Do you think there will be any trouble tonight?' he asked hopefully.

The Inspector stopped in the act of picking up her briefing papers. She could never tell what her assistant was thinking. She suspected that he wanted her to fail in her attempts to become a chief constable, and would be secretly delighted if she made a hash of tonight's operation. Speaking slowly and with deliberation, she replied.

'Consider, Sergeant, our position. Inside the Town Hall is a tournament organised in part by Jady Enterprises, a company owned by your friend Jady, the biggest con-merchant in Spawater. Outside the Town Hall, a demonstration against those infernal ID cards organised by one Joanna Wilkins, who just happens to be the company secretary of Jady Enterprises and indeed lives with the aforementioned Jady.' She picked up her briefing notes and continued.

'Added to this, there will be major upheavals next door at the Baths as they are removed for cleaning or maintenance or whatever. We are under strict orders to ensure that this is done discreetly so as not to alert and upset rice-munching conservationists who might think the Baths were being vandalised or sold on the quiet, so we have to ensure the Baths are moved efficiently and without fuss. For reasons beyond me, this has to take place tonight at the same time as the other two events.' Signalling to an optimistic Detective Sergeant Mathews that it was time to go, Inspector Brewe wound up the case for the prosecution. 'And you ask me if I expect any trouble?'

'So Hanif, now that we have cracked your security systems, how about showing me the prototype for the national database?'

Hanif stared forlornly at his mutilated desk draw. He would never have expected it from Joanna - Jenna, yes, Joanna never. Weakly, he put this point to her.

'Well,' Joanna replied nonchalantly, 'normally I would agree. Jenna's general attitude is that for getting things done, you can't whack violence. My view is 'needs must when the devil drives', and you have to admit, Han love, it worked.'

Joanna retrieved Hanif's passport by the simple process of jemmying open the desk draw using a spanner found in the caretaker's cupboard. Showing it to Susan allowed her to give Hanif access to his computer and the network without compromising security regulations. A triumphant Joanna, resolving to keep the gloating down to human tolerance levels, now encouraged Hanif to show her what all the fuss was about.

Hanif had mixed feelings; happy to be back in control of his life, in as much as he ever was, but slightly shell-shocked at Joanna's direct methods.

'Let's face it, Han,' gloated Joanna, breaking her resolve, 'a piece of plastic and a bureaucratic database State are no protection against a spanner wielded by someone not afraid to use it.' Warming to her theme, Joanna elaborated. 'The trouble with you computer types is that you are so mesmerised by new technology and biometric bullshine that you forget the basics. Building a database State using identity cards for security is like building a house using playing cards for bricks. One joker and it all falls down.' She tut-tutted in sham sympathy at Hanif's desk draw. 'Do you see what I am getting at?'

Hanif did. Seeing his office building and computer system broken into by use of simple initiative and a spanner had knocked the stuffing out of his once sated ego, which now resembled Winnie the Pooh during the year of the Great Bee Strike.

In lacklustre fashion Hanif went through the motions of demonstrating the prototype national database as originally agreed. He entered his security codes on-screen and arrived at a demonstration page designed for training purposes.

'While you are here, I might as well show you how it works.'

Like an overbearing aunt dragged away from her knitting by an eager nephew, Joanna sat beside Hanif and asked him to pray, continue. For want of anything better, Hanif did.

'So you see,' said Hanif presently, 'when information on the ID card clashes with information held in the database, the bottom of the screen goes red, alerting the operator.'

'What if the operator is colourblind?'

Hanif paused. He was tired.

'Look, Joanna, I don't make the bloody rules. I am simply showing you how the thing works, ok?'

‘Sorry, Han, you go on.’ A chastised Joanna couldn’t resist adding, ‘But what then? Is the ID card wrong or the database?’

‘I really do not know. Sometimes one, sometimes the other, I suppose. Now, let me show you what happens if the person is on restricted movements.’

‘What?’

‘Restricted movements. Like house arrest. If someone is confined to, say, their hometown and their card is used somewhere they are not allowed to be, the lower screen will go purple. Don’t ask me why they chose that colour.’

‘So this will be another way to control people?’

‘Of course. If suspected terrorists and their friends and families have to produce ID cards everywhere they go then the people controlling the database will know where they are and what they are doing at all times.’

Shocked, Joanna interrupted.

‘And you don’t object to this?’ In fact, Joanna knew all about the desire of the government to use the excuses of terrorism and ‘security’ to gain knowledge and control over people’s movements. It was still a shock to hear Hanif saying it so bluntly.

‘I’m beginning to,’ muttered Hanif with meaning. Hearing himself casually admit to being part of the problem was proving revelatory.

The intercom buzzed. Susan’s voice intoned a message for her employer.

‘Mr Singh? Mr Dauntliffe is here for his appointment.’

Joanna reacted first. ‘Great. Show him in; I want to meet the man who thinks he has the right to fingerprint and spy on me for the rest of my life. Show him in now.’

Hanif was in an emotional mess - Mary Poppins would have needed at least a couple of bags of sugar to straighten out the mess in his mind, but he was compos mentis enough to not wish to sacrifice his company’s best ever contract. ‘Spare no taxpayers’ expense’ cried the government. Conned by the consultants, the government would fight to the last taxpayer for the creation of a database State that would render democracy redundant.

'No, you cannot stay here. Oh my goodness!' Hanif realised the equivocal position he was in, entertaining the National Campaign Against Identity Cards local organiser in the heart of the identity card headquarters whilst the head of the identity card project waited outside. The day was becoming increasingly unreal. 'He mustn't see you!'

'Why not?'

'Because you are campaigning against him! You are organising the demo outside the Town Hall. He will know all about you.'

'How?'

'Never mind how; if he finds out who you are he will smell a king-sized rat and will cancel the contract. I will be fired and possibly prosecuted for allowing unauthorised people illegal access to the database.' Hanif stared around the room as if seeing it for the first time. There was only one door in and out and Mr Dauntliffe was on the other side of it.

'Shall I send in Mr Dauntliffe now?' interrupted Susan impatiently, 'and then go home?' she added with sarcasm in off the cushion. Susan disliked most of her boss's clients and Mr Dauntliffe was hardly an exception. She did not intend spending Saturday afternoon in his presence.

Mimicking Hanif, Joanna looked around, with greater effect.

'The broom cupboard.'

'What?'

'The caretaker's cupboard. I could hide in there until he's gone.'

Hanif was no great fan of farce. The Importance of Being Ernest was as a closed book to him. Brian Rix looked down from his angelic drawing room and smiled approvingly. Now someone else would discover the joys of cupboard concealment. Hanif did not agree. However, desperate situations call for desperate measures. Surely the day could not get any madder.

'Go on then. And for goodness sake don't cough.'

'Let's hope the caretaker keeps the cupboard free of dust,' grinned Joanna, thinking happily how the girls would enjoy this one. A three-drink giggle at least. Moving purposely cupboardwards, Joanna vanished therein.

'Mr Dauntliffe,' announced Susan moments later, making it obvious by her tone that it was no fault of hers. 'And good afternoon.'

'Charmed to see you again, Mr Singh,' intoned Mr Dauntliffe charmlessly, entering and greeting Hanif with the firm handshake and steady look deep into the other's eyes as learned at public school. A steady eye and a firm handshake designed, of course, to denote honesty and trustworthiness. Hanif, whose own untrained, and consequently genuine, handshake made lettuce leaves seem like the 'after' in a bodybuilding advert, simpered in agreement.

Sitting down uninvited with his back to the caretaker's cupboard, Mr Dauntliffe looked up at his host.

'I have had a dry journey; a cup of tea would be most appreciated.'

'Of course,' Hanif buzzed for Susan, but Susan was gone. 'Sorry,' he apologised, 'I will have to make it myself. My secretary has gone home and there is no-one else in the office.'

In her cramped quarters, Joanna suppressed a snigger. Poor Hanif, trying to conduct high-powered business talks with his biggest client knowing he was a cough away from embarrassment and ridicule. It was lucky she did not smoke. Not that Joanna was concerned for herself or worried about Hanif losing his job. Should her presence be discovered the worst that could happen was that his company would lose the contract. This Mr Dauntliffe character could hardly reveal the true reason without bringing the whole database security matter into disrepute, making it the laughing stock it deserved to be. In fact, she considered, it might even be worth revealing herself on purpose to achieve this end. Not just yet, though, she thought; let's hear what Mr Dauntliffe has to say.

‘Thank you, Hanif. Sorry to put you to trouble, but we have much to discuss and a good cup of tea always lubricates the brain, don’t you agree?’

‘Oh yes,’ replied a slightly bemused Hanif. This was more friendly than usual; could Mr Dauntliffe have a human side after all or did he want something?

Joanna too, was slightly bemused, but at the suggestion that they had much to discuss. Hanif had led her to believe that Mr Dauntliffe was only in Spawater to observe the activities at the Town Hall and check up on his precious ‘security’ systems. What did they have to discuss?

Mr Dauntliffe indeed had a serious matter to discuss with Hanif; he wanted to initiate him into the true database project.

Identity Cards
Chapter Twenty-Seven

'Welcome, welcome and thrice welcome. You came, you saw, you played Pool. Salutations one and all and welcome again to the grand finale of the Great Spawater Pool Tournament. My name is Alison Smedley and I am your mistress of ceremonies, as it were, for tonight's fun and games.'

Late afternoon at the Town Hall saw the beginning of the tournament finals; Alison compèring, as usual. The Hall was crowded enough to give any passing Health and Safety officer the heebie-jeebies. Friends and family of the previous heat winners contested the available floor space with an inspirational eagerness the contestants were stimulated to follow. Screens were erected outside on the Green so even greater numbers of Spawaterians could follow the action over cold refreshments. Pubs and clubs throughout the town, and in particular the town centre, had similar arrangements, hiring the screens and the coverage facilities from Alison's company via Jady Enterprises. Also in the pubs and coffee houses were assembling members and supporters of the National Campaign Against Identity Cards, waiting to surround the Town Hall with protest banners in order to make their point via the national television coverage and garner publicity for their cause. It was arranged that Joanna would address them later. Boom time for Spawater.

'You know the rules,' continued Alison, 'so I shan't detain you longer than absolutely necessary. This is a knockout competition between the winners of the previous rounds. We begin with sixty-four winners and over the course of the afternoon and evening will whittle this down to one. This Grand Winner, as you know, will challenge the Masked Pimpernel himself for the five thousand pound prize.'

Some heckling from the floor deja vue'd stagewards.

'All right then, ten thousand pound prize.' Alison giggled, causing Marilyn Monroe to gaze down from her beatific boudoir expecting to see a repeat of one of her films. 'Some like it copyrighted,' she pouted reprovingly.

'The Masked Pimpernel is not here right now,' Alison continued, 'having injustices to put right elsewhere. He will be along for the latter stages. Between you and me,' she added conspiratorially, 'the Masked Pimpernel is dropping candle wax on the biometric eye scanners and CCCT lenses down at the police station. Police are looking for that evil supervillain, Lightbulbhead Man.'

At the back of the Hall, Inspector Brewe glared at her smirking assistant.

'It is bad enough having irresponsible local would-be celebrities demeaning our authority, Sergeant, without you laughing along. Show some dignity.'

'Sorry, Ma'am,' replied Sergeant Meadows unapologetically. Changing the subject, he added, 'It is all pretty routine here, shall we go and check on things next door?'

'Thank you, Sergeant, I had not forgotten. Next door it is, then.'

Next door, the Baths were just closing to the public for the day. In the staff area, Jenna and Arnie were finalising operational details.

'All right, Superman, first you will do the decent thing by saying goodbye to Michael and his pals as they finish their work here, then I will accompany you to the staff changing rooms and apply some quick slap to your face. Then it's hi ho for the tunnels to the Hall next door and you can do your stuff on the Pool tables. Ready?'

'As I'll ever be.' Arnie smiled weakly. He knew it was pointless arguing with Jenna. Mules maybe, Loki and the gods of Asgard certainly, but Jenna? No.

'That's my little Boy Wonder. Now,' Jenna rummaged through her bag, 'take this walkie-talkie and stuff in it your utility belt. I got it from Alison and I have its partner. Any problems, give me a call by pressing the buzzer. Don't use your mobile as it can be traced.'

‘Are we all set then?’

Michael, Marlene and Erich were on the steps to the Baths prior to entering and beginning work. Louise was back at the ranch, staffing the computer to ensure no last minute hitches and to process the code for releasing the money when the deal was done.

‘Fine,’ Erich replied. ‘As expected, no sign of our friends yet.’

‘Friends’ was a cavalier way of describing the people hired by their employer to remove and deliver the Baths to the wolf-ridden Russian Steppes. Their mothers may have found them adorable but then so do Black Widow spiders find their offspring adorable, unlike their fathers. Objective observers would place them in the file named ‘people to cross the road, and possibly country, to avoid.’

‘No. They won’t be here until it is dark.’ Michael lowered his voice and continued seriously. It was the closest the others had seen to nervousness. ‘All we need to do now is ensure that the parts of the Baths are labelled ready in the correct order for loading before their arrival, then it is a quick swap; the Baths for the password, confirm with Louise and out of here. The less time we spend in their company, the better I shall like it.’

These were sentiments Harold Wood would have echoed in relation to Michael et al, as he stood in the ticket office glowering balefully at the intruders’ ID cards being waived as they were waved through the barrier by one of his underlings. All pretence of bureaucratic harassment had been dropped after the emergency services imbroglio in times best forgotten. Now, thought Harold despondently, Jenna’s rabble came and went as they pleased. And a fat lot of good the police were, he noted with the satisfaction of a vindicated miseryguts, watching the arrival of Inspector Brewe and Robin, or whoever, being delayed by the necessity of having their identity cards scanned at the turnstiles. The police are held up and the rabble goes straight through,

Harold observed. He didn't suppose the workmen who would shortly be arriving to collect the Baths would have their bona fides checked either, if that Jenna had her way.

Well, he concluded, we shall see, we shall see.

'How's it going so far?'

'Swimmingly. Jenna called; she and Arnie are next door at the Baths saying goodbye to the architects. All is well, she said, or words to that effect, and the Masked Pimpernel will be here anon. The tournament is underway, as you must have noticed, so everything is going according to plan.'

Jady had arrived at the Town Hall to find the competition in full swing. Each Pool table hosted two contestants per go adjudicated by an umpire, and condoned off from the supporting throng by the thick red rope that may only be crossed by celebrities. Having nothing to do at this stage of the proceedings - a hired professional snooker commentator was supplying the voiceover for the television coverage - Alison was relaxing backstage by sipping some bottled water - no caffeine on duty - when Jady found her. This meant nothing, Jady knew, as Alison could be relaxed in an earthquake. 'Look at the buildings wobble, aren't they funny? Fancy jelly for tea?'

Jady was thankful to hear that things were indeed going swimmingly so far, as it might not last. When the Grand Winner was declared, he was going to offer him or her a bribe to ensure that the Masked Pimpernel won the final duel. In the unlikely event that the winner proved honest, this could cause more than a storm in a teacup. Thank the gods the best snooker players had misspent childhoods.

'When the Masked P arrives we must keep him in his dressing room and make sure one of us is with him at all times. I will wait for him there now but I have to see Joanna outside when she turns up to check on Hanif and the anti ID card demo. Then you will need to guard him. Don't let anyone talk to him, or worse, don't let him talk to anyone.'

'Apart from you, of course?'

Jady laughed. Alison's insouciance had always baffled Arnie and kept him from worrying. 'Apart from me and you. You keep him calm and that's what we want.'

'All right. Let me know when you are going to see Jo. I'll stay with him except when I am needed on-stage.'

Jady looked admiringly at Alison.

'You know something, Ali? Arnie isn't the only person you reassure. I'll go and baby-sit Millado now and call you when I have to go.'

'Goodbye then, young Arnie, and thanks for your help.'

Michael took Arnie's hand with an integrity that Mr Dauntliffe would have recognised from his own schooldays before counting his fingers. 'We will look you up along with Jenna when we return.'

'I will see young Arnie off the premises,' said Jenna, 'then help you with your labelling.'

'Bye all, and thanks,' concluded Arnie, shaking hands with the others before allowing Jenna to lead him to the changing rooms.

Watching them go, Michael felt a twinge of guilt, like skipping to the second layer in the chocolate box before the soft-centres had gone. I'm getting too old and sentimental for this, he reflected; after this job I will open a bar and sit in front of it for life.

The three soon-to-be-ex architects started the chore of labelling. Out of sight, Jenna and her charge slipped into the changing room and, facial makeup applied, Arnie drew aside the loose shutter, shook off Jenna's hearty backslap and entered the tunnels leading to his dressing room backstage in the Town Hall. And the awaiting Jady.

.

'A big hand for the merry losers! Don't be downcast, in sporting contests there can only be one winner, except in the mixed doubles. Now, there are thirty-two down and thirty-two to go, or thirty-one if you insist. We will have a quick break for sober reflection and drinks, after which the Masked

Pimpernel will arrive and make the draw for the second round. If we are lucky, and I think we will be, he will give us a brief display of his talents to remind us what the competitors are aiming at. After that, we will have another quick break so we can all reflect on what we have learnt, and another quick drink. Then break for the second round and down to the last sixteen. Happy? Good. See you after the break.'

To her customary round of baffled applause Alison exited stage left, à la Snagglepuss, and disappeared into the depths beyond. She fetched up outside the Masked Pimpernel's dressing room, smiled at the security guard Jady had stationed outside and entered just in time to see Arnie clamber out of the maintenance tunnel.

'Hail fellow, well met,' greeted Jady swiftly as Arnie brushed himself down. At least the tunnels were dry. Speaking Shakespearily, Jady continued, 'Now is the summer of our content.'

'Hail what?' croaked Arnie, dusty of mouth and short of breath, besides being more of a post-modernist.

'It's good to see you,' continued Jady, skipping a few centuries, 'fancy a cup of tea or bottle of water?'

The important thing, Jady knew, was to keep things as mundane as possible so as to prevent Arnie worrying. A well-read man - libraries invited him to their Christmas parties - Jady could not think of a single example personally, fictionally or historically where worrying helped anything or anybody. If the good Lord had intended us to worry, thought Jady, he would have made worrying as worthwhile as wishing.

'Of course he does,' broke in Alison, slamming the dressing room door, thereby shedding the last of the dust from Arnie's superhero outfit. 'Hello, Masked Pimpernel, how are you? I'll get some.' As quickly as she arrived, Alison about-turned and departed waterwards.

'Know something, Millado?' mused Jady, hand on chin to assist thought, 'we should make a film of this. The unique selling point is that you could play yourself as the

Masked P without revealing your true identity; it might be useful for tax reasons too.'

Arnie looked at Jady wide-eyed; no matter how much he thought he understood his mentor, Jady always had a new angle. Pythagoras would have liked him.

'You must be joking, chief!' Arnie retorted heatedly. 'As soon as tonight is over I am burning my outfit. I never want to see the Masked Pimpernel again!'

Jady grinned; this was what he wanted. An annoyed Arnie was not a nervous Arnie. You cannot be annoyed and nervous at the same time, just ask Samson. Jady decided to let the gag run. Donning his mock-surprised voice, he continued.

'At this rate you will be thrown out of the Kryptonite Club. What would Batman think? Or any of the other superheroes?'

The door opened and a tray entered.

'Water up.' A cheerful Alison followed the tray. 'I do love fresh water from our Spa, fit for a superhero.'

Arnie sat down dully. He seemed to have shrunk a little. 'Superhero,' he muttered absently, 'I'm no superhero, I'm just a kid in a silly costume who can do Pool tricks. After tonight I will just be another kid in the dole queue, or starting a useless government training course to keep the unemployment figures down.'

This was serious. Underneath Jady's grasping wallet beat a warm and compassionate heart. Arnie had quit his job out of loyalty to Jady and his Joanna; Jady had a moral duty to look after him. Jady's conscience creaked into action, slowly, painfully yet unstoppably, like a stately steam engine awakening in the dead of night and busting out of the museum.

'No, you won't. After this you will get your job back with Hanif's company. I'll make sure of that.' As he said the words, Jady hoped fervently that they were true. If not, Arnie's would not be the only broken heart in Spawater. Besides, Joanna would hit the ceiling.

'Don't worry, young man,' added Alison complacently, 'you have friends. We all love you and we won't let you go on a nasty government training course.'

Of course! Jady could have kissed Alison with relief. Hanif would do anything for Alison. She only had to ask and Arnie would be reinstated. He might even get a pay rise. Jady mentally proposed Alison's honorary membership of the U.S. Cavalry. A proposal Big John Wayne, had he been in town, would have seconded sure as shootin'.

'I can't go back,' countered Arnie, opening his bottle.

'Why not?'

'Because Hanif is in charge of the national database and your Joanna is against it. I can only go back if he and Joanna make up.'

'But they have.' Jady seized on this with the enthusiasm of a fly in a pitcher plant. 'They met at Hanif's office to sort things out.'

Arnie drank deep and brightened.

'Well, if they are friends again, then I want my old job back. But did it work out ok? Hanif can be stubborn, even though he is a good boss.'

'Bound to, you know how persuasive Jo is. Ali, have you heard from either of them?'

Despite almost universal pressure, Jady still resisted the siren calls of the mobile telephone serfs. His love for the English language with all its nuances and essential shared understandings precluded the use of text messaging, 'Orwellian Newspeak', as he derided it, while maintaining that one cannot keep a cool head with a fried brain. Then again, for quick results, mobiles had their uses.

'Not this afternoon. Jo's is unattainable.'

'You can't use them at work,' interrupted Arnie; 'Hanif won't allow them for security reasons. The glass in our windows blocks out the signal.'

'Five minutes. Your escort is ready.'

'That's our signal, Mr Masked Pimpernel.' Alison responded to the knock on the door and the time check. 'We are due on stage shortly, time to make the draw. Your bodyguards are waiting. You need to limber up for your action shots.'

That will do, thought Jady complacently. Once Arnie had a cue in his hand he would be as fearless as a shark in a swimming pool. Jady wouldn't stay to watch as his presence made Arnie nervous.

'Yes, and I must find Jo. She should be outside somewhere, arranging the anti ID cards and national database demonstration.' Turning to Arnie, Jady patted him heartily on the back. No handshake – it would make things look serious. 'Well, good luck, Millado, not that you need it. Jenna will collect you later for debriefing at our place and we will celebrate properly tomorrow. I'll remind her before I look for Jo. Meanwhile, you look after Alison for us, won't you?'

'Of course,' grinned Arnie, donning his helmet. Being masked boosted his confidence. 'And I will do my best to beat the contest winner later on.'

'Certainly you will beat whoever wins,' replied Alison matter-of-factly.

'I'm sure you will,' added Jady, just a bit too casually whilst turning towards the door. 'Good luck, Ali; see you both later.' Jady departed, saluting Arnie's escort, and made his way towards the staff corridors leading to the adjacent Baths. Alison and the Masked Pimpernel limbered up to advance stagewards.

Arnie was not the world's quickest thinker - Hagrid replaced him in the Hogwarts Arms quiz team - but close contact with Jady over the past year and more had honed his suspicion muscle to Olympic standards. As they stood at the side of the stage, Alison preparing to march ahead and introduce him to the multitude, he tapped her shoulder and whispered.

'Why is everyone so confident I will win?'

Alison smiled knowingly. 'Trust Jady.'

'What time do you expect them?'

'Expect them, Inspector?' Michael smiled affably and shrugged. 'You know what removal people are like. Still, they are a reliable firm, I am reliably informed, they are due just after it gets dark so as to attract as little attention as possible. We want this operation to be discreet.'

Michael always found it amusing that he rarely lied to anyone, just one big lie to the fledgling national database covering the whole deal like a force field, with scrupulous honesty inside. Discretion was the least of it.

'You are aware,' Inspector Brewe continued, 'I take it, that there will be a demonstration tonight outside the Town Hall, as well as the activities therein?'

'Oh yes. They shan't disturb us.' But they will keep you and your friends busy, he thought cheerfully. It's an ill wind...

'Hi there, Michael; evening, Inspector, you people are never of duty, thank goodness. It is a comfort to know you are here to protect us twenty-four seven, or whatever they call it.'

Jady's pleasant manner, clearly concealing total scorn, never failed to rile the Inspector. One of these days she would catch him with his wagon broken and she would have her toolkit ready.

'Very good, Mr Lehmann. You have my number, let me know if there are any problems. Carry on, Sergeant.' With the briefest of nods to Jady, she and a sniggering Sergeant Mathews departed.

'Sorry to disturb you, Michael, I know you are busy. I am looking for Jenna. Is she about?'

Michael directed Jady to where Jenna was labelling sections of the Baths according to Marlene's written instructions. No, she had not heard from Joanna; the number was unobtainable. Nor Hanif. Yes, she thought Arnie would be fine, Alison she had not worried about work-wise for years; life-wise she had given up worrying as Alison seemed to survive willy-nilly. The police were not a problem; Harold Wood was still a peckerhead; Michael and friends had things under control, awaiting the firm to collect the

Baths; the demonstration was going ahead so far as she knew; the lark was in the sky, the snail was on the thorn, God was in his heaven and all was well with the world. 'Anything else?'

'That'll do for now,' Jady smiled cheerfully.

'Ok. Well push off and let me get on with my work. When this lot is ready for transit I'll join you in the Hall - after I've gone on the demo, of course. We must get our priorities right.'

'All right. I will just say goodbye to Michael and then wander about to see if Joanna's in town. If she rings tell her I'm outside somewhere.'

Jady moseyed over to where Michael was attaching labels. 'Well, goodbye for now, Michael old pal. Shame you and the others couldn't have a last drink in Lifeboats'. We will be celebrating tomorrow so there should be quite a party.'

'Yes, your competition has been a great success. I am pleased for you. It is a shame that our schedule won't allow us to be here tomorrow, but there we are.' Michael intended to be well out of town by tomorrow; somehow he did not think he would be terribly popular in Spawater by then. Still, he wished Jady well, recognising in him a kindred spirit with whom, had things been different, it would have been a pleasure and doubtless financially rewarding to work alongside. Max Biallistock and Sergeant Bilco would have approved.

Erich and Marlene approached them and both shook Jady's hand with real affection.

'I'll see you when you bring back the renovated Baths. I am sorry your colleague Louise isn't here. Say goodbye to her from me.'

'We will,' responded Erich matily.

Marlene peered over Jady's shoulder and pointed towards the turnstiles. 'We won't need to. Michael, look.'

A flustered Louise shook her way through the barriers in a manner that would have stricken the heart of Harold Wood had he seen it, and ran towards them. She pulled up alongside. Ignoring, or not noticing Jady in her disorder, she blurted out her message.

'It's all gone wrong. It is a disaster. We are all in big big trouble.'

Michael was on duty instantly.

'Excuse us please, Jady. Calm down Louise, relax, take a deep breath and speak slowly and carefully. And quietly.'

Louise gulped a few times like a goldfish over its ant eggs; then, remembering she was a professional, coolly stated the position. Her few words took seconds but seemed to age them by years.

Jady, withdrawn out of earshot and standing stock-still, puzzled at this bewildering development. But before he could make any sense of it he received an urgent tap on the shoulder. Glancing round he saw a rare sight, an agitated Jenna. Ushering him gently yet quickly a few steps away from the others, she whispered softly but firmly into his ear.

'Houston, we have a problem.'

Identity Cards
Chapter Twenty-Eight

'That's better. I do like a good cup of tea; it steadies the nerves, don't you think?'

Placing his cup carefully in the middle of the saucer, Mr Dauntliffe sat back in his chair and looked searchingly at Hanif. Nature knew best, of course, but Hanif couldn't help thinking that Mr Dauntliffe should not really have been a human being; a bird of prey, one of the larger varieties, would have suited his temperament to an iced tee. Spilling a drop or two, Hanif clattered his own cup down and waited anxiously for the blow to fall, like Johnny Appleseed facing a by-pass.

'Tell me, Hanif. Do you really and truly support what we are trying to do in Spawater?'

Oho, thought Joanna, snug in her nook. What have we here?

Hanif knew the answer to this one. After all, he had helped set the bid to win the contract in the first place.

'Of course, Mr Dauntliffe, identity cards and a national database are vital tools for twenty-first century Britain and long overdue, in my view. Our Spawater experiment is an essential part of implementing such tools nationwide. I support it wholeheartedly.' As the words he had used in so many speeches spilled automatically out, Hanif wondered if he really believed them anymore. His tidy world of theory had bumped into the haphazard world of practice and been found seriously wanting. Still, a contract was a contract.

'Wholeheartedly?' Mr Dauntliffe pressed. 'You support a national database wholeheartedly?'

'Yes, of course.'

'Why?'

Joanna nearly fell out of the cupboard. Why? What a startling question! If Moses had hired Mr Dauntliffe to introduce the Ten Commandments the tribes would still be wrangling in the desert. 'Thou shalt not kill? What, anything? Even plagues of locusts?'

'We must set up a Commandments Sub-committee to report back on this one in, say, forty years.'

It didn't do Hanif's equanimity much good either. 'Why?' he repeated, bewildered.

'Yes, why? Why do you support the introduction of a national database?' Mr Dauntliffe edged forward. This was a vital moment; Hanif's answer would determine his future as Mr Dauntliffe's technical boffin.

'Well,' stalled Hanif, playing safe, 'it will assist us in the war against immigration, and prevent illegal terrorists using our Health Service...I mean,' Hanif spluttered, 'if you have nothing to hide you have nothing to fear and the national database will help in identity management and, oh, be useful for all manner of things...'

'No, no,' interrupted Mr Dauntliffe impatiently, 'not the nonsense we use to sell the national database to Parliament and the public, I mean the real reason. You say you support the national database. I am asking you why.'

Hanif paused and absorbed these words. Obviously Mr Dauntliffe wanted more than the party line, but what? Hanif tried a new tact.

'Well, the national database is more than simply a way of streamlining the country. It will also encourage people to alter their behaviour. After all, if they can be stopped at any time and their records accessed, it will be much harder for them to break the law, for example.'

Mr Dauntliffe sat up encouragingly. 'Go on...'

Hanif felt he was on the right track. 'If people know that everything they do or say is recorded, and can be held against them, they will be unlikely to do or say anything that could get them into trouble.'

'What about people who oppose the national database?'

Yes, thought Joanna, what about them?

Hanif was acutely aware of his equivocal position regarding the contents of the caretaker's cupboard. From his position as heavenly arbitrator, Solomon sympathised.

'You would need the wisdom of me to keep both parties happy, old boy; eggshell treading is deuced difficult. Now, who wants half a baby?'

Back on Earth, Hanif shrugged hopelessly. 'I suppose they will just have to lump it.'

'How about protests in general; demonstrations, campaigns, strikes, that sort of thing? How will the national database affect those activities?' Hanif was beginning to see the light. 'Of course, with the national database in force, such activities would become well-nigh impossible.'

'Why?'

'Because people could be traced. Attending a demonstration would be tantamount to an act of insurrection. Their cards would be marked and, for example, they would never work again.'

Mr Dauntliffe clapped his hands and nodded enthusiastically in agreement, fuelling the theory that humans are descendents of the chimpanzee.

'Exactly, Hanif. That is precisely what will happen with the introduction of the national database. We will have total control over the population. Not for a week, not for a year, but forever.' He raised his teacup in triumph, missing link personified. 'And you, Mr Singh, are going to help me, us, my colleagues and I, achieve this.'

Joanna's ears pricked up like Brer Rabbit in the Briar patch. Keep talking...

'History shows that power devolves downwards; from all-powerful demigods via emperors, kings and barons down to universal sufferage, votes for all. Power is diffused. As time goes by and the universal benefits of added wealth are strewn amongst the ordinary people, they become autonomous and learn to hold authority in contempt. Governments cannot govern such unruly people. Anarchy threatens and with it, the destruction of the natural order of leaders and led. That way leads to the destruction of society.

To prevent this and maintain the natural order, people must be controlled, and the national database backed by Identification Cards is only the beginning.'

In his enthusiasm, Mr Dauntliffe was going too fast.

'You will think me a dullard, Mr Dauntliffe, but I am not quite with you. Could you go over that again, please?'

'Of course, Hanif, of course. I sometimes take these things for granted and forget that others are not so aware. Allow me to simplify it.'

Letting this monstrous condescension pass, Hanif nodded. He wondered what Joanna was making of it and hoped she could keep her temper and the caretaker's cupboard door under control.

Mr Dauntliffe sipped his tea carefully, replaced the cup just so, and, skipping the 'Once upon a time,' began.

'Since the birth of mankind, humans have been divided into two groups; the leaders and the led. The leaders, a small elite, are obliged to shoulder the burden of governing the majority who are incapable of governing themselves. Without the leaders there would be anarchy.' He looked at Hanif to see how he was taking this. Hanif's mind was racing but he returned the look with a serenity any swan would have recognised in one. Reassured, Mr Dauntliffe continued.

'Throughout history, this system has worked. Certainly there have been hiccups; revolutions, uprisings and so forth, but these have invariably ended in chaos and a return to the natural order. The leaders lead and the rest follow.'

Had Joanna been sharing her confinement with Ghandi or Gandalf or the Dalai Lama, she would have been awarded instant Nirvanadom for her silent self-control. She listened on in road-crash fascination as Mr Dauntliffe continued.

'However, a new century brings new challenges. Up until now, the majority have known their place; leaders, kings, emperors and more recently parliaments, have been able to rely on the support and obedience of the many, thereby maintaining the natural order and consequently preventing confusion and mayhem. But no longer.'

'No longer?' Hanif felt he ought to say something to show he was paying attention.

'No longer. You see, modern technology, particularly in communications, added to universal education and, in the west at least, an unprecedented increase in wealth for the masses, has bred discontent. For the first time in history, significant numbers of people are free from the day-to-day struggle for existence. They lead comfortable, affluent lives.'

Hanif risked a minor objection. 'But that's good, isn't it? Surely that is what progress is all about? All the political parties promise prosperity as the main reason to vote for them, don't they?'

To Hanif's relief, Mr Dauntliffe nodded.

'Correct. Prosperity, leisure, an easy life as far removed from the struggles of their grandparents as from the caveman, that is what the masses have been promised and that is what they expect. But what does this lead to? Disappointment and disillusion. Life, they discover, consists of multi-channel television, junk food, all day drinking and foreign holidays. The masses have the freedom to do as they desire and they spend this freedom becoming obese couch potatoes. They are dissatisfied, but instead of blaming their own lack of imagination and limited ambition for their dissatisfaction, they blame their leaders. They blame society. And what does this lead to?'

Hanif waited; it seemed a shame to interrupt when Mr Dauntliffe was so clearly enjoying himself. He had no idea Establishment discussions were so animated.

'To the breakdown and destruction of society. If the people lose respect for their leaders and their system of government, they will look for alternatives. They may even try to govern themselves or live without rulers entirely. Order will be lost and the country, and ultimately the world, will dissolve into anarchy.' He thumped the desk for emphasis. 'This must not happen.'

A sound from behind resembling a sharp intake of breath distracted him. 'What was that?'

'What was what?'

'Never mind. The point is, Mr Singh, are you with me? Do you agree that order must be maintained and antisocial elements must be weeded out and destroyed for the good of all?'

If Mr Dauntliffe had asked Hanif to agree that the Moon was made of cheese, Hanif would have asked green or blue. It is seldom advisable to argue with an enthusiast, particularly one who is a member of the ruling Establishment. It hurts their feelings.

'Well,' Hanif parried, acutely aware that he was addressing two audiences, 'certainly there is less respect around these days. People do not automatically trust the authorities as they did in the past, and plenty of them do not agree with the current political system, but when you say weeded out; don't you think you may be going a bit far? After all, letting people have their say is a tried and trusted safety valve. It convinces the majority they are living in a free and fair society.'

A client is a client is a client. Hanif would not normally cared or dared to put up even such minimal criticisms in the face of Mr Dauntliffe's arguments, let alone his actual face, preferring instead the line of least resistance and picking up the cheque. However, his conscience, knowing it had the support of Joanna in the cupboard, put up unexpected resistance. For the good of its owner it wanted out.

So did Joanna. Taking up residence in the caretaker's cupboard brought to mind the old saw that the children of the village cobbler traditionally have the worst shoes; the point being that there is no-one to pay the cobbler for repairs. In similar vein, Joanna was discovering that the caretaker's cupboard packed enough dust to give a passel of ravenous vacuum cleaners galloping indigestion.

The happiest of the Musketeers - admittedly against poor competition - Mr Dauntliffe was not looking for a yes-man; he had plenty of those already. What he needed was a computer expert who shared his vision and belief in maintaining the natural order of leaders and led, whilst knowing his own place. Hanif's mild criticisms showed him to be intelligent without being arrogant or overly ambitious. That was Mr Dauntliffe's job.

'Thank you, Hanif, I respect your views. At one time I might have agreed with them. However, a fortuitous combination of circumstances has changed my mind. One, technological advances. When Orwell wrote Big Brother is Watching You, it was a futuristic fantasy. Now it is an understatement. Big Brother can watch, listen, analyse, predict and prevent. Two, the Civil Liberties lobby,' his face contorted like a soul contemplating sin, 'was able to influence politicians and public opinion. The nation would not, in the past, have tolerated assaults on individual freedom and would have rejected at the ballet box any political party that proposed them.' He straightened up for emphasis

'This has now changed. Thanks to the events known as Nine-Eleven, political parties are falling over themselves to be tougher than the others in the so called 'War on Terrorism.' Useful idiots. In twenty-first century Britain, freedom is out of fashion.' He paused for a sip of tea then wrapped up the case for the prosecution.

'Now, as you implicitly agree, people are getting above themselves. They put their individual freedoms above the survival of the State. They no longer accept the wisdom of their betters. They argue and dispute everything and insist on their so-called human rights. Human rights! They mean the right to do exactly as they like and the Devil take the hindmost. They have gone too far and are threatening the very fabric of society. Human rights have replaced human responsibilities, in particular the responsibility of obedience and loyalty to the State.'

He took another satisfied sip. From the Heavenly zoos, where the digestives have chocolate on both sides, chimps looked down admiringly.

Joanna stopped breathing, partly to avoid inhaling more dust than was strictly required in a balanced diet and partly to make sense of what she was hearing. Clearly this man was deranged. Was he really a powerful member of the ruling Establishment? More to the point, where was he going with his argument and what did it mean? One thing was certain; Mr Dauntliffe must not discover that she was eavesdropping. Hanif losing his job? If this man could walk the walk as decisively as his braggadocio suggested, that was the least of it.

Mr Dauntliffe, refreshed, continued as though talking to himself.

'Yes, antisocial elements will be weeded out. Already we have persuaded the government to introduce laws making it possible to imprison people without trial and without explaining to anyone why we are doing it. If we do not like someone, they disappear. More important deviants face house arrest to prevent them travelling and spreading their unwanted views.'

'You have the power to introduce internal exile?' Hanif gripped his desktop. He wanted a drink.

'Effectively, yes. Under national database law, everyone will have to register his or her address. We can keep them there, incommunicado, without reason. Also, Mental Health regulations let us lock up people for life for having 'personality disorders' without evidence, on our say-so. Best of all...' Mr Dauntliffe could not resist a smile; if only those who had bullied him at school could see him now. Perhaps, he reflected with satisfaction, the worst of them would soon be forced to cancel their travel plans permanently. 'Best of all, we have 'acts preparatory to terrorism', a catch-all whereby we can imprison anyone for life without having to produce any evidence to anyone, ever.'

Hanif's conscience rested its case. 'Surely only for suspected terrorists?'

'That's what we tell the ministers and they tell Parliament. Of course, once it is on the statute books we will simply expand it to cover all malcontents and troublemakers. Anyone who objects will be treated accordingly.'

Mr Dauntliffe paused and looked keenly at Hanif with a gimlet eye any eaglehawk would call brother. 'You do approve, don't you? You agree that antisocial elements must be constrained for the good of the majority?'

Blue, green or polka dot, Hanif was not about to start arguing. Mr Dauntliffe was no shilly-shallying politician; his words held no ambiguities. Malcontents and troublemakers as decided, doubtless, by Mr Dauntliffe and the Establishment in general, would be 'disappeared' in fine totalitarian style. Unlike Joanna, who preferred to stay in her cupboard, Hanif did not wish to appear antisocial. Best bet was to pretend to agree with his client and hope Joanna understood.

'Of course, Mr Dauntliffe, of course; I agree entirely.' Hanif nodded vigorously. 'The common good must be paramount and people who cause problems must be dealt with one way or another, it is just that you are going a bit fast for me. You said earlier that the national database is only the beginning. How do you see things progressing and what would my role be?'

Mr Dauntliffe relaxed. This was what he had been hoping for; a top technician who would keep him abreast of technological factors whilst having no say in managerial decisions. The fate of the middle classes throughout the ages, Hanif could have responsibility without power.

'Well Hanif, I am glad we understand each other. It was a fortuitous choice of mine to select Spawater and your company for the trial period. Now, you ask how I see things progressing and what your role would be.' He breathed in, noisily, slowly and deeply, like a walrus finishing the night shift. 'What do you see on the pavement outside this building?'

Seeing Hanif flummoxed, Mr Dauntliffe answered his own question. 'Chewing gum.'

'Chewing gum?'

'Yes, chewing gum. Just one of the low-level crimes perpetrated by low-level people. There is also litter, litter everywhere; graffiti-strewn streets awash with cast-off rubbish, beer cans, plastic bags, dog mess and worse. And Spawater is one of the cleaner towns; we have untidy, scruffy streets all over Britain. And what do untidy streets produce?'

Fortunately, Hanif had grasped by now that Mr Dauntliffe was speaking rhetorically and kept his peace. Joanna wished Spawater had some of the cleaner cupboards to match the streets, but otherwise kept hers.

'Untidy minds. If people live in squalor they will think the same way. People must smarten up on the outside in order to smarten up on the inside.'

It seemed to Hanif that Mr Dauntliffe was putting up an argument for the public ownership of road sweeping and interior decorating, but this did not seem the time to say so.

'Quite right, of course. We do need cleaner streets and a sloppy environment means a sloppy mind.' Hanif hoped Mr Dauntliffe had not checked out his own bachelor flat or he would be off the case quicker than the time it takes to grow mould in a coffee cup.

'That was just an illustration,' replied Mr Dauntliffe imperiously. 'Now, let's suppose we have the DNA of everyone in the country. We will have soon enough. We can analyse chewing gum and find out the irresponsible waster who dropped it. We can arrest them and see that they do not do it twice.'

In her dark room, Joanna saw everything. She felt dizzy. So did Hanif, but he had the advantage of a seat.

'Yes, that would be possible, but would it not be an overreaction?'

'Not at all. You see, once a few examples have been made, the littering will stop. As will the graffiti and the drunkenness.'

Mr Dauntliffe struggled to contain his excitement. He was going to make his mark in history; the man who defeated Original Sin.

'For example, anyone who abuses alcohol will be forbidden it. They cannot buy more as their DNA is checked before any purchase. Equally they will be banned from all public houses until we decide they have learnt their lesson, if ever. Friends cannot purchase it for them as we will have records of everyone's spending habits and any variance will be noted and acted upon. In this way we will wipe out all antisocial behaviour. In time people will not even think of misbehaving. Future generations will accept that the common good is all and individuals are dispensable. We will live like the ant; eschewing hedonistic individualism for the common good.'

Mr Dauntliffe drained his cup. The tea was cold but he was hot.

'Look back, Hanif, at the five principles. We can watch, listen, analyse, predict and prevent. We no longer have to wait for an offence to take place in order to react; we can act pre-emptively. With cameras everywhere allied to satellite monitoring, and miniature, unmanned low-flying surveillance drones, we watch. Our latest cameras also listen, and are programmed to recognise forbidden words such as 'bomb', 'protest', 'meeting', and any such words we see fit to add.'

Like 'freedom' or 'fair-trial', fumed Joanna in disgust.

'We will know everything about everyone. Full spectrum. Every financial transaction they make, every penny they spend, where they go, who they meet, what they do, what they discuss, what they think, their health, life expectancy, education, potential for rebellion, everything.'

He glanced, pleased, at his empty cup.

'We can analyse words and body language, including crowd behaviour, and use this analysis to predict likely events such as protest marches and anti government campaigns. Knowing this in advance enables us to prevent such deviant behaviour and dispose of the ringleaders. Minor deviants can be fined automatically, deducting funds from their bank accounts at source, prohibiting them from travelling except where we allow them to go, such as their place of business, prevented from buying petrol or train tickets, loss of citizen privileges, and so on.'

Joanna resisted the urge to punch the cupboard door.

'With a biometric integrated national database containing everyone's DNA and Citizen Value, we will have total control. This will enable us to set a Citizen Value for every unit of society. Behave and your Citizen Value increases, misbehave...'

'Citizen Value?'

'Naturally. All citizens will be given a value according to their worth to society. Proper behaviour, speech and attitude will raise their value. Deviant behaviour,' he frowned, 'lowers it. Low value means loss of privileges such as freedom to travel. That part of the Identification Card will be deactivated so travel will be impossible except in ways we approve of, such as travel to work or to the correction centre.'

'So...' a shocked Hanif followed the thread, '...once such a system is in place it will remain forever. The government which controls it can remain in power permanently, as any attempt by the people to rise up and revolt will be discovered and quashed before it can spread. That means parliamentary democracy is dead.'

'What is parliamentary democracy? The choice between Tweedle Dee and Tweedle Dum. We can allow an illusory 'choice' between two major political parties and a few minor ones in order to keep the majority contented. The minority of malcontents we can deal with quietly and justify on the grounds of 'security'. You see, Hanif,' Mr Dauntliffe leaned forward conspiratorially, 'we have the technology, all we needed was the excuse, and thanks to our friends in Al Qa'ida, we have it. Now it is simply a matter of implementation.'

Had he sprouted a forked beard, sported a pointy hat and sung 'gunpowder treason and plot' Mr Dauntliffe could hardly have inherited the mantle of Guy Fawkes more convincingly. All he needed was a barrel of finest and a fuse.

'Your friends in Al Qa'ida..?'

'Inadvertently. Well, we trained them, and now we use their existence to frighten Parliament into supporting our objectives. For the price of one criminal action in America we have shattered centuries of bogus 'liberties' and can today bring total control to Britain. Then Europe, then the world.'

Mad as a Hatter, Joanna hoped. This joker would be laughed off a pantomime stage for being too absurd. Oh no, he wouldn't, of course, if it were true. Total control, total control over everyone, always. Order would be maintained, but at what cost? It would be the peace of the morgue, the stability of stagnation. No more crime except the biggest crime of all: the emasculation of the human race.

'Forgive me playing Devil's advocate,' dared Hanif, as if in tune with the conscience in the cupboard, 'but what would this total control do for human progress and enterprise? Surely, if people know that everything they do is under surveillance, they will not do anything. No risks, no bending the rules, no inspirational long-shots; Britain will fall behind the rest of the world as we stand still and they progress.'

'Not when the rest of the world takes our route, as it inevitably will.'

'Then the whole progress of the human race will be frozen.'

Even as he said it, Hanif knew the nature of the reply as though it was a line in the type of play Shakespeare produced when his liver was playing up.

So did Joanna. She recalled her many conversations with Jenna, agreeing with her that any nation that surrenders its privacy surrenders its freedom. Jady agreed, insisting that giving up liberty in the name of security leads inevitably to the midnight knock, the cattle wagons and the death camps.

However, listening to Mr Dauntliffe through the cupboard door gave Joanna a different perspective. Perhaps life in the database gulag will not be so dramatic. The uncertainties of life will disappear under the dead diodes of the automated world. Excitement will be replaced by routine.

No more fear and no more hope. No more anxiety and no more dreams. History will be distorted then forgotten; the future will never happen.

Objectors will be instantly discovered and eradicated until all humanity accepts as natural the immutable status quo. No free spirits, total acceptance by the masses. No cattlewagons, just drab, grey conformity and spiritual decline. Joanna understood. The surveillance state means a continuation of the present. Forever.

She found herself unexpectedly jolted back into the present. The dust had finally succeeded in its task as surely as though it consisted of malevolent Nanobots. She was going to sneeze.

'Better frozen than onwards into anarchy. We are quite developed as it is. The next stage would be rampant individualism and a total breakdown of the natural order. Now,' Mr Dauntliffe placed his open palm down with a finality that brooked no further discussion, 'Mr Singh, are you with us, or...'

'Absolutely, sir, of course.'

Hanif was no longer worried about Joanna's displeasure. Clearly she must realise his client was spiritually joined at the hip to Hitler, Stalin and Doctor Strangelove, and would know Hanif was only humouring him until he could put in an order for the white jacket.

'You have opened my eyes. The sooner we can achieve full national database implementation alongside compulsory ID cards, the sooner we can live like the ant.'

Mr Dauntliffe leant over and grasped Hanif's right hand. 'Congratulations, Hanif! I knew you were a sensible chap. Welcome to the future.'

'Thank you.'

Mr Dauntliffe leaned back in triumph, a chimp with a crown. Singh was on board. He was only a pawn, certainly, but an important one, assisting in humanity's greatest aim; the eradication of individualism and with it, Original Sin. Much to be done, of course.

'And now, to the present. We have the Town Hall to attend. At your convenience we must proceed thither.'

'Of course.' Hanif stood up and felt the tension ease like kicking off tight shoes after break-dancing at the annual Stasi Ball. First, he thought, get this man out of my office so Joanna can escape. Then play it by ear. 'Do you have transportation or would you like me to arrange a car?'

'I left my car at my hotel.'

'Fine. I will arrange transportation. If you care to step this way?' Hanif buzzed the concierge at reception. 'Have a car ready, please. Five minutes.' Turning to Mr Dauntliffe, he continued. 'We can wait in the outside office.'

Together they exited into the adjourning anti-room usually housing Susan. Hanif tried to make small talk.

'When I shut the main door the rest will lock automatically.' No, it wouldn't, thought Hanif, but he did not want Joanna locked in the office all weekend. Some people get upset about that sort of thing.

But he needn't have worried. Fate would solve his problem.

'Hold on, Hanif, I have left my case in your office.'

Without waiting for a response, having left his manners in the last century, Mr Dauntliffe strode back inside the main room. Returning to his place at the desk, he retrieved his case and turned to leave.

Hanif, following his client instead of his better instincts, arrived in time to see the cupboard doors fly open and Mr Dauntliffe sped on his way by an unexpected and violent shove in the back.

Joanna had sneezed her way to freedom.

Identity Cards
Chapter Twenty-Nine

'Dead? What do you mean, dead? How can he be dead?'

The team were alone, having politely excused themselves from Jenna and Jady.

'Be quiet, Erich,' snapped Michael, 'this will take some thinking about.' The important thing, Michael knew, was to keep calm. Problems are opportunities, someone once said. If so, they had just been handed the opportunity of a lifetime.

'Go over it again please, Louise. Tell us exactly what you know.' Louise, once more her professional self, reiterated her story.

'It was on the evening news; it said a major breakthrough in the fight against international crime had been made by the Russian authorities last night. Following a series of raids throughout the former Soviet Union, with cross-border co-operation, one of the largest, richest and most powerful criminal gangs in the world has been broken up. The raids met with armed resistance in many areas, particularly the remoter ones. The man reputed to be the leader of the entire outfit was killed in one such raid.'

Louise paused for effect.

'The man named is our employer.'

'Or,' Marlene remarked dryly, 'our former employer.'

'Where is he now?'

'Who knows? He simply marched backstage and vanished, according to Ali.'

'Where's Ali now?'

Jenna's mobile crashed into life with the cannon of Tchaikovsky's 1812 Overture. It seemed appropriate.

'She's here.' Jenna proffered it Jadywards. Forgetting his own scriptures about mobile phones being the cancerous spawn of Beelzebub, Jady clasped Jenna's dohickey to his face.

‘Ali, where’s the Masked P? Jenna says he’s gone AWOL.’

‘Oh hello, Jady, I was about to ask Jenna where you were. How are tricks?’

‘Tricks? What about you-know-who’s tricks? His trick shots? Jenna says he’s done a runner. What is happening?’

Alison faltered. ‘Yes, I am afraid you-know-who is a bit upset.’

‘Why? What happened?’

‘Well, we reached the final rounds of the finals. The last sixteen and the standard was high. The Masked Pimpernel did his trick shots.’ Alison stopped for air. ‘Oh, you should have seen him, Jady,’ she enthused, ‘he was magnificent. He held the audience in the palm of his hand.’

‘And..?’

‘He wowed them. They were begging for more. Everyone was going wild.’

‘And..?’

‘And so I wound up for another drinks break. You have to be mean to keep ’em keen, as we promoters say.’

‘And..?’

‘They will soon be playing the final round. Afterwards you-know-who is due to play the winner and reveal his sponsors, whoever they may be. And you have to be here to relay the Pimpernel’s victory speech. You know, the one about human progress depending on universal freedom and the database State, a threat bigger than Hitler. Or did you do that one last time? I know; it is the one about governments being secretly pleased about terrorist attacks as it helps them bamboozle Parliament into surrendering to fear and totalitarianism. Or something like that.’

Jady was a patient man but did not see why he should waste any more patience on this chatter. Job nodded sagely, ‘wise decision.’

‘Alison, could you please tell me where Millado is now and what the precise problem is?’

‘Oh yes. I was coming to that. You see, after we went backstage he said that the remaining players were all too good for him - he was watching progress on a monitor - and he could not hope to beat any of them. I reassured him he had nothing to worry about as you trusted him so he should trust you. Jady, I said to him, would never let you lose in front of all these people. He must have a card up his sleeve.'

Jady shuddered. He could see where this was going. Noah, tuning in to the weather report and hearing that there was a slight chance of showers, would have reached for his boarding pass.

'Then what happened?'

'He sort of froze, then he seemed to see the light. At least, he said he saw everything and how could he not have realised before. Then he stomped down the backstage corridor and into one of the dressing rooms. Then my phone rang.'

Jady was used to Alison's non-linear thought processes and let her continue. 'Go on...'

'My cheeses belled and told me to encourage him to do even more tricks. They said the prospective sponsors were drooling and were falling over themselves to be the inspiration behind the Masked Pimpernel. The price is going up by the minute.'

This, of course, was the whole point of Jady's enterprise, to create a bidding war between top-of-the-range businesses for the right to claim sponsorship of the Masked Pimpernel. By maintaining his secret identity and cocking a snoot at the soulless database demagogues, the Masked Pimpernel had caught the imagination and admiration of the nation. He was the symbol of freedom, privacy and human dignity, one in the eye for nosy, timorous, control-freak governments the world over.

Jady's scheme had brought home enough bacon to repopulate Animal Farm. It should have been his moment of triumph, prior to prising a large cheque from Alison's company for services rendered. Such a shame the symbol of secrecy had scarpered.

'But what about Millado?'

'The call held me up. By the time I reached the dressing room he had gone.'

'Gone? How? Where?'

'How he usually leaves the building. He removed a maintenance panel and left by the tunnel. Well, in his costume he could hardly have used the front door.'

Like Arnie, Jady saw the light.

'Of course! He has run away from the contest but has to go via the tunnel in order to collect his clothes. They are beside the changing rooms here. He means to change into his civvies and leave through the Baths. That means we can head him off at the pass. What's his mobile number?'

'He's not carrying his mobile.'

'Why not?'

'Security.'

That weasel word again. Bandied about like a 'Get out of jail free' card, Jady swore he would throttle the next person who said it.

'It was your idea, remember? Calls and texts can be traced.'

'Oh yes, of course.' He choked back warm humble pie. Jady was seldom flustered, but the prospect of all that sponsorship evaporating like rolling mist on a summer morn scrambled his brain to mush. Top Cat had a similar experience with the Ziamboosie diamonds.

'He carries a walkie-talkie, though. Jenna has its partner.'

'Brilliant.' Jady relaxed slightly. Hard work, but progress was being made.

'You keep things going at your end, Ali. We will find Millado and restore him to comparative sanity. Call us if there are any developments.'

'Will do.'

Jady turned hopefully to a waiting Jenna. 'Can you call him on the walkie-talkie?'

'I have been trying. The problem is, his end does not ring. I've set it so a light flashes when I call and it doesn't show up in his utility belt. We have to wait for him to emerge from the tunnel, or call us.'

'Why doesn't it ring?'

'Security.'

Jady reappraised his options. 'Security?'

'Well, we cannot have noises in the tunnel, can we? Look, I'll set my walkie-t to trace; then his one will flash quicker as he gets nearer to us. That way he might get the hint and call in.'

Jady had to admit there was something in this security lark; real, practical security, that is, as opposed to government paranoia.

'So we wait in the changing rooms by the tunnel exit?'

'Sounds good.'

Approaching the changing room, Jenna asked Jady what news Louise had brought that caused such disconcertion.

'I don't know, but it certainly upset the others. Big big trouble, she said. I know how she feels.'

Jenna agreed. 'Well, they shoo-ed us away smartly enough; my guess is it concerns money.' Jenna laughed softly. 'Michael is nearly as fond of it as you are.'

Before Jady could respond to this monstrous slander, Jenna's walkie-talkie lit up, signalling communication from Arnie. She handed it over. 'You take it.'

'Hello, Millado? Where are you?'

'Is that you, chief?' A disembodied voice crackled thinly through the ether.

'Yes. I'm with Jenna. Look,' Jady spoke sympathetically, softly softly catchee Arnie, 'Alison tells me you are upset. Don't worry. We'll meet you in the changing rooms and I will put your mind at rest.'

'I can't.'

'Yes you can, Millado. No worries, just get here and I will sort things out.'

'No chief, I can't.'

'Yes you can, Millado, I have faith in you.'

'I mean I can't, chief,' persisted Arnie pathetically, 'I don't know where I am. Everything is pitch black; I am lost in the tunnels.'

The demonstration began. Demonstrating the natural cooperation and enterprise inevitable when people take control of their lives instead of passively accepting government and State dictat, the members and supporters of the National Campaign Against Identity Cards scrubbed round the non-appearance of Joanna and massed peacefully and determinedly around the Town Hall and its environs. The publicity generated by the Campaign and the dawning realisation of the true cost and implications of the national database had swelled their ranks to war-protest proportions. Had the public known the State's true aims as personified by Mr Dauntliffe, they would have massed in revolutionary ones.

The media, detecting the sweet smell of political scandal, had assembled accordingly. Resistance to Identification Cards and the database State flowered with the inevitability of nature breaking through concrete. The streets were blocked and an increasingly anxious Inspector Brewe, surprised and concerned by the numbers, ordered the local streets closed to traffic. Under strict orders to avoid trouble, there would be no confrontation on her watch; she would do any confronting that needed doing.

'All units, stop all traffic entering the area with one exception, there is a fleet of lorries expected at the Baths any time now. Escort them through.'

'Drop me off here, driver. I will walk.'

Mr Dauntliffe beckoned to the driver to stop the car. The driver did so and Mr Dauntliffe was decanted on to the far side of the Baths, in walking distance of the Town Hall.

'Very good, Mr Singh, we will continue our discussion later.' With a curt nod to the driver Mr Dauntliffe took his leave and proceeded towards the Town Hall and his rendezvous with its chief of security, Harold Wood. As he strode alongside the Baths, eyeing the throng of demonstrators ahead with malevolent distaste, he noticed that not all traffic had been barred; a series of industrial trucks was caterpillering its way towards the Spawater Baths delivery entrance.

'Whew!' Hanif reflected on his day; first, losing his identity card which led to embarrassment outside his office, then the embarrassment inside his office when he could neither open his desk nor access his computer. This was followed immediately by the most frightening conversation he had had in his life, not helped by the fact that he was concealing his client's greatest opponent in a cupboard. Only temporarily, though, as said opponent burst out from her confinement just in time to commit assault from behind. What a day, could it get worse?

'Where to, sir?' asked the driver.

'Anywhere. No, park around the corner somewhere. And stop calling me sir.'

'Ok, Han Sahib,' replied Joanna cheekily, 'but I have to admit; you were magnificent, truly inspirational. How on earth did you think of it?'

Despite his shattered nerves, Hanif permitted himself a self-congratulatory smirk. Not known as a rapid thinker - bright but slow usually summed him up, like a Hippo with a degree - when Joanna burst forth from the caretaker's cupboard into the small of her opponent's back, Hanif rose to the occasion with a fleetness of mind and foot that could only be described as Bilkonian.

As Mr Dauntliffe clambered up off the floor and into his dignity, Hanif bounced into action. In three strides he slammed the cupboard doors shut, retrieved Mr Dauntliffe's dropped case and turned to Joanna reprovingly.

'Ms Almari, I appreciate your enthusiasm and accept that I did ask you to get here as quickly as possible. However, when I say hurry I do not expect you to rush in here like a herd of elephants. What would Health and Safety say?'

Turning to Mr Dauntliffe, Hanif continued.

‘I do apologise, sir, for the eagerness of my staff. Not hurt are you? Good. This is our driver, Ms Almari. Not just a driver, of course, but also one of our highly trained personnel with a background in personal protection. Personal personnel protection, you might say.’ Hanif paused to see how this was going down, while Joanna, getting the message, played up.

‘Joanna Almari, sir, private personal protection. Regret inconvenience, but security, you know...’ Joanna tailed off enigmatically. She knew the word ‘security’ was seldom challenged. For killing discussion and switching off the brain cells, ‘security’ rocks.

‘But you came out of the cupboard!’

‘Of course sir, the cupboard...’ Joanna agreed earnestly.

‘Cupboard?’ Mr Dauntliffe was seldom at a loss. He was seldom leapt at from cupboards either.

‘That’s right,’ added Hanif, confidence bubbling though his veins like pure oxygen. This was going to work. He nodded significantly, ‘Cupboard...’

‘Oh, cupboard!’ Mr Dauntliffe saw all. He was seriously impressed. ‘Of course! Well, Mr Singh, it certainly had me fooled. And you, Miss, er...’

‘Ms Almari, sir. And with all due respect, should we not be on our way?’

For diverse reasons, all three were eager to get to the centre of town and go their own separate ways, and minutes later Mr Dauntliffe found himself in the back seat of a most un security-like car, nestling uncomfortably amongst chocolate wrappers, CD cases and similar in-car flotsam.

‘Convincing, don’t you agree, sir?’ leaned Hanif from the front passenger’s seat. ‘Anyone would think we were just three friends going for a drive.’

Mr Dauntliffe winced at the thought of the two in front ever being equals, let alone friends; even Mr Pettifogg was preferable. Nevertheless, he had to concede despite himself, this car was a perfect disguise. A far cry from the usual government vehicles, he intended never to use such a low-life means of transport again and it was a relief to reach the centre of town and journey's end. Not before time, as far as all three were concerned. Mr Dauntliffe made his excuses and left.

'Well, Joanna,' said Hanif, back in the present, 'desperate thingies call for desperate remedies. Now, let's park somewhere and see what on Earth is going on.'

'Good evening, sir, and may I say what an honour it is to have you here once more. How was the journey?'

'Have you ever travelled by car?' replied Mr Dauntliffe, releasing Harold Wood's hand with pleasure.

'Why yes, sir, of course,' answered Harold, mystified.

'My journey was like that.' Mr Dauntliffe was not in the mood for provincial forelock tugging. He had not forgotten that this miserable specimen waving him through the security systems and the crowd, like Igor ushering his master into the vampire's Ball, was the simpleton responsible for drawing nationwide scorn down on his database project and allowed that mouse Pettifogg to nip him on the ankle. Mr Dauntliffe wished to see how a municipal building coped with an unruly mob such as the public, and how individuals within mobs could be singled out, where necessary, for individual processing. Then he would return to London and sanity.

'Now, I want you to show me how you have implemented my security requirements and what you have learnt from your earlier false alarm. By the way,' he added sternly, 'you failed to demand my identity card.'

'So it is agreed. I will talk to their boss and offer him and his gang half the money if he will hand over the code and cancel the operation.'

'If the money still there,' added Erich.

'If it is still there.'

As the lorries backed carefully through the commercial entrance into the rear of the Baths, escorted by a police officer, Michael prepared for confrontation.

The logic was simple. With the demise of their employer, the deal was off. There would be no-one to pay the gang at their destination and the authorities might well be waiting for them with open handcuffs. Better all round, thought pragmatic Michael, to share the release code and Michael's fee than face Russian justice. 'I'd sooner head-butt an ice-pick than face Russian justice,' agreed Trotsky from his workers' paradise. 'Or face another lecture on dialectic materialism from Hegel,' added Marx; 'That's a concept of alienation too far.'

'Take care, Michael,' warned Louise anxiously, 'you know what kind of people they are.'

Michael was touched by Louise's concern. 'Don't you worry. They may be amoral thugs who will cut off your hands and use your biometric fingerprints to empty your bank account or steal your car, but they are not stupid. When they know the jig is up they will do a deal with us.' He grimaced. 'They might not settle for fifty percent though, we may have to take a punch in the pocket.'

'If that's the only punch we take, I'll be happy,' agreed Erich philosophically. A morsel of the pie was better than starvation in his humble opinion. Unlike Oliver Twist, Erich was not going to ask for more.

One last smile. 'It will be ok, you'll see.' Michael reassured them, if not himself, and made towards the new arrivals. 'Here goes.' Looking back he added, 'I'm sure they will see reason.'

The leading truck stopped across the way and a man who had 'Boss' metaphorically written through him like seaside rock, leapt from the cabin and curtly dismissed the saluting police officer. Donning his finest bluffery, Michael sauntered over to greet him.

Over at the Town Hall, Harold Wood was beginning to feel the strain. There was no pleasing his superior, Mr Dauntliffe. Finding themselves amongst the throng of Pool aficionados, the latter found fault with all poor Harold's security arrangements, from the eye scanners that needed constant monitoring due to disrespectful elements making faces at them or winking at the wrong time, all the way to malcontents insisting there was no reason to demand proof of identity to a Pool competition in the Town Hall in the first place. Others seemed to think that driving licences were a perfectly good substitute for identity cards and said so loudly and aggressively. These troublemakers just would not take security seriously; in vain did Harold try to explain for the umpteenth time that the forces of terror were invisible and everywhere, and honest folk must endure some slight inconvenience if they were to be free to go about their lives. In front of Mr Dauntliffe himself objectors nitpicked that if terrorists were invisible how did he know they were everywhere, and why would they attack the Town Hall when they could be bombing the bank?

The trouble is, as Harold was slowly beginning to realise, total security and real life do not mix. Unlike Harold, the general public and similar troublemakers preferred taking their chances in reality. Faced with identity checks for a trivial amusement in the Town Hall, they recognised the dire, doom-laden warnings of the politicians as the demented control freak moonshine they always were.

'I am sorry, Mr Dauntliffe, sir,' pleaded Harold, 'we do not have these problems on an ordinary working day; it is just that there are so many people here. We have not had such numbers in the building since we implemented the new security regime. The system works perfectly when there is nobody here.'

But Mr Dauntliffe was not too bothered. These were early days and the full database spectrum had yet to be attained. When every subject of the State was on the DNA database and liable to have their citizens' privileges withdrawn at the press of a button, they would learn not be so unruly. That goes double, he affirmed silently, for the demonstrators outside. Such actions - indeed any actions - against the State would not be tolerated.

No, Mr Dauntliffe's apparent displeasure was simply his automatic attitude towards the hoi polloi such as Harold

Wood. He would not need the support of such low-lives for much longer.

'How may I examine your system away from all these people?'

Harold perked up. The system worked perfectly well without the random interaction of humans.

'I know, sir. We can go through the connecting corridors, avoiding the hooligans outside, and inspect the Baths.'

'Is there not maintenance work taking place there this evening?'

'Yes, but it will not effect us. We can ignore it.'

'Very well, Mr Wood, lead on.'

Back at the Baths, Jady and Jenna were ignoring the faint sounds of altercation echoing between Michael's people and the large visitors with the trucks. They had troubles of their own. Using Jenna's mobile, Jady phoned Alison.

'Ali, what is happening your end?'

'Everyone wants the Masked Pimpernel, especially my cheeses and the sponsors. They want to see him perform more tricks during the next break. We are almost down to the final four contestants. I have to go out and supervise the draw for the semi-finals.'

Jady and Jenna were sitting in the dressing room used by Arnie when travelling incognito to the Town Hall. They had broken contact with him for the time being as talking could do no good and was hampering progress. There was nothing further they could do barring entering the tunnel themselves, which, they agreed, would be a last, desperate throw. None but a long term residence of Colditz could view such a prospect with equanimity.

'All right, Ali, keep in touch. We'll let you know when we have found him.'

'Ok. Speak soon.' Alison's unruffled voice ceased.

Jenna reclined lazily on the wooden bench. 'They seek him here, they seek him there...'

'Thank you, Jenna.'

'Those cheeses seek him everywhere...'

Too deflated to protest, Jady gave her back her mobile and stared at her walkie-talkie, willing it into life.

Jenna continued. 'Is he in the municipal maintenance tunnels...'

'No point in him calling, I suppose?'

'...or is he in Hell...'

'Jenna....'

'That dammed elusive Pimpernel.' Jenna righted herself. 'The third line is a work in progress. Not really, Jady, all we can do is wait. Leave him alone and he'll come home...'

'Know something, Jen? You missed your vocation in life.'

'What was that?'

'You could have been the Poet Lauriat of lost causes.'

Before Jenna could protest that surely the Great Jady of Jady Enterprises, no less, did not countenance the notion of lost causes, evidence to support Jady's view presented itself. Heavy footsteps along the back corridor heralded the approach of an individual who was not a candidate for Slimmer of the Year. They halted at the open door of the changing room.

Taking a step inside without invitation, the creator of the footfalls made a gesture that brooked no argument. A pistol, levelled at the two incumbents.

Identity Cards
Chapter Thirty

'Ladies, gentlemen and lovers of the seven ball game, let us all join together and give a Spawaterian round of applause to the worthy semi-finalists.'

Alison held court once more in the main Hall, addressing the assembled sports lovers and media representatives. The siege mentality generated by the presence of large numbers of demonstrators outside the Hall added to the sense of exclusivity, and the atmosphere would have had Benjamin Franklin reaching for his kite. All that was missing was the star attraction himself, the Masked Pimpernel. Doubtless, thought the more thoughtful Town Hall johnnies, he was being held back for reasons of suspense; Hitchcock, they told themselves over cool refreshments, would give Alison the thumbs up.

Michael, looking up at Jady and Jenna as they were frogmarched into the boiler room underneath the Baths, was less inclined and less able to do the same, as he was currently tethered to the radiator pipe alongside Louise, Marlene and Erich.

'Let me speak to the boss; I'm sure we can work this out.' Michael's plea to his captor was articulate but the grunt he received in reply conveyed more information. It said 'nothing doing' in anyspeak. Following grunt with action, the new additions were handed over to the radiator gang. Willing hands ruffled Jady and Jenna pipewards and before Jady could say 'Habeas Corpus', prisoners were they six. Jady's jacket and Jenna's bag, containing her mobile and Alison's walkie-talkie, were thrown onto a pile of similar bags and clothing belonging to Michael's group, well out of range.

Motioning to one man, if man he was, to remain with the captives, the others left. Jenna, Jady and the four architects of fantasy were left to their own devices, leaning up against the wall, hands tied behind their backs and around the radiator piping. Their feet were bound together in front of them and their guard, perched on a janitor's stool, sat quietly as though this were an everyday occurrence. Leaning forward with difficulty, and turning her head towards Michael, Jenna broke the silence.

'You realise I want double time for this.'

'Overtime rates; money for old rope so far.'

'So far, yes. But it is much too soon to relax. Besides,' added Inspector Brewe heatedly, 'the job is not just about money. We are here to keep the peace and allow honest citizens to go about their lawful business.'

The two officers were behind the scenes, in the surveillance room allocated to them by Harold Wood. Outside, the demonstration was continuing peacefully, with most demonstrators watching the large video screens displaying the Pool tournament. The tournament itself was also running smoothly as the patrons awaited the final rounds and the reappearance of the Masked Pimpernel. It was as if Mother Nature had set the weather dial to Lull.

'Of course,' replied Sergeant Mathews hastily. 'We are here to serve the great Spawater public.' Ideals and ambitions make awkward bedfellows and he kept forgetting that Inspector Brewe had both. Perhaps that was what annoyed him most about her. 'I just meant that it is quiet so far, that's all.'

'Yes, quite. Now, the most likely time for trouble is when the Masked Pimpernel plays the winner. I want all officers kept informed of his whereabouts at all times.' She looked up at the large monitors where Alison was congratulating the four semi-finalists. 'On the subject, where, exactly, is the Masked Pimpernel?'

'You see, Jenna, and you, Jady, the truth is; we have not been quite honest with you.'

Michael decided to come clean. Whether they liked it or not, all six were in this together. While the Baddies escaped with the Baths, the radiator six faced an uncomfortable weekend at least, followed by all kinds of embarrassment when someone eventually called in at the boiler room. The Baddies had chosen their prison well. The boiler room was totally out of earshot and on Michael's instructions the Baths were now closed to staff and public alike, the irony of which he failed to find amusing. On eventual discovery, Michael had a feeling that despite their bogus, biometric authority, questions might be asked by inquisitive police officers; officers less gullible than New Age politicians who put greater faith in biometrics than the evidence of their own senses.

You can fool all the people some of the time, and all the databases all of the time, but you can't fool all the people all of the time. Michael did not wish to be in the neighbourhood when common sense came a'callin'.

'The truth is, we are not who or what we appear to be.'

'Hah!'

'Go on...'

In response to Jady's encouragement, Michael did.

'So, Pool lovers, the final draw for the semi-finals has been made. The winners, as you know, will meet in the final, and the final winner will win the opportunity to meet the Masked Pimpernel himself in the final final. Got it? Good. Now,' Alison looked sidelong at the stage manager. He was signalling the non-appearance of the Masked Pimpernel by an official shoulder shrug with accompanying arms appealing to the heavens. 'We will take another break so our remaining contestants may savour the moment, and resume afterwards.'

There was some grumbling from the assembled sports fans about the way the tournament was being eked out, and cynical suggestions that the Masked Pimpernel must be sponsored by a drinks company as they were given so much drinking time, but the majority were happy and the bar was busy. The evening moved merrily on.

'And that,' concluded Michael, 'is how things are.'

It is difficult to register indignation when tied to a radiator. Dignity and radiators do not mix. Jenna did her best, though, and submitted Michael to a stream of invective unsuitable in company. Even the guard looked hurt, and beyond the occasional threat to dismember them if they did not keep the noise down, left them to it. Jady on the sidelines winced in sympathy despite his main emotion being admiration. What rotten luck, the Russian Boss coming unstuck on the big day!

'Yes, Jenna,' Michael conceded humbly when the maelstrom abated, 'you have been treated shabbily and have every right to be angry. But when you look at it, no real harm would have come to you. You were clearly an innocent in all this, as your continued presence in Spawater after the removals would have demonstrated. When things had quietened down I was going to credit your account with a bonus. If we get out of this, that still holds.'

'*If* we get out of this,' Marlene added. 'I'm sorry too, Jenna, Jady. We all are. The question is, what do we do now?'

'Someone's coming,' interrupted Erich hastily.

The door flew open in the abrupt manner only Baddies have mastered, and their captors reappeared. With them, in body but not spirit, were Joanna and Hanif.

'Here we are then. Everything seems to be in order,' announced Harold Wood with a strained cheerfulness that would awaken the suspicions of Bambi. His attempts to ingratiate himself with Mr Dauntliffe fell on the customary stony ground reserved for all who, in Mr Dauntliffe's considered opinion, were not 'One of Us'. Harold would have been flattered to know in whose company he was bracketed. Backbench MPs, junior ministers, and even the Cabinet had they but known it, were as irrelevant to the scheme of things as Spawater's Chief Security Officer. Pawns all, with their minor, uncomprehending roles to play, while He, Mr Dauntliffe, and his associates, ruled. The establishment did not need nor want the votes of the ignorant masses to enable or entitle them to rule; it was their birthright.

Ignoring Harold's twitterings, Mr Dauntliffe took in the scene. There were workmen removing various artefacts under supervision from a supervisor who was clearly in a hurry. Mr Dauntliffe was impressed; these workmen had the right hardworking attitude. Gazing further afield, he noticed a large, well-dressed man and what appeared to be a few assistants arriving from the main staff buildings. Noticing Mr Dauntliffe and Harold, one pointed at them.

'I see we have been noticed,' said Mr Dauntliffe, turning to Harold. 'Go and check their security credentials.'

'Don't worry, Jo,' reassured a concerned Jady, 'we will be fine; they can hardly murder us all, it would look like the Alamo and start a worldwide manhunt.'

Suitably unreassured, Joanna tried to make sense of her altered circumstances. One moment - how long ago? Minutes or another age when the world was young - she and Hanif were letting themselves through Harold Wood's security turnstiles using a Jenna-supplied multipass. The next moment they were rounded on, bundled downstairs into the depths of the staff building and tied to a radiator in a room already full to bursting with close friends and colleagues. Even by living-with-Jady standards, this one was a lulu. Little Red Riding Hood hardly raised more eyebrows on discovering Grandma was a furry, crazy-eyed, big-toothed transvestite wolf.

Hanif, on the other hand, accepted his fate with equanimity. After all, it was just what the day needed to round it off. The knowledge that he was tied up and events were, like his mobile, out of his hands, meant that he could relax and await fate's next whack of the wet kipper in the gizzard, knowing that there was nothing for him to do but lie there and wait. Sleeping Beauty had a similar experience and things turned out fine.

Less fatalistic, and sensing that the guard had little interest in the proceedings, Joanna spoke out, keeping fear out of her voice as though radiator surfing was her hobby.

'What's going on? Why have we been kidnapped or whatever this is? What is happening?'

'Micky-boy will explain, won't you, Michael, or whoever you are.' Jenna replied evenly, handing Michael the metaphorical floor to accompany the real one. Sitting up as far as possible, he began.

'You see...'

Like the dwarves gathering around Snow White to enjoy a good fairy tale after a hard day's work, all seven listened keenly to Michael's explanation. Even those who had heard it before did not seem to tire. Like a favourite song, it could be sung over and over without causing ennui. Hi ho. Hearing it for the first time, Joanna felt her stomach unknotting at the knowledge that it was nothing to do with her Jady. Well, nothing actionable.

Hanif took it big.

'See! I was right! I told you, I told Alison that there was something fishy about this lot. Architects? Con artists more like.' Hanif was delighted, his body was in the basement but his ego was in the clear. To be proven right in the end made the day worthwhile. Fate knew what it was doing after all; shame on him for doubting. Now he could bask in the sunny rays of self-righteousness like Samson in the rubble.

'What a pity your biometrics didn't spot them too,' retorted Joanna bitterly, 'then we wouldn't be in this mess.'

The clouds massed over Hanif once more as he realised the import of Joanna's remark. He had been suspicious but his biometric database system had given Michael's people the thumbs up. He had not voiced his qualms to officialdom because the biometric system would not back him and his fears would have been dismissed as paranoia or jealousy. Perhaps they were, but they were also correct; in fact, human.

‘Don’t blame Hanif,’ spoke up Jenna unexpectedly, ‘he was only doing his best. You cannot expect a computer system to outsmart clever con artists.’

‘No,’ Joanna agreed sarcastically, ‘computer systems are only human.’

‘They are designed by humans,’ added Jady, who felt he ought to say something, ‘so they are fallible. Humans can break anything designed by other humans. Con artists can study computer systems, find their weaknesses and exploit them to their own advantage.’

‘But,’ persisted Jenna, ‘to continue my point, if con artists are so clever, why are they tied to a radiator?’

Michael shifted uncomfortably. He was used to being in control. Being talked about as though he was not in the room was beginning to grate. It was like being on trial which, now that he thought about it, was an uncomfortable comparison.

‘One thing is certain,’ confessed Hanif with deadpan finality, ‘the national database is finished. Once this gets out it will be a national joke.’ He turned to Michael and laughed softly. ‘So it was the national database and identity cards that allowed you to get this far, and also allowed your friends outside to double-cross you and get away with the Baths.’

‘I am afraid so,’ agreed Michael. ‘I offered my, er, friends the opportunity to split our fee for the job but they would not see reason. They decided there was more money in stealing the Baths and selling them to the highest bidder.’

‘How were you going to collect the fee if the man who hired you has been killed?’ Jady asked curiously.

‘By using your national database.’ Despite her straitened circumstances, Louise could not suppress a smirk. “The thugs outside were going to supply Michael with the relevant code in exchange for the Baths. He would relay this to me. I would input this code along with our complementary one into the prototype national database and, having established our credentials, electronically access a certain bank account. The bank would transfer the funds therein to a joint account in our, er, false names. Simple.’

'Surely the account would be frozen now that your boss is dead and his gang arrested?' Jady protested. He hated to see good money go to waste - or bad money, come to that - but it seemed to him that the account would have been frozen as soon as the boss was iced.

'That is what those thugs outside thought, which is why they declined Michael's offer to share, but it is not necessarily so,' countered Louise. 'You see, the Russian police would need the cooperation of the international banking system and your prototype national database here in Spawater to sort things out. The world's financial institutions do not trust your national database, with justification,' - Hanif squirmed - 'so it will take weeks, perhaps months, to link the two. Perhaps never. The bureaucracy is such that nobody can be sure which trans-national accounts are linked to which or owned by whom; nor do their owners want them to.' She turned to Hanif. 'Your government has upset a lot of powerful interests, my friend. Your national database will contaminate the British banking system like a virus that the world's superrich do not want to spread. They will obstruct what they see as a global threat to their control, so no, the account will not yet be frozen.'

Hanif groaned. Fate had decommissioned the wet kipper and gone nuclear. 'Whatever happens, everyone will blame me.'

'Why you?' asked Marlene. 'You were just a local guy hired to implement a government policy. Your government is responsible for all of this.'

'When do governments take responsibility for anything? I am in charge of the local prototype. Of course everyone will blame me, I have access to everything.'

Michael and Jady stiffened in their bonds, glanced at Hanif and looked at each other. Two minds; one thought.

The conversation was interrupted by a ruckus in the outside corridor. Mr Dauntliffe and Harold Wood were about to join the throng and were taking the news very differently. The Marcus Aurelius school of thought holds that if aught befalls you, it is good. It is part of life's great web and should be accepted gracefully. Harold Wood, silent, knew his place. Others believe that one should rage, rage against the dying of the light. Mr Dauntliffe was of the second school. Having been unceremoniously jerked into the staff building and manhandled into the depths and away from civilisation, Mr Dauntliffe took the view that it was better to get problems off one's chest than suffer in silence.

'Don't you know who I am?' he roared, awakening the ghosts of lions and gladiators past. 'I'll have you put away for life for this. This is treason; attacking me is tantamount to attacking Britain. I will have you hanged.'

Possibly his haranguers believed that the European Union did not consider attacking Britain to be a serious offence, and the only hanging they recognised was hanging baskets, which were, of course, banned under Health and Safety. Possibly they simply did not take seriously the threats of a man with a sock in his mouth. Either way, all Mr Dauntliffe's protestations had earned for him was a place at the hot end of the pipe and his own sock, for a mercy, as a gag. This seemed to inspire the Baddies. In short order all ten prisoners had an assortment of socks tickling their tonsils and a more conventional rag tied around their mouths in the traditional manner.

The boss delegated his foreman to check the gags, who, satisfied with their effectiveness, grunted approval. On that signal, the Baddies about turned and went about their business.

'At last, at long last. The search for someone worthy to challenge the Masked Pimpernel is nearly over. We have our two finalists, the cream of Spawater Pool Hall society. Let's have a colossal, Applauses Maximus Spawaterium, for our gladiators of the green baize, champions of the cue ball, conquerors of the cushions; our two finalists who will shortly play for the privilege of challenging the Masked Pimpernel, no less, for the ten..?' Alison paused, raising a titter amongst the cognoscenti, '...no less, yes, ten thousand pound prize and perhaps more importantly, the glory, honour and fame of victory. I give you our two finalists, let's hear it for them.'

They heard it for them in fine style. Looking down on Alison in admiration, Nero, who made it to Heaven as he had the Latin, remarked, 'now that, Stradivarius,' is how to fiddle.'

In her communications room, Inspector Brewe studied the monitors covering both the inside of the Hall and the demonstration outside with growing relief. Both were peaceful and good-humoured, if a spot exuberant; it looked like a successful outing all round.

'Now, it is time for a break,' continued Alison smoothly. 'Not a Pool break but a break for refreshments. Enjoy. See you afterwards.'

'What about the Masked Pimpernel?' shouted a heckler. 'He is supposed to give a show between rounds.'

Some grumbling and agreement accompanied the outburst; the natives were restless. Alison glanced sideward. The stage manager gesticulated the international distress signal - open palms outwards with matching shrug - and continued contemplating a career change.

'Who demands the presence of the Masked Pimpernel? Who presumes to tell the Masked Pimpernel where to be and what to do?' Alison stepped back from the mike, shook her head sadly and resumed. 'It is not for us to determine the whereabouts of one who is a greater Pool player than us all, one who defies the authorities and refuses to be data processed, registered or controlled by The Man. Can you say the same?' Alison looked down at the heckler. 'Come here. Step up here on to the stage.'

Embarrassed and showing it, but encouraged by his beer bucked buddies, the heckler complied.

'Now,' Alison demanded, 'show me your identity card.'

The man reached inside his jacket pocket.

'Stop.' Alison turned to the crowd and winked. 'Well, we know one thing; this man here is not the Masked Pimpernel. He was about to show me his identity card simply because I asked him. No questions, no arguments, just simple obedience. Tell me,' she added, turning to the former heckler, 'why were you about to show me personal information about yourself?'

'Because you asked.'

'Precisely, because I asked. And you asked where is the Masked Pimpernel. Let me tell you that the Masked Pimpernel does not answer just because he is asked, and neither should you. The Masked Pimpernel will be here when necessary and not before. Now,' she turned to the audience, a crowd no longer, 'this man has been a good sport so, to show there are no hard feelings, the next round is on the House. There will be a free drink for everybody, then on to the final. Thank you.'

Alison had bought drinks; with them she had bought time.

Time passes slowly when you are tied to a radiator. A calm, tranquil hue covered the radiator ten like a comfort blanket. French aristocrats, awaiting madam guillotine, shook their heads across the ages in sympathy while they still could. Outside, the faint, distant, rubble-strewn sound of the Spawater Baths being loaded onto industrial trucks, stone onto steel. Inside the boiler room, the hum of the machinery masked the slight chaffing sound of those with unscratchable itches.

'All quiet on the Western front.'

'Pardon?'

'I mean things are quiet all over, Ma'am,' replied Detective Sergeant Mathews. 'There have been no arrests so far and the monitors show everyone watching the final. My money is on the big bloke.'

'Never mind your money, the time to watch out is after the final. When we are down to the winner against the Masked Pimpernel is the most likely time for trouble.' Inspector Brewe looked away from the monitor bank directly at her sergeant. 'Enjoy the peace now. I have a feeling it might not be peaceful for long.'

Screams of fright muffled through gags paid poor homage to the stupendous crash and splintering of false ceiling that heralded the arrival of a newcomer to the boiler room.

Body and bits obeyed the iron laws of gravity and kersplatted over the caretaker's stool, ricocheting onto the floor with a dull thump, replaced by a winded groan, subsiding slowly into a whimper. Several of those present, led by Mr Dauntliffe, contested the radiator high jump handicap; excepting Hanif who was beyond caring - 'you've had it mate' lamented Saint Jude - and Jenna, who knew the walkie-talkie in her bag was still emitting its homing signal.

'Saved,' she exulted, as the dusty figure extracted itself slowly and painfully from the debris. 'Saved by the Masked Pimpernel.'

Identity Cards
Chapter Thirty-one

'They said it could never be done. Never, they said, would anyone earn the right to challenge the Masked Pimpernel on equal terms. The Masked Pimpernel stands alone, they said, alone and above us all. For who else, they said, can come and go as they please without carrying their life story on a piece of State-owned biometric plastic, forced to reveal all to any jumped-up Hitler in a peaked cap on impertinent demand? Who can raise the banner of human freedom, dignity and responsibility, in other words true security, aloft and above mere card-carrying mortals? Why none, of course; none but the Masked Pimpernel. And yet, here is a challenger; a worthy challenger who has proved his mettle by beating the best and the rest of Spawater's citizenry, earning the right to challenge the Masked Pimpernel for the honour and glory of our fair city. Ladies, gentlemen and good citizens of Spawater, I give you our winner; the winner of the Pool tournament to end them all, and one worthy to challenge you-know-who for the cash prize itself. Let's raise the rafters for our winning challenger. Hip hip hip...'

Alison held aloft the winner's arms. As the room echoed to the cheers, she took the opportunity to make the least surprising announcement of the night.

'There will be a break for the winner to enjoy his moment and prepare for the challenge ahead. See you afterwards.' With that, she shepherded the stage-struck winner from the dais and into the wings.

'The final will be under spotlights so you will need special make-up.' She signalled to the waiting make-up team who were armed with slap provided by Jady especially for the purpose. 'Walk this way.' On cue, the make-up team gently dragged the winner into the depths.

'Any word?' asked Alison briskly of the stage manager.

'Nope. The number you gave me is still switched off.'

Alison tutted philosophically and looked out at the mob.

'What are you like at Pool?'

'Is it a bird, is it a plane, no, it's the Masked Pimpernel, flying in from the heavens to save us all.'

On Jady's mute instruction, Arnie first ungagged Joanna and Jenna. Joanna spluttered slightly, her larynx caught up in sock-fluff, while Jenna spoke up for the multitude. Jady was next.

'Untie my hands. Then we can both release the others.'

Taking a blade from his utility belt, Arnie slashed Jady's bonds and, with a single bound, he was free.

'Never mind the gags, Millado, just do the hands.'

Inspired by his superhero status, Arnie adroitly cut free Joanna, Jenna, Michael, Erich, Marlene and Louise. While the aforementioned ripped off their gags, spat out socks and regained breath and composure, he paused, knife in hand, beside a bellowing but thankfully muzzled Mr Dauntliffe and a perspiring Harold Wood, awaiting instructions.

'What are we going to do about these two?' he asked, forgetting his superhero status and reverting to his mild-mannered alter ego.

'Those two?' Hanif replied heatedly, looking down on the face down forms of Harold Wood and Mr Dauntliffe. 'I know what I would like do to one of them, at least. I will probably end up prison over this, and it is his entire fault. Leave him to rot, I say. As to that caretaker, he is just a pawn. You might as well untie him.'

Arnie made towards Harold Wood with the knife.

'Hold it, Masked Pimpernel,' cried Joanna, staying his arm. 'I have an idea.'

Jenna smiled at Joanna's assertiveness. Marlene, Louise and Erich looked on, wondering. But Michael clasped both Jady and Hanif's arms at the shoulder, cheery comrade style.

'So, gentleman, have I.'

'What shall we do?' said the floor manager. 'People are demanding that the Masked Pimpernel shows up and plays the winner. They are running out of patience.'

'As long as they don't run out of beer, we will be fine.'

'Well, I'm not taking responsibility, that's for sure. You hired us, and our time is up, so it's down to you. I quit. If anyone wants me I will be in the bar.' With that, the floor manager, who, had he but known it, had Pontius Pilate's blood coursing throughout his veins refusing to gather or distribute oxygen because its corpuscles didn't want to get involved, nodded his cares away and exited barwards. Had he a bowl, he would have washed his hands in it.

Alison's phone bleeped. It was a frantic senior cheese seeking guidance.

'Hello there. Sorry? Where is the Masked Pimpernel? I cannot answer that,' said Alison truthfully. 'On a mobile,' she continued disingenuously. 'After all, this call might be bugged.'

The cheese made forceful remarks about the potential sponsors and how this had all better be part of a deliberate scheme to build up suspense or the whole project would go the way of the Roman Empire.

'Don't worry,' replied an unruffled Alison before ending the call, 'as I was explaining to the floor manager just before he resigned, as long as the bar stays open the punters will be happy. Byeee.'

The tannoy crackled into life.

'Bars closing in five minutes.'

'Right, that's enough watching the monitors. I don't know what's going on but that Jady is bound to be at the bottom of it.'

'Bottom of what?'

'Bottom of whatever is going on,' replied Inspector Brewe tersely. 'He is the brains behind this nonsense and he is clearly up to no good.' She turned to the sergeant knowingly. 'Remember when we were trying to puzzle out how Jady could make money out of a free tournament? Well whatever he is doing he is doing it now, and whatever it is, we have to stop him.'

'But we don't know where he is.'

'Come on, Sergeant, he must be somewhere. You see that woman compère-ing the show? One Alison Smedley. She is a cohort of Jady; she will know where he is.' She stood up decisively. 'We are going to talk to her.'

To the tune of 'Oh come, all ye faithful', the Pool lovers of Spawater and assorted visiting media folk sang 'Why are we waiting' towards the empty dais. Even the most attractive people look ugly in a mob - ask Doctor Frankenstein - and despite their noble Roman ancestors it was only the fact that many of them had their hands full of beer glasses that stopped them forgetting the iron discipline of the Legions and storming the stage like Boadicea's boys on a bender.

'Miss Smedley?' Inspector Brewe was on her finest, briskest form. 'I want to talk to you about the whereabouts of your friend Jady and the Masked Pimpernel. Don't try to deny you know Jady. Where is he?'

'You should never deny your friends or they might deny you,' replied Alison deadpan. 'Of course I know Jady, officer. Last I heard he was over at the Baths, but he seems to have vanished.'

'And where is the Masked Pimpernel?' Even as she said it, Inspector Brewe wondered what the world was coming to. In all her police training courses and seminars she had never been told how to react when a superhero goes AWOL.

'Good question,' chuckled Alison merrily. 'I wish I knew. Listen to the audience; they want to know too.'

'What are you going to do about it?'

'Go and talk to them, I suppose. Excuse me.'

Recognising the early stages of mutiny - she had been here before - Alison about-faced and strode out onto the stage to face the mutineers. Horatio could have used her on the bridge.

'That was a great help to our enquiries.' Sergeant Mathews struggled to keep the sarcasm out of his voice.

'Mind your manners, Constable,' replied the inspector tersely. 'And don't let Smedley out of your sight.'

I'll try not to lose her while she is on stage, thought the sergeant, wisely keeping it to himself.

'Hello again,' announced Alison blithely. 'Glad to see you are all still keen. I do so like a keen audience. Sorry about the bar closing but there is more to life than alcohol. Don't you agree?'

From the Crow's Nest, Captain Bligh looked down anxiously on Alison. 'I tried that one,' he said knowingly to Long John, 'and they threw me overboard.'

'Arrr... she should tell 'em there be buried treasure under them thar floorboards. Never fails.'

The roar of denial swamped the singing, such as it was, and enabled Alison to regain the initiative.

'I expect you are wondering about the whereabouts of the Masked Pimpernel,' she said brightly.

'Yes, where is he?' replied a voice from the crowd. The dam broke. On the principle that the best way to get something is to shout loudly for it, the Hall erupted.

'We want the Masked Pimpernel!'

'Masked Pimpernel! Masked Pimpernel!'

'Where is the Masked Pimpernel?'

'Here I am,' piped up the Masked Pimpernel.

'Here we are then, what do we do now?' Jenna looked at the others, gently massaging her chafed wrists.

Leaving Mr Dauntliffe and Harold Wood tied, and in Mr Dauntliffe's case, fit to be, the others left by the fire escape and were safe in the corridor leading to the Town Hall and the staff exit.

The hasty discussion conducted by Joanna as they fled the basement concluded that the police would take some convincing and it would be quicker to raise the mob. Or two mobs. Joanna would raise the anti identity card militia while the Masked Pimpernel and his loyal assistant Jenna shanghaied the Pool-lovers.

'Masked Pimpernel,' voiced Jady steadily, the better to preserve his secret identity from flapping ears, 'now that you have done your duty here, there is a higher duty you must discharge. I mean, of course, the tournament in the Hall. You must return there immediately.'

The Masked Pimpernel had never claimed the gift of flight, leaving that to his Kryptonese cousin and the Wright brothers, but fancy took wing; golden opinions raining on him like mist-strewn sunbeams swept his feet from the ground, boosting his confidence from nought to sixty and had the world cowering in its corner, towel in hand.

'You are right, of course, sir; I shall return to the Hall and win the tournament.'

Joanna looked at the two of them incredulously.

'Do you realise our situation? There's a bunch of thugs stealing our Baths and you talk about Pool competitions?'

Jady could mix chalk and cheese if pushed; saving the Baths and the competition was child's play; Arnie being the child in question.

'We can all leave here now by the staff exit and avoid trouble. Jo, you can raise the demonstrators on the Green and get them to block the roads. Millado and Jenna can reach the Hall through the connecting corridor and get the Pool crowd onside and outside to stop the Baths going down the plughole.'

Nero looked down on Jady approvingly. 'Keep fiddling, my son.'

'What about the police?'

'Not straight away, give us a ten minute head start.'

'Why a head start? What will you be doing?'

'I will be with Hanif and Michael and the others sorting out bank accounts.'

Later in Lifeboats', Joanna and the others would have much to say on the subject of General Jady giving orders like Napoleon's dentist; but the Uzbeks would have approved, and besides, like eighty percent of Jady's plans, it seemed a good idea at the time.

'Ok, but we have to act quickly,' snapped Joanna in businesslike manner. 'We must stop those friends of Michael's escaping with our Baths.'

'They are no friends of mine.'

'True enough, Michael,' Joanna conceded. 'No friends of the world either. So let's stop them.'

Silence descended on the Hall as the Masked Pimpernel strode confidently towards Alison centre stage.

'Ladies and gentlemen, beer lovers, Pool lovers and others, I give you, arriving like the seventh cavalry at the eleventh hour - that's why they named a shop after them - I give you, the Masked Pimpernel.'

From the sidelines, Inspector Brewe peered out at the new arrival amid the ecstatic applause.

'Sergeant, I want an all points alert put out. Whatever is going to happen is going to happen soon and I want us to be ready for it.'

'Ready for what?' quizzed Sergeant Mathews. 'What shall I tell our people to be ready for?'

'Ready for trouble,' interrupted Jenna.

The two police officers swung around like one police officer.

'You!' gasped Inspector Brewe, who did not need police training to know trouble when she saw it. 'Where's Jady? You're one of his lot, aren't you? What's going on? What trouble?'

Jenna peered stagewards; the audience were hushed as the Masked Pimpernel held them spellbound. Witches and wizards looked on enviously. Like the Good Fairy, Alison stood by. Turning back to Inspector Brewe and Sergeant Mathews, Jenna kicked off.

'Listen to the Masked Pimpernel, officers. There is dirty work over at the Baths and your assistance is required pronto.'

'Ladies and gentleman, campaigners against identity cards and the national database, may I have a minute of your time? My name is Joanna Wilkins. Thank you for coming here today and registering your opposition to the imposition of the database State on a free people.'

As one of the local organisers of the Town Hall protest, Joanna had no difficulty in joining the speakers occupying the raised platform on the Green outside to make her announcement. Centralism leads to Stalinism, and as an open, democratic outfit, The National National Campaign Against Identity Cards was happy to leave local action to local groups.

Cheers from the crowd. Joanna was known to many of them only as a name on an email and it was good to see her in human form.

'Now, the threat of the national database may seem to many of you a threat some way off in the future and not a danger today, not yet. Well, I have to disabuse you of that belief. The threat is real and the threat is now. Criminals hiding behind biometric nonsense are at this very moment stealing the Spawater Baths and it is up to us to stop them. Now.'

'What is to stop us?'

Jady looked beseechingly at Hanif as he pondered Michael's question.

'Now let's get this straight.' Hanif stalled, not because he missed it the first time but because he needed to let the enormity of it sink in.

'You are saying that I should hack into the database to establish your authority to withdraw funds from your former boss's account, then destroy the database to cover your tracks.'

'Not any of his traceable accounts,' egged on Louise, 'one that was set up abroad purely for the purpose of paying our fee for the job.'

'The job of lifting our Baths!'

Michael gave a grin that would have had Little Boy Blue blowing his horn like Sachmo and throwing him out of the meadow.

'Well...yes. But that's all changed now. Whatever happens, Hanif, you have to destroy the database or we all suffer, not just me. There is bound to be an enquiry. There is Jady and Alison's Masked Pimpernel; your security company managing a database that allowed fraudsters to stroll into the Town Hall and lift Spawater's main attraction when Boadicea failed, and the growing resistance to identity cards as shown by the demonstrators. We will all be caught in the middle of it unless you destroy the database. Once it is gone, no enquiry can prove a thing.'

'But why should I let you use the database to access your boss's account?'

'Why not?' cried Jady. 'Don't you think we all deserve a little something after the trouble we have been brought to? What will happen to the money if we don't?'

Louise answered.

'It will rest there forever. The account was set up purely to pay us when the job was done. Empty it and the account will be closed automatically. It cannot be traced.'

'Remember, Han, it is not just us. Millado will be caught up in any investigation too. And Alison. Is it fair on them?'

Hanif considered. An honest man, it took a greater dishonesty to push him from the path of righteousness. Mr Dauntliffe's dishonesty in promulgating the national database to vainglorious politicians for his own, dishonest ends supplied that push.

'We will have to be quick, before the police start asking questions. It means going to my office.'

'Great!' Jady slapped Hanif on the back adding physical discomfort to his mental anguish. The others relaxed; if Hanif was on side they were home and dry. 'Well done, Han, you know it makes sense. Right,' Jady continued, 'no time to lose; let's get to your office and sort things out.'

At the repeat of the word 'office' Hanif turned, thought, frowned and halted.

'No, wait. I can't do it.'

They all froze as though Father Time was on strike for shorter hours. Jady was first to respond. 'Why not?'

Hanif sighed. He wondered if he perhaps had died and was in a personal Hell where it was one damn' thing after another. Hamsters on the wheel knew how he felt.

'I cannot get into my office because I have lost my Identification Card.'

'People of Spawater, I am sorry for not being here sooner. I was unavoidably detained.'

'Doing what?' yelled an amused voice from the crowd, provoking various suggestions of a nature that made Arnie thankful he was anonymous. He tapped the side of his full-face mask for moral support, inadvertently implying the hecklers were loopy and raising his stock still further. Now that he had arrived, the audience were prepared to forgive his tardiness and enjoy the show.

'I need your help.' Arnie glanced at Jady's hastily jotted note, noted the contents and continued. 'Spawater needs your help. At this very moment, criminals are next door loading up the Spawater Baths onto industrial trucks. They mean to take the Baths out of the country and sell them to the highest bidder. Only you can stop them. I want everyone to race over to the Baths and prevent them being stolen, now!'

Telling a large, impatient group of heavily refreshed Pool lovers to leave a building and go and fight crime causes a mixed reaction. Some like the idea, some do not, some believe it, and others beg to differ.

'Are they armed?' asked a worried voice, possibly a teetotaller. Others listened out for the reply.

'Armed? Of course they are!' Arnie was irritated by the question. Previously finding the centre of attention a scary place to be, repeated outings as the Pimpernel, public speeches and generally being in the limelight had infected

Arnie with mild celebrityitus. Added to the fulsome praise from the people he respected most, Arnie was operating considerably above par. The Masked Pimpernel would take nonsense from nobody.

'Silly question!' he snorted. 'As if international criminals would not be armed. Even the Saturday night heroes in the town centre are armed. Now, go and stop them.'

'What about the Pool tournament?'

This opened up a new avenue of thought. Was it all a ploy to avoid meeting the tournament winner? The Pool lovers took up the chant, momentarily nonplussing the superhero on the stage. Taking the opportunity to get a word in, Inspector Brewe turned to Jenna.

'What's all this, then?' she demanded without irony. 'What are you all up to?'

'It is what it says on the tin, officer. As we speak the Spawater Baths are being loaded onto trucks and taken away.'

'Of course they are; they are being taken for refurbishment. It is in arrangement with the Council.'

'Sort of.' Now that her friends were safely out of their basement prison, Jenna was beginning to enjoy herself. 'You see, officers, those architects chose the wrong removals company. Instead of taking the Baths for refurbishment, they are taking the Council to the cleaners. They used fake biometric identities to fool the Council into allowing them to remove the Baths. They fell out with their leader, apparently, and left him tied up along with that retard caretaker who seems to think the leader is from the government. He certainly pretends to be. It is not the architects' fault,' she added hastily, 'they were taken in the same as the Council.'

Inspector Brewe took a deep breath and wondered what she had done to deserve Spawater. One of her previous lives clearly had some explaining to do.

'Remind me, what is your name again?'

'Jenna. Jenna Wilkinson-Baart, but you can call me Jenna.'

'Well, Ms Wilkinson-Baart, I have heard a few in my time, but this one takes the biscuit and the cake too. Do you really expect me to believe that moonshine?'

'Not really,' Jenna conceded amicably, 'you prefer biometric bullshine; that's why we are appealing to the crowd instead. Where they go you will follow.'

Inspector Brewe, who did not believe in biometrics, preferring to trust her twitching nose, peered stagewards. Arnie, morally supported by Alison, was standing stock-still, weltering under a fusillade of catcalls and demands that he play the competition winner as advertised. Jady and Alison had done their work too well; saving the Baths took second place to the Pool competition. Satisfied, the Inspector turned back to Jenna, nose twitching as though it was about to discover an underground river.

'Think again, Jenna,' she gloated. 'Your crowd don't seem to be going anywhere.'

'Here we are then,' announced Jady cheerfully, 'Hanif Towers, headquarters of the national database, local version. Wave us through with your magic card then, Han, and we will give it its just deserts. I wish my Joanna was here to see this.'

'Don't rub it in, Jady, please,' begged Hanif, 'I am having a bad enough day as it is.'

'Sorry.'

'Come on, let's get it over with,' instructed Michael seriously. A future in front of bars or behind them; this was the crunch.

'All right, follow me.' Hanif swiped his identity card through the series of readers from the outside door onwards and presently Jady, Michael, Louise, Marlene and Erich stood beside him in his office. Putting his ID card safely back into his wallet after accessing his machine, he stared curiously at Louise.

'Look, just tell me. I know you didn't just find it on the floor, so how did you come to have my ID card?'

'It is as I said,' said Louise with mild exasperation, 'I found it under your table in The Lifeboat Club when I reached for my bag to go home. I thought it was my own temporary card fallen out of my bag somehow amid all the drinking. They do that sometimes, you know.'

Jady interrupted before Hanif could prevaricate further.

'Never mind that now, Han, the sooner we do the deed the sooner we can relax.'

'Relax? I will never relax again. Take a seat, everyone. Come on then, Louise, I will need your help with your bank and its codes.'

Michael smiled warmly as Louise sat beside Hanif at the terminal. Turning to Jady he raised his eyes reverently to the sky.

'God bless biometrics.'

Identity Cards
Chapter Thirty-two

Joanna's call to the anti identity card protesters hit the spot. People who felt strongly enough about the threat to the country from a control-freak government to take part in a protest felt equally strongly about threats to the country's heritage. The Roman Baths belong here, demanded the protesters, and here they stay. Period. Looking down from Valhalla, Lord Elgin turned to Socrates and raised a glass of nectar. 'See, Soc? When governments lose their marbles you can always rely on the people.'

As the world's most hardworking removals company - no job too dishonest - rushed to finish craning the Baths onto the lorries, it became aware of a tremendous clamour without. The forces of protest were loudly disputing the opening of the gates to prevent the lorries making their getaway, fortunately not by sitting down, which could have added injury to insult.

Over at the Hall, the Masked Pimpernel stood transfixed by the crowd's catcalls. They were here to see the Masked Pimpernel face the winner of the Pool contests and Bath time could wait.

'Well?' Inspector Brewe looked gloatingly from the stage to Jenna. 'Your bluff has been called, I think. Now perhaps you would like to start telling me the truth before I start the arrests.'

'Arrests for any particular reason?'

Inspector Brewe snorted in triumph. She had long wanted revenge on Jady for unspecified crimes against humanity - hers - and he and his gang were surely up to their necks in something. Arrest first, think of the charges later, about summed it up. She yelled her reply above the clamour of the crowd.

'Don't worry Jenna; we no longer need a reason to arrest people anymore.'

But Alison reacted first. She had been standing on stage beside the Masked Pimpernel, giving moral support and drinking in the situation. It looked like an impasse but the solution, like most things in life - to Alison, anyway - was simple.

'Ladies and gentlemen, here is the deal. First we have the final, then we all pop next door and save the Baths. Is that ok?'

Things were most certainly not ok next door. Corralled inside the gate were the gang, guns and ignition keys in hand, awaiting orders from their leader. Outside, the protesters milling around the area were taking orders from no-one. The police, in the middle as usual, watched apprehensively. Wat Tyler looked on approvingly.

'You must listen,' pleaded Joanna to the senior officer present amid the tumult, 'those people are trying to steal the Baths. You must stop them.'

'Sorry, miss, we have our orders. Those lorries have full authority to be there and remove the Baths. When they are ready to depart we will ask you to move your protestors.'

'My protestors?'

'Well, you told them to assemble here so you are responsible. If they refuse to move we will have no choice but to make arrests. Starting with you.'

'But they are stealing our Baths.'

'They are removing them for cleaning, miss. That's all.' The officer rattled his handcuffs threatenly. 'Now, will you move your protesters?'

Rattled but defiant, Joanna stood her ground.

'Will you at least call your boss, Inspector Brewe? She is inside the Hall and is being told about it too.'

'No can do, miss; if you were as informed as you think you are, you would know that we cannot make calls to mobiles in the Hall from outside during public functions.'

'Why not?'

'Security. A mobile signal might be used to detonate a bomb. The security chief insists only emergency calls are made, and this is not an emergency.'

Wondering what on Earth was, Joanna cursed Harold Wood. Like the government, his paranoia about security was totally counter-productive; safer to go to sea with Jonah.

'Well go to the Hall then,' she shouted, grabbing his shoulder and crying out in exasperation. 'Find out for yourself.'

'You're nicked.'

'All set? Right. Referee at the ready, here it is, ladies and gentlemen, the moment you have all been waiting for...'

'Too right' cried a heckler.

'...let the joust begin!'

Winning the toss and to the cheers and roars of the multitude, the Masked Pimpernel strode up to the table.

Whistling appreciatively, Louise eyed Hanif with a new respect.

'What a vehicle for corruption! There has never been anything like this, ever! Do we really have to destroy it? This national database of yours is a con merchant's dream!'

Hanif winced.

'You mean we've got access to the codes?' asked Michael, trying to keep the childish exhilaration out of his voice but still sounding like an unusually animated Peter Pan.

'Yes,' replied Hanif, less Peter, more dead. 'Here is the code you need to release your funds.' Rising from his seat and turning to Louise, he continued seriously, 'There you are, Louise, you know what to do.'

Louise leaped eagerly into the hot seat and began the process of accessing the special account.

'So,' said Jady, looking Hanifwards and trying not to sound triumphant, 'the national database is not such a good idea after all, then? Joanna and the others were right all along?'

'Yes, I'm beginning to agree,' agreed Hanif. 'If dishonest people were able to infiltrate the database they could wreak havoc.'

'Then it's lucky only honest people like you have access,' Jady laughed. 'Otherwise who knows what would happen?'

'Give it a rest, Jady. All right, you win. A national database is a bad idea. Now don't rub it in.'

'Ignore him, Hanif,' Marlene piped up. 'He is just being childish. Now, what is the position?'

Hanif turned away from Louise at the screen to address the others.

'It is simple enough; I used my administrators' codes to tell the database to reveal the access cipher and identity numbers required to satisfy the bank. Louise is now entering them into the bank's system...'

Louise shrieked with joy. 'It's done it! It's transferred the money! We've won!'

Dignity forgotten, Michael, Erich, Marlene, Louise and Jady jigged around the room like pirates when the shovel strikes metal.

'...which transfers the money to your joint account and then permanently deletes the transaction record,' persisted Hanif above the uproar. Yo Ho Ho.

'Now, Hanif,' cautioned Louise seriously, reason returning and addressing the task in hand, 'we need you to order the database to wipe itself out, source code included, and then we can get out of here.'

'I've said it before and I'll say it again,' gloated Michael merrily, visions of luxurious, bar-owning retirement welling up before him like surf on a summer swell, 'God bless biometrics.'

'I don't believe it.'

'Seeing is believing, Sergeant. Or may I call you Inspector?'

Jenna's insistence eventually wore down Inspector Brewe sufficiently to delegate Sergeant Mathews to investigate her claims. With the onset of the Pool challenge final, peace returned to the Hall as the crowd simmered down and focussed on the Pool table. The Inspector decided she could humour Jenna; after all, it was only Sergeant Mathews.

Traversing the corridor to the Baths and quietly entering the basement, Sergeant Mathews was astonished to find Jenna's claim true.

'I know him,' whispered the sergeant eyeing the cowering Harold Wood, 'but who is the other fellow?'

'Like I said, it's the gang leader. It seems they fell out over the spoils; you know how these criminals are. They just left him for you to find. He's lucky they left him alive.'

'Look, he's trying to say something. He looks very angry.'

Mr Dauntliffe was indeed trying to communicate, grunting like a poked pig seeing an applesauce delivery van. Jenna offered up a quick thank-you to the god of cotton socks for keeping him gagged and replied authoritatively.

'Don't untie him yet; you never know what he might do. Remember, his ex-colleagues are just outside. I suggest we leave them both for now and return quickly with reinforcements.'

Harold joined in the desperate grunting, forming a contrasting falsetto to his accomplice's bass as the sergeant agreed with relief. Confronting a gang of Bath robbers was lower than vacuuming the hallway on his to-do list. Seldom, outside Las Vegas, was a buck passed so willingly.

'You're right, Jenna. I'm over my head here; Inspector Brewe must be informed. She can deal with this.'

'Too right, Sarge.'

They looked at a struggling Harold, a clearly furious Mr Dauntliffe and each other.

'Yes, it is Inspector Brewe's problem.' They laughed in unison, adding baritone and quavering fortissimo to the ensemble. All they needed was a conductor and baton. 'Let Inspector Brewe deal with it.'

‘Hush, please.’

The audience hushed. Silence ruled as they watched the Masked Pimpernel lay off a simple safety shot and sit down. The challenger rose to take his turn under the lights.

Inspector Brewe turned to Alison, now in the wings. ‘Remind me, just who is the Masked Pimpernel?’

Alison clasped her hands in supplication. ‘He’s my hero.’

Oh well, thought the Inspector, worth a try.

‘I’ll find out eventually, you know; he must have done something I can arrest him for.’

‘You should arrest his opponent; did you see that foul shot?’

The audience certainly did, alternately groaning and yelling encouragement as if watching a life or death struggle like the good old days.

Up in the gods, Cleopatra turned to Mark Anthony and his friends in wonderment. ‘This beats your gladiator games all ends up. Cheaper too, I shouldn’t wonder. Why didn’t you think of it?’ ‘Ides more pressing priorities, Cleo,’ replied Julius. ‘Et tu, Brutus?’ ‘Don’t start all that again,’ Brutus replied, absently wiping his knife, ‘just watch the game, the challenger is losing maximus horribilis.’

Brutus was right. In earlier rounds the challenger had played with a confidence that was merited, sweeping all aside with aplomb. Now under the spotlights and up against the Masked Pimpernel, he seemed ill at ease, out of sorts and only capable of miscues. Arnie, rising from his seat again as the referee gave him another free penalty shot, could only marvel at how simple it was. The self-confidence forever oozing out of Jady and Co., allied to the compliments they had recently rained upon him in his Pimpernel mode, had banished all nerves and nervousness. Popeye might quiver with spinach withdrawal; Samson could shake at the prospect of attack by hairdresser, but the Masked Pimpernel, that aristocrat of superheroes, like Krakatoa’s big brother, quaked at nothing and nobody.

This was easy.

'Inspector! Quick! It's all true!'

Normally laconic, Sergeant Mathews looked out of sorts himself as he breathlessly delivered the news. From Valhalla, Phidippedes looked on scornfully. 'Out of breath from a little run like that? Ha!' he snickered, 'hardly a marathon.'

'True? What do you mean? What is true?'

Recovering his breath with suspicious haste, the sergeant told her. As she listened, the words of her boss came to mind. 'I want that Pool contest to pass without incident and unnoticed by the rest of the country...I will bust you so low you will be saluting traffic wardens.' If this was Jady's doing she would find him, so help her, whichever stone he hid beneath, and bring him to justice. And after he had served his fifty years in the slammer, she would be waiting outside and would nick him for wasting police time - hers.

Putting such pleasant thoughts aside, she reached for her radio before realising it would be jammed, cursed Harold Wood for a security obsessed moron and exited stage left.

'Right. I want these people cleared out of the way now, and the gates opened.'

The senior officer outside the Baths had been patient, keeping the police presence low-key in accordance with Inspector Brewe's instructions, but enough was enough. Arresting Joanna, far from intimidating the protestors, had simply given them one more thing to protest about.

Through the loudspeaker the officer addressed the protesters.

'This is the police; by obstructing the gates you are all in breach of the peace. I must ask you to remove yourselves peacefully and allow us to open the gates. Anyone who obstructs the gates will be arrested. Move out of the way immediately.'

While the protesters were distracted by the voice from the loudspeaker, two battle groups comprising of the heavier officers drove in from acute angles to the gateposts in a pincer movement that had Rommel taking notes. Careers spent reclining in police cars and behind desks eating megaburgers paid off as the weighty officers swept all before them. Possession is nine tenths of the law, and once the law possessed the gateposts it was a relatively simple matter to obtain the final tenth by hurtling towards the middle of the gates, brushing vegetarians and other well-meaning folk aside in their wake.

The gates were won.

'Open the gates,' hailed the voice behind the megaphone. Through the grille in the side of the police van and above the crowds of police and protestors, Joanna could see the wrought-iron gates slowly creaking open. Above the chanting of the protestors and the general hubbub could just be heard the sound of lorries starting up their engines. The gang leader, seeing the gates begin to open, had his trucks revving in readiness. The police action would enable the trucks to get out of town. Once away, they would disguise the trucks and split up according to prior arrangements, rendezvousing at the coast.

'What's happening?' Inspector Brewe raced up to the back of the action. Lines of riot police stood awaiting orders to the backdrop of 'Close the gates, close the gates!' reminiscent of Saltley in the seventies. As the protesters chanted and the gates wavered to and fro - mainly fro - like the incoming tide, inch-by-inch they widened. The protestors were slowly driven back.

'It's all right, Inspector,' announced the senior officer. 'It is all under control. The rioters are trying to prevent the egress of the vehicles collecting the Baths for repair, but our officers are opening the gates as you can see. Just give the word and I will order a baton charge to clear the lot of them.'

'Baton charge?' The Inspector was appalled. 'What do you mean, baton charge? I want those gates closed and I want them closed now!'

Cheers erupted from all sides as the crowd witnessed the scene; black ball into corner pocket for an easy victory.

‘Congratulations to the Masked Pimpernel, champion of Spawater and consequently the known world. Three cheers for the winner and the noble loser, hip hip hip...’

The Great Spawater Pool contest was over. The Masked Pimpernel vidi, vici and vini-ed like a good ’un, triumphing easily and comprehensively. Julius could only look down admiringly. ‘That’s how it’s done, Jules,’ laughed Cassius, ‘three sets and it’s over.’

‘Yes,’ Julius agreed amicably, ‘but that challenger was the biggest disappointment since Daniel’s lion. What a wuss; crying because it had a thorn in its paw. Now Boadicea, she was a handful; you should have seen her get out of snookers...’

Seizing Arnie and the moment, Alison manoeuvred him on stage and called out for silence.

‘No time for speeches, I’m afraid,’ Alison addressed the audience, ‘the Masked Pimpernel has an announcement to make.’

‘I do?’ whispered Arnie.

‘Yes.’

Aloud, Alison continued, ‘The Spawater Baths are being stolen and the Masked Pimpernel needs all of you to save them right away.’

‘Oh yes,’ Arnie agreed, ‘right away.’

‘So he wants all of us to rush to the Baths now.’

‘Yes, now.’

‘So what are we waiting for? Let’s go.’

‘What are we waiting for, let’s go.’

The audience did not need telling thrice. The bar was closed, the competition was over and the fun had shifted next door. Had gold been discovered in them thar Spawater hills the Hall could not have emptied faster. The crowd, in flagrant disregard for Health and Safety’s nagging scriptures on running in enclosed spaces, battered Harold Wood’s biometric controlled turnstiles to buggery, crashed through random doors and fire-escapes out into the open air, and hurdled towards the Baths. They were ready for anything.

'Close the gates, close the gates!'

With choir-like unison the riot police took up the protesters' chants. As a diversionary tactic it exceeded all expectations; the protesters, caught between the large police in front trying to open the gates and the riot police behind demanding they stay shut, were momentarily at a loss. They slackened their efforts, allowing the pro-open police to make progress; the gates were opening wider. The pro-shut riot police advanced, squishing the protestors like sandwich filling.

Inside, the gang leader revved his engine to signify readiness to the other trucks.

'Shut the gates, shut the gates!' yelled Inspector Brewe through the megaphone. The message began to reach the pro-open police who slackened, allowing the gates to swing back closed.

'There they are, let's stop 'em!'

From behind the police lines and Inspector Brewe came the charge of the Pool brigade. Seeing is believing and the Pool lovers saw the riot police wrestling a large group of people towards the Bath gates. Obviously the police were trying to prevent the Baths being stolen, so clearly their opponents were the thieves. Alcohol-fuelled courage plus the camaraderie grown by winning a Pool competition together lent them the espirit de corps their ancestors used to such advantage at Agincourt. Without pausing for breath or sober consideration, they plunged heroically into the fray.

'Shouldn't we be doing something?'

'Jenna wants you to wait here. Don't worry, young Masked Pimpernel, she said she wouldn't be long. And congratulations. We are all proud of you.'

Under cover of the general mayhem as the Pool lovers decamped to the Baths, Alison gathered in a dazed Arnie and propelled him to his dressing room.

'What's going on?

Alison sat opposite the mirror above the sink and began removing her stage slap.

'Jenna has gone to collect your clothes and will meet us here. You can change into your civvies and she will take you back to Jady and Joanna's flat. Then you can relax and enjoy your victory.'

Arnie was still shell-shocked.

'I won! I beat the winner!' he mumbled. 'It was easy.' Arnie stopped, light returning to his eyes. 'How come he was so easy to beat? Was it fixed?'

Alison stopped wiping her stage make-up and turned seriously to Arnie. 'He is next door. Let's ask him.'

'I want three officers to accompany Sergeant Mathews. Sergeant!'

'Ma'am?'

'Take three officers and bring back the gang leader. Oh, and that fool of a caretaker.'

'Right ho.'

Confusion reigned in Spawater far more comprehensively than the Romans, but even through the chaos Inspector Brewe could see the future, and it looked bleak. Her chief's exhortations for the evening to be kept low-key had fallen a little short. Her one consolation was that she had at least caught the gang leader. That would go some way in mitigation. And, she realised brightening, she had saved the Baths. For it was becoming clear that whatever else occurred, the trucks were going nowhere. Mayhem still ruled but shouted reports reached her to the effect that the trucks were now driverless. The gang leader had realised that the trucks could only escape over the crowd's dead bodies, leading to the mother of all car chases to the docks, and ending inevitably in the Dock. Reluctantly, he gave the order to abandon the mission, dived into the melee and disappeared forever.

The great Spawater Baths Robbery was over.

'Come on then, laddie; the sooner we are out of here the better.'

Arnie looked pained.

'Oh for heaven's sake,' chortled Jenna. 'All right, we will look the other way. Promise. Come on, Ali. Now hurry up.'

Mollified, Arnie climbed out of his Masked Pimpernel robes, having allowed Alison to remove the facial slap he wore for confidence beneath the mask.

'It was not a fix, you know,' said Arnie, struggling into his clothes.

'Of course it wasn't,' agreed Alison. 'You were the better player under pressure, that's all.'

'Why, who said it was?' asked Jenna over her shoulder.

'Nobody. I thought it was because it was so easy, but I spoke to the loser and he was not got at to lose. He said it was just nerves under the lights that made him come over all uncomfortable and itchy, and he really tried to win because he would have made a fortune in sponsorship as the man who beat the Masked Pimpernel.' Arnie grinned. 'I beat him fair and square.'

Jenna turned, Arnie's modesty forgotten, and faced him.

'Of course you did, and when things quieten down we are taking you out on the night of your life. You did a great job and we are all proud of you. Especially Jady.'

'Where is Jady? I haven't seen him all night.'

'He's been busy. You will find out all about it in due course. You dressed? Now, let's get out of here before that nosy Inspector turns up. I have a feeling she will not be very happy with us.'

'Right, you. What's your name and where are the rest of your gang?'

'What are you talking about, officer? How dare you address me in that manner? Why have your men handcuffed me like this? Release me! Release me at once I say!'

Ignoring Mr Dauntliffe, Inspector Brewe turned to her sergeant. 'Have you arrested him properly?'

'Yes, Ma'am.'

'Very well. What about this fellow?'

They looked down at a cringing Harold Wood. Squatting on the floor in a vain attempt to avoid the roving helicopter-borne television cameras, Harold saw his dancing cruise holiday waltzing over the horizon. What, he thought miserably, would Mrs Wood make of it all?

'Him too.'

'Good. Throw them in the wagon.'

Mr Dauntliffe was incandescent. To be attacked, marshalled into a basement and tied to a radiator by criminals was bad enough. To be released only to have handcuffs applied to his already chafing wrists by the police was worse; but to be talked about in one's presence as if one were a bag of coals was beyond the pale.

'How dare you!' he shouted, struggling gamely between two officers. 'Do you know who I am? Release me at once, you babbling cretin, or I will have you transported! Release me I say! Release me or I will ruin you! Ruin you, do you hear!'

Incensed, Inspector Brewe stuck her face into his. 'Ruin me, you say? Look around you.' Using main strength she shook him brusquely round by the shoulders to face a free-for-all Pool-lovers, protestors and police punch-up of John Wayne proportions, intermingled, had they but known it, with fleeing removals men, one tiptoeing, hooded Jenna and one superhero (retired). Above the backdrop of sirens, searchlights and helicopters she shouted, 'Look at this mess! You and your gang are responsible and you and your gang are going to pay when we catch them. Release you? I've got you, sunshine, right where I want you. Sergeant!'

'Ma'am?'

'Throw him in the van.'

Identity Cards
Chapter Thirty-three

'To absent friends.'

A week is a long time in political cover-ups. By the following Saturday, the only unusual thing about Spawater was Jady breaking his 'Saturday night is amateur night' rule and joining the others for a celebratory drink in The Lifeboat Club.

During the previous seven days, armies of government hirelings had descended on the town centre like lawyers on expenses and swept away the debris and the evidence. The government that demanded to know the whereabouts and behaviour of its citizens at all times showed an understandable reluctance to shine the light of publicity on its own activities. Under the catchall of 'security', the area was sealed off and the government's sins wiped clean, or at least wiped. Julius Caesar would hardly have recognised the place.

This caused national rumours but little stir in the old Roman town itself, as Spawater had seen many disturbances in its time and was accustomed to them. The previous week's contretemps was small vino by comparison; no one eaten by lions, mown down by chariots, enslaved back to Rome for the Gladiator Games Handicap or even exiled to guard Hadrian's Wall. Spawater returned to normal.

'Be upstanding and raise glasses, please, to Michael, Marlene, Louise and Erich. May they live long and prosper, wherever, and whoever, they may be.'

'And the Masked Pimpernel, saviour of us all, wherever and whatever he may be also.'

The merry tinkle of celebration echoed annoyingly around the main lounge, bouncing off the rafters in The Lifeboat Club, causing its principle Internet poker-broker to miss his opening bid.

Glancing round from the interactive gaming machine at the passing Ron, Bullet looked peeved.

'What are they celebrating this time? Another get rich quick scheme? I don't know why they bother, Ron; the only way to get rich is to work hard and not waste money.'

'Too right, Bullet,' Ron replied sagely. 'They never learn. Another drink?'

It was not the birth of another scheme, but the satisfactory closure of a chapter in their lives that merited incurring the wrath of a respected fellow Club member. One week after the debacle in the town centre, they had been given the all clear.

'So the police are not going to investigate?' Arnie, more worried even than Hanif once the adrenaline had worn off, could not quite grasp, like the government, that there are some things it is better not to know.

'That's right,' Jady confirmed, 'our local neighbourhood Police Inspector announced, in the presence of Joanna here and my solicitor, that the whole matter has been dropped and we must never mention it again. Or words to that effect.'

'Not in those words, I'll bet,' guffawed Jenna over her glass. 'When she interviewed me she said they should bring back hanging just for us.'

'The case is going, going, gone,' Jady responded smugly, planting his glass firmly on the table in the manner of an auctioneer, 'kaput, and gone with the wind.'

'But Inspector Brewe was very angry,' Joanna added seriously. 'I should keep out of her way for the next lifetime or so.'

'I think we all should,' added Hanif, siding with Queen Victoria on the subject of amusement. 'If she ever gets the chance she will throw away the key.'

'Indeed so,' Jady nodded. 'I think getting out of town for a while might be just what the doctor ordered when he was sober. I certainly intend to and I think we all could do with a break.'

Jenna poured herself another livener and laughed in agreement. 'We can certainly afford it. Cheers.'

'So what did the Inspector say, exactly?' Arnie had endured the most frightening week of his life; alternating between his bedroom and Jady's flat for reassurance, he was convinced that the police would discover the Masked Pimpernel's secret identity and arrest him for goodness knows what, subjecting him to embarrassment, humiliation and ruin. The police simply dropping the investigation seemed far too easy.

'Drop the investigation? Now?'

'Orders from on high. Whatever went on last Saturday, there are people in the government who want it forgotten and buried. All arrests and cautions are hereby disregarded. Officially, the whole thing is dropped.'

'Why?'

'Security.'

'What goes on my record?'

'Nothing,' replied the Police Chief ruefully. 'So far as we are all concerned, Inspector, none of this ever happened. Now, you tell everyone concerned to forget the whole thing.'

Inspector Brewe left her boss's office with mixed feelings. On the one hand, dropping the case meant that she would not be held accountable for handcuffing, assaulting and insulting a senior establishment figure with unimpeachable credentials. On the other, it meant that Jady and his associates escaped scot-free. Pontius Pilate felt the same when Barabbus burgled his villa.

Sergeant Mathews accepted the news philosophically.

'Is that it then, Ma'am? All over? Just as well. Now we can get back to proper policing.'

'But don't you realise, Sergeant, it means that Jady and his gang have got away with it again! Especially that Jenna with the surname, who told us Mr Dauntliffe was the ringleader. They made fools of us and I for one am not going to forget it.'

Made a fool of you, you mean, thought Sergeant Mathews happily, mentally raising a glass. Aloud he replied, 'I don't see what we can do about it, Ma'am, if we have been told to drop it. After all, the identity cards and national database scheme has been dropped too. I suggest we do likewise and forget the whole thing.'

Forget, agreed the Inspector, but not forgive. Once again Jady and his associates had not only evaded justice but also avoided being accused of any wrongdoing whatsoever. Inspector Brewe knew Jady had committed any number of offences, but what, exactly? They nailed Al Capone over tax evasion but everyone recognised his real crimes. Equally, the Inspector knew that Jady held as many guilty secrets as Cap'n Flint's sandpit, but without a map they remained a mystery. Agatha Christie would have approved. She turned, furiously, to her assistant.

'I'll get him one day, Sergeant, you see if I don't, so help me. Him and the whole passel of them.'

Gazing serenely through the porthole, Harold Wood reflected upon the ups and downs of his week. It had hardly been a promising start; gagged and tied to his own radiator with a man he had been anxious to impress but who subsequently turned out to be the leader of the Russian Mafia, or something of that ilk. Being arrested by Sergeant Mathews did little to improve matters and having his DNA taken forcibly from him under the eyes of a contemptuous Inspector Brewe just about put the tin lid on a Saturday best forgotten.

Things could only get better - give or take a riot on his watch - and after being bailed and summoned to the office of the Council Head the following afternoon, things did. The Council Head, seemingly under great strain - if the shaking hands and perspiring forehead were anything to go by - explained the official position.

There had been a conspiracy, the Council Head explained, to steal the Spawater Baths under the cover of a Pool competition. Characters who could blend in seamlessly at a James Cagney convention had, it appeared, conspired with foreign powers in a plot that DaVinci Code breakers would reject as farfetched. A concerned Council Head, still under the ether following his morning meeting with Mr Pettifogg, congratulated Harold on his part, Milligan-like, in the plot's downfall.

Harold who, like Sleeping Beauty, did not always know what was good for him, asked what, precisely, had been his contribution. The Council Head looked pained but explained that Harold's security measures had foiled the plot. Obviously, British Intelligence wanted it kept under the rose, but essentially, without Harold, none of last week's activities could have happened, and the government wished to thank him for his contribution. Of course, now that the conspiracy was broken, Harold's security measures had done their bit and would be dismantled. Human vigilance was the new watchword; technology was out.

'A holiday, Harold, that's what you need. Take the wife on a cruise; you deserve it. And don't worry about the cost, the government have authorised me to release Council funds to cover everything. First, er, business class.'

He called me Harold, thought Harold.

Brushing aside all of Harold's objections - time off not booked through proper channels, Town Hall in a mess, reports on Pool tournament to be written, Health & Safety analysis, evaluation of security systems and a whole myriad of tasks of equal importance - the Council Head insisted that he and Mrs Wood leave for a round-the-world cruise, the long way, that very minute. Don't worry about his Hall, insisted the Council Head; government forensic agents were foraging for evidence and it was closed to all. With the public, the biggest irritant to the smooth and efficient running of Council services, barred, Harold could relax and contemplate the challenge of adapting his Two-Step Shuffle to the southern hemisphere.

When he returned - no hurry, the Head assured him - he would find an important new role waiting for him. A promotion. He would be promoted to Tsar. Harold Wood, the Spawater Environmental Tsar, would be responsible for recycling, lowering carbon dioxide emissions and all other Green issues. Harold's enthusiasm, the Head insisted, was just what was needed to save the environment from mixed bin bags and smoky bonfires. The planet, the Head felt assured, would be safe in Harold's hands.

Finally, concluded the Council Head hastily, the whole earlier matter was subject to the Hundred Years Secrecy Rule; it never happened and must never be referred to again.

Harold understood.

'You would be wise to forget the whole thing and think yourself lucky to be alive and in one piece.'

Mr Pettifogg was enjoying himself. Once again he was able to lord it over his superior with impunity.

'More tea?'

Mr Dauntliffe would have preferred arsenic, but with the Press and busybody taxpayers' organisations questioning the vast sums of money wasted on the abortive database and identity card project and lobbying to vet the accounts, expenses were being kept to a minimum.

'Thank you,' he replied, with a humility he did not feel.

Mr Dauntliffe had had a difficult week. The pomposity he had displayed in Spawater police station when threatened with ninety days incommunicado detention for starters disappeared like a manifesto promise when Mr Pettifogg brought to his attention the current state of affairs.

'Without the prototype national database that you had been instrumental in imposing on Spawater, the attempted theft of the Baths and the ensuing riot could never have happened. When the cabinet were told that the database was to blame, they dropped it overboard with the identity card scheme alongside.'

'But it was the Home Secretary's proposal,' Mr Dauntliffe protested feebly. 'I was merely the conduit through which the government's wishes were formulated.'

Mr Pettifogg raised his eyebrows against which, Mr Dauntliffe knew, all protest was futile.

'The government,' continued Mr Pettifogg, enjoying himself more than ever, 'has spent a taxpayers' fortune both on the pilot scheme itself and propaganda to persuade the people to surrender their freedoms in the name of security. Now the unfortunate events in Spawater have driven a coach and horses through the very notion that enslaving everyone to a computer system enhances security. It is now a non-subject, buried under the Hundred Year Secrecy Rule.'

'There is no such rule.'

'There soon will be.'

Mr Dauntliffe sighed his sigh of superiority. Through the cowardice of government and the unauthorised, riotous actions of the very subjects the database was set up to control, his dream was dead.

'I see. So the scheme has been dropped.'

'Of course.' Mr Pettifogg poured out the tea, magnanimous in victory. 'The government, the Home Office and more importantly, the State,' here Mr Pettifogg frowned directly at his superior, wondering why he had ever feared him, 'have been made to look foolish thanks to the shenanigans last Saturday. The government washes its hands of the whole affair. Least said soonest mended is its approach.'

Indeed, with an alacrity that would have wounded Judas, the Cabinet disowned the national database and everyone involved with it. Mr Dauntliffe was far too experienced to suppose it could be otherwise. A discredited scheme has no friends.

'You were lucky that quick thinking database manager in Spawater had the good sense to pull the plug,' Mr Pettifogg continued, 'and fortunate that the town's CCTV cameras were integrated into the surveillance system alongside the biometric data. He wiped the lot and now nobody can prove a thing. Of course, we still had to honour the contract with his employers, but in return his employers are obliged to protect customer confidentiality.'

'What reason have they given their shareholders for dropping the scheme?'

'Security.'

'What reason have they given to the newspapers?'

'Security.'

Mr Dauntliffe sipped his tea meditatively. Secrecy is security for the rulers; liberty is security for the masses.

'So what happens now?'

'To the national database and identity cards? Abandoned, of course. All is forgotten and the taxpayer picks up the tab.'

'No, no, no,' harrumphed Mr Dauntliffe scornfully, 'not to identity cards.'

'To you? Well,' Mr Pettifogg sipped his own tea and savoured the moment. He had been looking forward to this. 'How's your garden?'

It could have been worse. Gardening leave, thought Mr Dauntliffe. A period of silence and reflection while the story died down. Yes, he agreed, probably the best thing. Time to reflect on the whole sorry episode. Time to discover exactly what had happened to destroy his plans. What and why, and mainly who, was to blame?

'It could use some attention,' he replied, playing the game. 'Yes, some time to recharge my batteries would be the best thing, I agree.'

'Good. It is agreed then.' Mr Pettifogg drained his cup and placed it firmly in the centre of the saucer, signalling the end of the meeting. 'I shan't detain you further, I am sure you have arrangements to make.'

'Well,' said Mr Dauntliffe, rising, 'it has been a useful little chat.' He turned to leave.

'One more thing,' said Mr Pettifogg, escorting him out, 'what happened to the so-called Masked Pimpernel? He seems to have vanished.'

With the malicious yet impotent glare of an ousted dictator boarding the plane to Switzerland, Mr Dauntliffe did likewise.

The disappearance of the Masked Pimpernel created conspiracy theories sharper than Occam's razor. Kennedy, Pope John Paul One and Princess Di chewed Shergar-burgers at Elvis's interstellar hotel and, like the King's horses, could not put all the pieces together. The general belief was that the Masked Pimpernel had been the brains behind the plot to steal the Spawater Baths. When the plot misfired and the anti identity card protesters surrounded the building, he knew the jig was up, so he sent the Pool lovers to the Baths in order to escape in the confusion. Others added that the entire competition was rigged and the Pimpernel did it all with mirrors and magnets.

'Close, but no coconut,' laughed an ebullient Jady as the friends conducted their debriefing.

'I won it fair and square,' cried Arnie vehemently. 'There were no magnets, were there, chief?' He tailed off. With Jady, he could never be sure.

'Of course not.'

'It seems we will never know the whole truth of the matter,' commented Jenna, wistfully. 'The Masked Pimpernel has gone to that great fortress of solitude in the sky.'

'Well, good riddance,' stated a determined Arnie. 'I could have ended up in prison or six foot under. I never want to hear that name again.'

'You are in good company, young Arnie,' added Alison. 'My company never wants to hear that name again either.'

The losing finalist, accused of accepting a bribe to throw the match, had threatened to sue Alison's company unless they produced the Masked Pimpernel and made him deny it publicly. Unable, and most certainly unwilling to do so, they had settled out of court, giving the loser the money originally earmarked for Jady.

Jady frowned in rueful remembrance. They had all taken a juicy share of the spoils from Michael's erstwhile employer - washing it via Jady's offshore account to evade money-laundering checks - and he could hardly complain, but the original scheme had backfired. The Masked Pimpernel no longer existed. Too many pointed questions hung over the entire episode for him to raise his cue in public. Damocles might have given it a shot, but Arnie, no. That was a spotlight too far.

'What did your company say?' asked Hanif, who had refused to accept money from the Russian Mafia and with Damascene logic had donated his share to the Campaign for Liberty.

'They said that the Masked Pimpernel could go back to whatever planet he came from and take Jady with him.' Alison giggled happily, champagne bubbles tickling her nostrils.

'You look happy; what is it this time?'

'Oh, hello Ron,' continued Alison. 'We were just talking about the Masked Pimpernel and saying how funny it all was. My employers are furious about the Masked Pimpernel vanishing because they can't use him to promote anything. They have lost a winner.'

'I thought you were his manager or something. Aren't they furious with you too?'

'Oh no. Thanks to me, our company is famous worldwide. Clients think we created him as a publicity stunt, which is nearly true.'

'Who was he anyway? I thought he was young Arnie at first, but he was too well built and his voice was too deep.'

'It looks like we will never know,' interrupted Jenna abruptly. With her share of Mafia money in the bank this was no time for loose talk. 'Now Ron,' she continued, 'getting back to serious matters; how about some more champagne?'

'Always with the champagne,' muttered Ron, his usual grumbling self. 'Life is just one big celebration, isn't it?'

'Too right.'

Ron scanned the group looking for someone on his own level. 'What about Joanna then, sitting quietly. She doesn't look in the mood for celebrating at all. What's wrong, Joanna? Not drinking?'

What was wrong was Ron. Sitting in a joyous reverie like Snow White the day they invented the dishwasher, Joanna was the happiest of them all. Her spirits floated above the earthly celebrations higher than alcoholic spirits could ever aspire as she contemplated the downfall of the national database and identity cards.

Joanna's cup, like her flute, was full. The menace of a national database and Identification Cards was gone forever. The protesters and the Pool lovers had demonstrated the public's refusal to be stamped, bar coded, numbered, labelled and generally mucked about by the control freaks of Westminster, and it was the government that now feared the people, as it should be.

That the scheme was aborted came as no surprise. The whole ruinously expensive, unworkable control-freak lunacy, the fetish of a long forgotten and disgraced former Home Secretary, was always a non-starter. Its sheer impracticability and ludicrous expense would inevitably scupper the scheme as sure as governments need votes and money. Joanna always knew that. No, the joyous surprise was the scheme being dropped because the people objected on principle. Once awakened to the peril, the people's instinct as always, was right. The government lay prostrate, its integrity in tatters and its very raison d'etre under question. Joanna's great fear, that one day a cheap and reliable way to enslave the people might be discovered and implemented, had proved baseless. The protesters had galvanised the people to such degree that no parliament in the foreseeable future would forget that the people are the masters, the people rule. The national database and identity card scheme was as dead as the soul of the government.

'What's that, Ron?' said Joanna, becoming aware that a response was called for. 'Sorry, miles away.'

'Are you alright?' Ron continued, hoping he had found a low, and therefore kindred, spirit.

'I've never felt better, Ron,' Joanna replied, dashing Ron's hopes on the rocks in grand, siren style. 'It is champagne all round. The threat, Ron, of ID cards and the national database, has been lifted; the Spawater Baths are safe and the police are not going to pursue anyone over recent events. That is most certainly worth a toast.' Joanna raised her glass. 'To life, and all who sail in her.'

'C'mon Ron,' interrupted Jenna impatiently, 'a girl could die of thirst here. Make with the champagne.'

'All right,' sighed Ron, 'but I am not doing deliveries. You will have to send someone up to the bar to collect it.'

All eyes turned to Arnie.

Accustomed these days to star treatment, Arnie was slightly put out by being relegated back to gopher.

'Why me?'

All eyes stayed tuned.

'All right then,' he grumbled, rising, 'back to normal, I suppose.'

'Can't be in the spotlight forever, you know,' commented Jenna. 'There's work to be done.'

'Speaking of spotlights, Jady,' interrupted Alison across the table, 'the girls said sorry, but that make-up you provided is no good under them. They have gone back to their old supplier.'

Jady paused for thought, and then replied casually.

'Ok, thanks Ali; tell them not to worry about it. Get some crisps, Arnie, too, please. Here, I'll come with you, ' and Jady hustled Arnie briskly barwards.

'What girls, Ali?' asked Joanna curiously.

'The make-up girls. Jady supplied the make-up for the contest. They used it on the winner and Arnie for the final, but luckily Arnie was unaffected as it was under his helmet. It itches under spotlights. The girls say they will stick with their old supplier.'

'Oh, right.' Joanna nodded, closing the subject forever. She turned abruptly to Hanif. 'Well Han, I'm honestly glad it's all over. Now that it is, does Arnie get his job back?'

'Of course.' Hanif beamed. 'It will be a pleasure to work with him again. I've already welcomed him back after he takes a holiday to get back to Earth.'

Hanif was a happy man. As the local database and identity card people, his employers had feared ruin, humiliation and ruin. Hanif's apparent quick thinking in destroying the evidence, coupled with the government abandoning the project, had saved them and their business. In addition, the government had settled the contract in full, leaving them quids in. Hanif had received a handsome bonus, which he accepted wry-faced. On a whim, he used it to open an internet casino account on the principle of easy come, easy go.

Also, he was friends again with Joanna and the rest of the gang, so all that was missing was a good gloat.

'I told you from the beginning Michael was not who he pretended to be.'

Joanna, her cup as full as Hanif's, was having none of it.

'And what made you suspicious, eh? His ID card? The national database? No. Biometric technology put him in the clear. Let's face it, Han; t'was good old-fashioned human intelligence that made you smell a rat. The kind of human intelligence the database huggers want replaced by dumb machines and bits of biometric plastic.'

Good old-fashioned human jealousy too, Hanif added privately. Still, all's well...

'Leave poor Hanif alone,' broke in Alison plaintively, 'he only did everything for the best.'

'That's true,' Joanna conceded amicably, turning to them both. 'How about a toast? To friends reunited.'

'I'll drink to that.'

They stood up opposite each other across the table and raised their glasses.

'Friends reunited.'

As they cemented their friendships, Jady returned ashen-faced and collapsed into an armchair.

'You are not going to believe it. You are just not going to believe it.'

Joanna groaned. Not déjà vu again?

'Ron has just had the results of the Health and Safety inspection on his kitchens.'

'Failed, of course,' shrugged Jenna. 'So what? We don't eat here anyway.'

'Failed, of course. The trouble is, the entire club must be closed while things are put right. It could take months to satisfy the bureaucrats. Ron cannot afford this. Lifeboats' will be sunk. At the same time, Ron has had a lousy offer for the club from a gambling outfit, the Deludo Supercasino conglomerate. He may be forced to settle for peanuts.'

'How did the gambling outfit know Ron was in trouble?' asked Alison curiously.

'How indeed,' retorted a suspicious Jenna.

Glass in hand and rising to his feet, Jady took a deep, Churchillian breath.

'We did not fight and destroy the government's identity card madness just to lose to Health and Safety. Or supercasinos. Up with this we shall not put.'

Joanna sighed. Just when things seemed to be calming down, Jady was about to go off on one of his adventures, doubtless taking her and the others along for the ride. Ah well, in a hundred years we will all be dead. What is the point of a boring life?

After the lull comes the storm.

The End

Made in the USA
Monee, IL
04 November 2026

67385520R00193